Unwelcome Strangers

# Unwelcome Strangers

## *American Identity and the Turn Against Immigration*

David M. Reimers

Columbia University Press

*New York*

Columbia University Press
*Publishers Since 1893*
New York   Chichester, West Sussex

Copyright © 1998  Columbia University Press

Library of Congress Cataloging-in-Publication Data
Reimers, David M.
    Unwelcome strangers : American identity and the turn against immigration /
David M. Reimers.
        p.    cm.
    Includes bibliographical references (p. 183) and index.
    ISBN 0-231-10956-3 (alk. paper).   —   ISBN 0-231-10957-1 (pbk.)
        1. United States—Emigration and immigration—Government policy.
    2. United States—Emigration and immigration—Public opinion.
    3. Immigrants—United States—Public opinion. 4. Public opinion—
    United States. I. Title.
    JV6483.R45   I. Title.
    325.73—dc21
                                                                97-52683
                                                                CIP

Casebound editions of Columbia University Press books are printed on
permanent and durable acid-free paper.
Printed in the United States of America
c 10 9 8 7 6 5 4 3 2 1
p 10 9 8 7 6 5 4 3 2 1

*To Rebecca, Kevin, Kat, and Daena*

# Contents

# Acknowledgments

IN THE COURSE of writing this book I have presented my findings to a number of academic audiences. These include the Population Association of America, the American Political Science Association, the Columbia Seminar on American Civilization, the Nordic American Studies Association, the Social Science History Association, the University of Illinois History Faculty Seminar, and the Concordia University History Seminar. I am grateful for the comments of the participants. One of the most helpful sessions was at my own history department's colloquium in March 1997. Neil Maher was especially astute in his critique.

A research grant from the American Philosophical Association made possible two trips to California and one to Washington, D.C., to consult materials and interview persons involved in the immigration debates. The American Council of Learned Societies gave me a travel grant to give a paper at the Nordic American Studies Association in Oslo in August 1995. I also wish to thank Dean Tom Bender for providing research funds, permitting the purchase of a new computer and other materials.

The libraries of several of the restrictionist organizations contained useful information, and I am grateful for the opportunity to use them. The New York Public Library also houses important materials. Most of my research was done at the Elmer Bobst Library of New York University; thanks to the internet newspapers, governmental documents and other materials are now available in the NYU library. The staff there was, as always, helpful. Special thanks go to George Thompson and Tom Crawford.

I have interviewed a number of persons active in the movement to change American immigration policy. They knew that my views and theirs differed, but they spoke candidly and gave me their time. I appreciate these talks for providing me with greater insight into the immigration debate. I hope that I have done justice to the many persons I talked to and quoted in the manuscript itself.

Three colleagues read a first draft of the manuscript. I am indebted to John Baick, Elliott Barkan, and Leonard Dinnerstein (again) for their suggestions. A later draft was read by George Lankovich and Alan Kraut. I wish to thank them for making this book more readable and the argument more plausible. Kat Morgan prepared the index. As usual my editor, Kate Wittenberg, has been supportive. Readers for Columbia University Press also provided helpful comments. I, of course, am responsible for any errors and interpretations. My wife, who never reads anything I write, has been nonetheless a great supporter, has discussed some of my ideas, and has given me insights into the way economists think about immigration.

# Abbreviations Used in Text and Notes

| | |
|---|---|
| ADC | Aid to Dependent Children |
| AADC | American Arab Discrimination Committee |
| AICF | American Immigration Control Foundation |
| APA | American Protective Association |
| CAPS | Californians for Population Stabilization |
| CCN | Carrying Capacity Network |
| CIR | Commission on Immigration Reform |
| CIS | Center for Immigration Studies |
| ELA | English Language Amendment |
| FAIR | Federation for American Immigration Reform |
| GAO | General Accoounting Office |
| INS | Immigration and Naturalization Service |
| IRCA | Immigration Reform and Control Act 1986 |
| MALDEF | Mexican American Legal Defense and Educational Fund |
| NAACP | National Association for the Advancement of Colored People |
| NIF | National Immigration Forum |
| NPCA | National Parks and Conservation Association |
| NPG | Negative Population Growth |
| PAI | Population Action International |
| PEB | Population-Environment Balance |
| PEG | Political Ecology Group |

| | |
|---|---|
| SSI | Supplementary Security Income |
| SOS | Save Our State |
| TEF | The Environment Fund |
| TRIM | Tri-Immigration Moratorium |
| VCT | Voice of Citizens Together |
| ZPG | Zero Population Growth |

Unwelcome Strangers

# Introduction

WRITING THIS BOOK was difficult at times. Many persons debating immigration resort to emotional and vague generalizations. Both sides use such appeals, which are not helpful in determining immigration policy. Just what does it mean to be called a "nation of immigrants"? The continuation of a generous policy? I believe so, but how generous? Currently about one million newcomers are coming to the United States annually. Is this the right number or should it be increased or decreased? Restrictionists believe the number should be substantially lower. They think that while illegal migration is especially burdensome, the problem is not undocumented immigration alone. Legal migration, they inform us, is three times the illegal flow, and to their minds it is the numbers that cause problems.

Restrictionists make four basic critiques of current immigration. They believe that the system is broken, that mass immigration harms the United States economically, that it is damaging the environment, and that it is changing American culture adversely. Some of the arguments used in the debate contain views I strongly disagree with. I am especially uneasy about the debates over assimilation and the impact of new immigrants on American culture. These arguments often sound too much like turn-of-the-century nativism. However, the explicit racist and religious prejudiced tones of those debates are absent today, and I do not label critics as racists. Racism is a much abused term, and

I have let the arguments speak for themselves; readers can make their own judgments. I support the current diversity of American immigration and believe that, on the whole, the new immigrants are enriching American society socially and culturally, much as past generations did. This preference is strengthened by the experience of living in the cosmopolitan New York City area the past forty years and by teaching at New York University since 1966.

While I believe the evidence indicates that immigration is a net benefit to the United States, economically as well as socially, it does not affect all groups equally. If evidence exists that immigration hurts particular groups economically, then the proponents have to acknowledge that fact and be willing to come up with programs to deal with this impact. Likewise, if we desire diversity among immigrants, then as a society, we must be willing to admit that there is a cost. Clearly, one of the tasks is to make certain that immigrants learn English as rapidly as possible. Making English our official language will not facilitate this task, but offering more English classes will. Bilingual education is a controversial issue, and programs have had mixed results in placing their students into mainstream classes as quickly as possible. The best programs should be studied to see if they can be emulated, and the ones with dismal track records should be scrapped.

The environmental critique of immigration is problematic, for the simple reason that the predictions of environmentalists have not come to pass, largely due to new sources of energy, better agricultural production, and tough environmental rules. However, America does have finite resources, and the relation of population growth, including immigration, to the environment needs to be probed more carefully.

Failure to deal with the problems of immigration can lead to a backlash. The pro-immigration lobby has too often been unwilling to admit that immigrants might be taking advantage of American welfare, such as Supplementary Security Income (SSI); as a result Congress passed a particularly harsh measure in 1996 that did not protect those already here. As Rick Swartz, a leader in fighting against immigration changes in 1996, noted: "We didn't address it. What happened is someone else addressed it. And what did they do? They cut if off completely."[1]

From the other side of the debate Mark Krikorian of the Center for Immigration Studies insisted that the Illegal Immigration Reform and Immigrant Responsibility Act of 1996 was passed to remedy faults in the system largely brought on by the pro-immigration groups: "Yet it was the very success of these groups that made the law necessary in the first place. For years, they tried to thwart enforcement of immigration laws by aggressively taking advantage of every legal crack in the system. Congress has merely pushed back by closing these loopholes."[2] Only belatedly did the Immigration and Naturalization Service (INS) and the federal government take stronger action to deport alien criminals. Alien crime is a real problem that must be faced. I also believe that sponsors should be held more accountable for those they assist in immigrating. Nor can I see any reason to permit immigrants (and their children for that matter) to be included in affirmative action programs. Such inclusion only prompts additional attacks on affirmative action, which is already besieged.

Proponents of immigration want the United States to maintain a humane and generous refugee and asylum programs. But how does one do this? Michael Teitelbaum remarked years ago that the immigration issue was a question of right versus right. This is certainly the case with asylum. How does one weed out frivolous claims without sending persons back who have legitimate fears of persecution? Or how does Congress deal with the ever contentious issue of illegal immigration? The INS estimates that 275,000 undocumented immigrants settle in the United States yearly. Tougher border controls have no doubt cut the number, and it could be reduced further, but at what cost? Is a national identity card needed? How much more money should be voted for the INS, an agency that seems incapable of solving its problems even under the leadership of the current able commissioner, Doris Meissner.

The reluctance of proponents of immigration to admit problems is due to their fear that such admissions will be used to cut immigration. But we do need careful debate, for immigration policy is mostly made in an ad hoc and uninformed way. Ultimately the nation must decide how many immigrants to admit and what criteria should be used. Unfortunately the debate does not always satisfactorily answer these questions.

# 1

## Toward Exclusion
### *American Immigration Policy Before World War II*

*"I say the class of immigrants coming to the shores of the United States at this time are not the kind of people we want as citizens of this country."*
—Representative James V. McClintic (D.-Okla.), *Congressional Record*, Dec. 10, 1921, 177.

FROM THE EARLIEST DAYS of European colonization, the colonies wanted settlers, but they were also uneasy about those who might follow them. Religious affiliation of prospective immigrants prompted the most opposition to newcomers. Members of the Society of Friends were often scorned and especially by the founders of the Massachusetts Bay Colony. The Friends were certainly persistent in their attempts to preach there, and they returned after being warned to stay away. In response Puritan magistrates "ordered that Quaker Cassandra Southwick should have her children taken and sold at public auction." Another Society of Friends missionary, Elizabeth Hooten, was seized and turned loose in the wood, but her fate was better than Mary Dyer who refused to leave Boston and as a result was hung in 1659.[1]

Boston was not the only inhospitable place for members of the Society of Friends. In 17th century New Amsterdam, Peter Stuyvesant banished several Quaker missionaries who insisted upon carrying on their religious ecstasy in the town's streets. But Stuyvesant liked few people other than members of the Dutch Reformed Church. He wanted to deny Lutherans the right to have their own church, and he despised Jews even though their numbers were few in the colony. The Reverend Dominies Johannes Megapolensis of the Dutch Reformed Church agreed with Stuyvesant. He believed that Jews had "no other God but the unrighteous Mammon, and no other aim than to get possession of Christian property." He wanted "these godless rascals" to be "sent away from here."[2]

The Dutch West India Company excised a restraining role, however, and permitted Jews, with restricted rights, to remain in New Amsterdam. The company's directors believed that intolerance was bad for business, and besides, several Jews had invested in the company. The West Indian directors told Stuyvesant that harshness to newcomers was a poor policy "at so tender a stage of the countrys' existence. You may therefore shut your eyes, at least not force people's consciences, but allow everyone to have his own belief, as long as he behaves quietly and legally, gives no offense to his neighbors, and does not oppose the government."[3]

Most colonists shared Stuyvestant's antisemitism, and Jews found their rights curtailed.[4] For the most part, they could not vote or hold office and had to care for their own indigent members. A few won respect as successful leaders in their communities, but Jews had to wait for the American Revolution to end most—but not all—civil disabilities.[5] Jews, for example, did not receive the franchise in New Hampshire until 1876.[6]

Protestants gradually won acceptance in the colonies, and of course Pennsylvania was especially welcoming as it was founded by William Penn, a Quaker himself, and a believer in toleration. The same can not be said for Roman Catholics, who like Jews were feared and distrusted. The vast majority of European colonists who claimed a religion were Protestants of one kind or another. Like so many Protestants of that era, they held strong beliefs about Catholics and the pope, sometimes identified as the Antichrist.[7] Maldwyn Jones wrote of the colonists' attitudes and treatments, "Most of the colonies levied discriminatory head taxes upon ship captains landing Roman Catholics, and even the colonies which attempted to promote immigration were careful to specify that only Protestants could qualify for the bounties or other inducements offered."[8]

Lord Baltimore founded Maryland in part for profit and also to establish a safe haven for Catholics. But not many Catholics settled there or elsewhere in the colonies, and when Protestants outnumbered Maryland's Catholics the latter found themselves less than welcome. It did not help that England fought wars against Catholic Spain and Catholic France. In time the small numbers of Catholics found more acceptance, but they did not receive full civil rights until the American Revolutionary Era.

If religion accounted for most hostility between those who got here first and those who followed, other issues periodically caused conflict. The colonists wanted good workers and offered incentives for persons bringing in white indentured servants. Eventually white southerners decided that slaves better served their needs. The colonists looked askance at some other potential workers. The English periodically shipped convicts to the New World to serve laboring sentences for misconduct, but not many before the 18th century. After passing the Transportation Act of 1717, England sent about 50,000 convicts to America for sentences of seven to eleven years and occasionally longer. Among these unfortunate persons were hardened criminals, thieves, rapists and thugs, but they also included "respectable tradesmen fallen on hard times, artisans who had forsaken their crafts out of desperation or dissipation or both."[9] Needless to say, the receiving colonies were none too fond of English policy.

Colonists worried that these felons would be found "repeating the same Crimes" for "which they were Sentenced at Home."[10] Benjamin Franklin asked in 1759, "What good mother would introduce thieves and criminals into the company of her children . . . ?"[11] Receiving criminals was bad enough, but the colonists also believed that the felons carried infectious diseases with them.[12] Attempts to outlaw this traffic were vetoed by the British.[13]

Religious, economic and moral issues lay at the bottom of colonial opposition to newcomers, but nationality was also a factor. Maldwyn Jones reminds us that at "one time or another immigrants of practically every non-English stock incurred the open hostility of earlier comers."[14] This hostility was even directed at small numbers of persons such as French Huguenots and Acadians from Canada. The large scale immigration of Scots-Irish and Germans after 1717 triggered the greatest uneasiness about non-English stock. The New England Puritans, while persecuting members of the Society of Friends, had no desire to see any non-Puritans reside in their midst, especially if they were poor. In 1729 a Boston mob attempted to halt the unloading of a ship of such immigrants. A few years later another Massachusetts mob nearly destroyed a Presbyterian church.[15] While religion and nationality accounts for some of this hostility, New Englanders also worried that the Scots Irish might be paupers who would become wards of the public. While still viewed at times with suspicion, Protestant Irish were more welcome in Pennsylvania and along the back country of the southern colonies.

The Germans, however, caused misgiving in Pennsylvania about their alleged clannishness and desire to speak their own language, prompting Benjamin Franklin's oft-quoted remark that "Palatine Boors" might Germanize Pennsylvania.[16] Didn't they have their own newspapers and churches? And what would eventually happen if interpreters were constantly needed to translate German legal documents? Anticipating future debates about language, Pennsylvanians looked to the schools to Americanize immigrants. The colony established charity schools "whose purpose it was to Anglicize the Germans." Because the Germans opposed the schools, the program was never fully implemented; the last such school closed in 1763.[17]

In spite of the misgivings of many colonists about particular groups of immigrants, European settlers discovered the colonies to be in fact more tolerant than the land they departed. The colonial labor shortage made the English and the colonists ignore differences among the immigrants. In 1740 Parliament passed a naturalization act that was liberal for its day. Persons who resided for seven years in the colonies and who took an oath as Protestants could become English citizens. Jews were exempted from the religious test and so were Quakers, who did not believe in taking oaths. Later other groups such as the Moravians, who also objected to oaths, were exempted.[18] There were limits to liberalization: the English still excluded Roman Catholics, few in number, from naturalization.

Ethnic factors played only a slight role during the American Revolution. One exception was the Scots who were mostly loyalist.[19] The Revolutionary era itself proved to be a victory for toleration. The new states disestablished churches, the Constitution outlawed religious tests for office, and minority groups like the Catholics now worshiped openly.

In drafting the Constitution, the founding fathers said little about immigration. No doubt many agreed with George Washington who wrote in 1785, "let the poor, the needy and the oppressed of the Earth,

and those who want Land, resort to the fertile plains of our west country, the Second Land of Promise, and there dwell in peace, fulfilling the
first and greatest commandment."[20] Some delegates were uneasy
about immigrants who might not share American values, and the
drafters of the Constitution debated whether foreign-born citizens
should serve in Congress, but in the end the Constitution permitted
them to be eligible. The only major limitation facing immigrants was
the Constitutional provision that the President and Vice-President had
to be "natural born." Nor did the first Congress seriously consider
halting immigration. The federal naturalization statute of 1790 permitted white immigrants to become citizens after two years residence
in the United States.

This does not mean that Congress took no interest in immigration.
A few expressed fears that the "common class of vagrants, paupers and
other outcasts of Europe" were coming to America, but no federal law
was passed to prevent them from doing so.[21] During the 1790s both
the Federalists and Republicans worried about particular groups. Federalists fussed about "wild Irish" revolutionaries entering, while the
Republicans feared that some exiles from the French Revolution
might not agree with American principles of Republicanism. However, the Federalist-dominated Congress did not enact large scale measures to restrict immigration. The legislators did raise the requirements
for naturalization and passed alien acts granting the president the right
to deport certain classes of allegedly undesirable newcomers. When
the Republicans won the elections of 1800 these laws were allowed to
lapse and the period required for naturalization was set at five years.[22]
Congress was content to allow the states to regulate immigration for
the next 75 years. Indeed, the federal government did not even begin
to count arriving newcomers until 1820.

Before the federal government began regulating immigration in
1875, several states enacted their own restrictive laws and established
immigration commissions to deal with the rising tide of immigrants.
These included bans on criminals. As early as the 1780s Pennsylvania,
Massachusetts, South Carolina and Virginia banned persons convicted
of a crime; but New York, the main port of entry, did not bar criminals until 1833.[23]

As for poor immigrants, states such as Massachusetts required mas-
ters of vessels to provide security for those mostly likely to become
paupers.[24] New York imposed a variety of restrictions to keep out per-

sons deemed undesirable, including criminals and those with certain diseases. New York, however, was not entirely opposed to immigration, only those thought to be unfit for residence in the state. In 1847 the state organized a board of Commissioners of Emigration to work with immigrant aid societies to help newcomers by protecting them from fraud and to develop a more efficient system to control immigration.[25]

As immigration grew after 1830 so did anxiety among native-born Americans. Before the Civil War incoming Irish prompted the most concern. The Roman Catholic Irish arrived in growing numbers even before the potato famine struck in the late 1840s. To many Americans the Irish seemed to be overwhelming their cities' poor houses and asylums. Nativists accused European governments of deporting their paupers so that "the burden of their support might be placed on the American people."[26] And in another economic charge, immigrants were alleged to drive down the wages and status of American workers. Worried Americans said that the "enormous influx of foreigners will in the end prove ruinous to American workingmen, by REDUCING THE WAGES OF LABOR TO A STANDARD THAT WILL DRIVE THEM FROM FARMS AND WORKSHOPS ALTOGETHER, OR REDUCE THEM TO A CONDITION WORSE THAN THAT OF NEGRO SLAVERY."[27] Maria Monk's *Awful Disclosures of the Hotel Deu Nunnery* (1836) added another reason for anxiety about Catholics. She claimed that her personal experience at the Hotel Deu Nunnery permitted her to witness a den of vice and iniquity.[28]

Historian Dale Knobel has traced the development of nativist groups during these years of increased immigration and rapid social and economic change. Many were older fraternal organizations that provided their members with a sense of brotherhood and tangible economic benefits. But many adherents grew anxious in the face of the new immigration, and they sought to define what it meant to be an American. They perceived alien threats to American society, especially the "menace" of Roman Catholicism.[29] Such fears were fed by the publication of pamphlets and books that insisted America faced a Catholic invasion and danger. In the 1840s Samuel F.B. Morse, inventor of the telegraph, echoed such concerns in published newspaper letters and a pamphlet entitled *A Foreign Conspiracy Against the Liberties of the United States*. Controversies erupted over Bible reading in the public schools, the ownership of parish property, and public support of religious schools.

Nativist fraternalism proliferated. "Its proven structure and ritual, its emphasis on mutual support and independence, and its identification of unrestricted immigration and naturalization with threats to personal autonomy gave midcentury nativistic fraternalism strong appeal," reports Knobel.[30] Groups such as the Sons of '76, the Order of United American Mechanics, and the American Brotherhood appeared and gained members, but the Know Nothings were largest and most important organization.[31]

The Know Nothings had a limited electoral success in some states, but eventually they split over the slavery issue. Moreover, while anti-Catholicism was strong, the nation still prized immigrants for their contributions to the growing economy. Even the fraternal orders and the Know Nothings did not advocate immigration restriction. Rather, they wanted to change the naturalization laws so that immigrants took longer than five years to become citizens. Historian Tyler Anbinder put it, "Most important, they believed that immigrants could not be sufficiently 'Americanized' in five years." They wanted a 21 year period for naturalization, though a few radicals wanted to bar the foreign born from voting.[32] Such a change required action by Congress, but the national legislature ignored such requests.

In 1875 the Supreme Court held state rules about immigration unconstitutional. As a result the federal government entered the field of immigration regulation. For the next twenty-five years, Congress barred certain classes of immigrants, such as paupers, criminals and the insane, and in the 1890s established Ellis Island as the main receiving station for the millions pouring into America in those years. These laws passed in the late nineteenth century kept out few immigrants.

Having a greater impact was the first major restriction aimed at a nationality group, the Chinese. Racism prompted this action. In 1875 Congress forbade the admission of prostitutes, a law in part aimed at Chinese women. Then came the 1882 ban on most Chinese immigration. Welcomed at first as desirable workers by the railroad builders and promoters, Chinese immigrants soon found themselves facing discrimination and a rising chorus demanding their exclusion. The depression of the 1870s, especially acute in California, gave birth to a Workingmen's Party, whose platform included halting Chinese immigration. The officers of the Workingmen's Party were blunt: "We have made no secret of our intentions. . . . Before you and the world, we declare that the Chinamen must leave our shores. We declare that white men, and women, and boys, and girls, cannot live as the people of a great republic should and compete with the single Chinese coolies in the labor market."[33]

The emergence of labor unions as a force in the anti-alien movement dates from the conflict in California. Even labor groups in the eastern states, where few Chinese lived, sponsored anti-Chinese rallies.[34] Anti-Chinese leaders also argued that these immigrants were socially and morally inferior to whites and that as a separate race they could never be assimilated into American society. Congress agreed, and barred most Chinese for ten years and periodically extended the ban until it was repealed in 1943.[35]

A new phobia emerged in the 1880s about immigrants: fear of the alien radical, which was fed by violence. When a bomb exploded during a labor rally in Chicago in 1886 it triggered anxiety about the danger of radicalism to America. Although Chicago authorities had no solid evidence on the identity of the bomb-thrower, they nonetheless arrested six immigrants and one American-born anarchist. They were convicted and sentenced to die.[36]

Anti-Catholicism and antisemitism by no means disappeared after the Civil War. Old stock Americans feared that too many Jews and Catholics were entering. In the 1880s and early 1890s the Iowa-based American Protective Association (APA), with its message of anti-Catholicism, gained strength, especially in the Midwest. The APA was not strictly anti-immigrant. Its members, for example, took an oath never to vote for a Catholic whether American-or-foreign born, never to hire one, and to promote the "American" language in the schools.[37] As it became more anti-foreign it lost some of its support among Protestant immigrants. Moreover, its message of blaming all economic woes on Catholics and warning of a Catholic seizure of power appeared too absurd to many Americans. Consequently it lost strength and collapsed in the 1890s.[38]

Jews were smaller in numbers than Catholics, but they too became the target of nativists. Populist agitators blamed Jewish bankers for their economic troubles, prominent Gentile clubs banned Jewish members, and fashionable resorts turned away Jewish guests.[39]

Beginning in the 1880s greater numbers of Jews and Catholics began to arrive from the southern and eastern regions of Europe, and by 1896, immigrants from those areas surpassed the numbers from northern and western Europe. This shifting pattern made critics of immigration search for a scheme to stem the flow. The Immigration Restriction League, founded in the 1890s by elite Bostonians, proposed a literacy test for incoming immigrants. Such a test would bar adults (those age 16 or older) from entering if they were unable to read and write in some language. Its proponents knew that potential immigrants from southern and eastern Europe were more apt to be illiterate than those from northern and western Europe; hence this was a way to keep out the former. As Senator Henry Cabot Lodge, a member of the League, said, "the literacy test will bear most heavily upon the Italians, Russians, Poles, Hungarians, Greeks, and Asiatics, and very light, or not at all upon English-speaking emigrants or Germans, Scandinavians, and French." During the economically depressed 1890s Congress listened to Lodge and passed the test, but it was vetoed by President Grover Cleveland, and the legislators did not have enough votes to override it.[40]

With the return of good times after 1900 xenophobia temporarily lessened but by no means disappeared. Racism directed at Asians was particularly strong. Japanese immigrants began to arrive in the 1880s, just as the Chinese were being excluded. Historian Roger Daniels points out that it did not take long for West Coast anti-Japanese sentiment to develop. With labor leaders; James D. Phelan, mayor of San Francisco; and the San Francisco *Chronicle* leading the way, pressure to exclude Japanese newcomers began to build. The Asiatic Exclusion League and trade unions urged federal action. When the San Francisco school board segregated Japanese pupils in 1906, President Theodore Roosevelt was confronted with a diplomatic problem. Not wanting to offend Japan, but willing to see immigration halted, Roosevelt persuaded the board to change its order and the Japanese government to stop giving visas to Japanese laborers.[41] Koreans, whose numbers were small in the United States, were also included under the ban because Korea was under Japanese domination.

Japanese wives of the immigrants could still come to Hawaii and the United States. Some were "picture brides," women who married by proxy Japanese male immigrants they had never met. Congress finally ended this flow in the 1920s when it barred further Japanese immigration. Japan and some American officials had suggested a quota, such as that given to Europeans, but the legislators rejected this proposal.[42] According to the 1870 naturalization act the only immigrants who were eligible to become citizens were whites and persons of

African descent. In 1922 the Supreme Court held that white meant "Caucasian" and that Japanese immigrants were not Caucasians.[43] Congress simply banned all persons ineligible for naturalization.Moreover, Californians passed discriminatory laws against the Asian immigrants. In 1913 California by a three to one vote barred these Japanese nationals from owning or leasing land.[44]

A few thousand Asian Indians had come to the United States around the turn of the century, mostly as agricultural workers.Yet even a few prompted protests against their presence. In Bellingham, Washington, white workers drove 700 Asian Indians across the border into Canada.[45] Finally, in 1917 Congressional legislation barred their entry. Moreover, those Indians, like Japanese immigrants, already in the United States were denied naturalization rights. Several had applied for and received naturalization before a test case reached the Supreme Court. In 1923 a unanimous court held that Asian Indian immigrants were not white within the meaning of the naturalization act and hence ineligible for citizenship or immigration.[46]

After 1924 among East Asians only Filipinos were untouched by the immigration restriction laws. Following the United States' annexation of the Philippines as a result of the Spanish American War, the Supreme Court declared that Filipinos were nationals, but not citizens, with the right of emigration to the United States. They were nonetheless not welcome in the West. They had begun to arrive in substantial numbers during the 1920s when there was a demand for western agricultural laborers. In time they found themselves excluded from movie theaters and other public facilities and they encountered discrimination when trying to find housing. Several incidents of violence occurred during the late 1920s and early 1930s. Finally, in 1934 at the instigation of labor unions and organizations such as the Native Sons of the Golden West and the Commonwealth Club, Congress granted the Philippines an annual quota of 50 until 1946, the date set for independence. Then they would be barred as were other Asians.[47]

Because the number of Asians was very small compared to Europeans, the exclusion of Asian immigrants did little to dampen the growing flow of immigrants coming to America, which reached record numbers between 1900 and 1914. These numbers were anxiously watched by those Americans who remained opposed to Jewish and Catholic immigrants. Playing upon the fears of Catholicism Wilbur Franklin Phelps founded a magazine called *The Menace* in 1911.

Historian John Higham reports that its circulation reached one million within three years. Another fanatical anti-Catholic periodical was *Watson's Magazine*, published by the former Georgia Populist leader Tom Watson.[48] As in the past anti-Catholic zealots portrayed the Roman Catholic Church as a threat to American values.[49]

The most famous incident of antisemitism occurred in Atlanta, Georgia, in 1915 when an angry mob lynched Leo Frank, a Jewish businessmen. Frank was arrested and accused of the murder of 13 year-old Mary Phagan who worked in Frank's co-owned pencil factory. Frank's innocence was clear to his supporters at that time, but the jury nonetheless convicted him. Much to the delight of Atlanta bigots, he was sentenced to hang. However, Governor John M. Slaton commuted his sentence to life imprisonment. This was too much for some Georgians, who stormed the jail and seized Frank. Within hours he was hung from "a tree near Mary Phagan's birthplace."[50]

The alleged tendency of Jews toward criminality raised again the association of immigrants with crime. In 1908 New York City's Police Commissioner, Theodore A. Bingham, wrote a piece for the *North American Review*. He singled out Jews, saying that, although Jews were only one quarter of the city's population, "half of the criminals" were Jews. He said, "They are burglars, firebugs, pickpockets and highway robbers . . . . but though all crime is their province, pocket-picking is the one to which they take most naturally."[51] Bingham's factually incorrect statement brought a storm of protest from the city's Jewish community, and he apologized a few months later.[52]

Many Americans believed that other newcomers were also prone to crime. Italians were believed to be violent; some were thought to be members of the mafia or the black hand that terrorized immigrant neighborhoods. In 1890 David G. Hennessy, police chief of New Orleans, was murdered. His last words were allegedly, "The Dagoes did it." Residents believed that Italian gangsters were responsible for the killing. When a jury refused to convict those put on trial, an angry mob broke into the prison and lynched eleven of the accused.[53] Newspapers across the land expressed regret at the incident but indicated their opinion that Italians were a particularly violent people. The *Baltimore News* reported, "The Italian immigrant would be no more objectionable than some others were it not for his singularly blood thirsty disposition and frightful temper and vindictiveness."[54] Such charges were repeated by other papers and public officials.[55]

As the anti-foreign voices grew in the late 19th and early 20th centuries, they found a new argument to restrict Europeans: racism. While prior objections had been based on economics, crime, health, morality, religion and fear of radical alien ideas, now the restrictionists argued that the peoples of southern and eastern Europe were distinct races who were inferior to the so-called races of northern and western Europe.

A variety of politicians, patriotic groups and scholars endorsed these ideas.[56] Madison Grant's *The Passing of the Great Race* (1916) warned against "race" mixing and the threat of continued immigration.[57] The Immigration Restriction League declared in 1910, "A considerable proportion of immigrants now coming are from races and countries, or parts of countries, which have not progressed, but have been backward, downtrodden, and relatively useless for centuries. If these immigrants 'have not had opportunities,' it is because their races have not made the opportunities; for they have had all the time that any other races have had."[58]

The latest newcomers, ran the argument, simply could not fit into American society. Harvard graduate and Boston Brahmin Prescott F. Hall, executive secretary of the Immigration Restriction League, told Congress in 1919, "The Italians, however fitted intellectually, have certain traits that unfit them for coming to our country for years to come because of certain traits known to all, that unfit them to receive the ballot or to be in any case recipients of American citizenship."[59]

Practically no public figure could out bigot Edward A. Ross, professor of sociology at the University of Wisconsin, in the belief that the latest wave of immigrants was inferior to the older ones. In *The Old World in the New: The Significance of Past and Present Immigration to the American People*, published in 1912, he declared that immigrants were bringing untold problems to America and that their mixing would lead to a decline of American intelligence. He concluded by writing that "the Mediterranean peoples are morally below the races of northern Europe is as certain as any social fact."[60] Ross even believed that the "frequency of good looks in the American people" would fall in the face of immigration: "It is unthinkable that so many persons with crooked faces, coarse mouths, bad noses, heavy jaws, and low foreheads can mingle their heredity with ours without making personal beauty yet more rare among us than it actually is. So much ugliness is at least bound to work to the surface."[61]

Ross was known as a progressive, a supporter of governmental programs to check American businesses' abuses and aid the less fortunate members of society. Many progressives shared his belief in immigration restriction, but many others such as Frances Kellor and Jane Addams, did not, and they formed organizations to assist the incoming millions with programs of "Americanization."[62]

Responding to the rising xenophobia Congress did add to the list of those barred. In 1903 the legislators prohibited among others, "idiots, insane persons, epileptics, and persons who have been insane within five years previously . . . professional beggars; persons afflicted with a loathsome or with a dangerous contagious disease . . . polygamists, anarchists."[63] The addition of anarchists was in response to the assassination of President William Mckinley by an anarchist, American-born Leon Czolgosz.[64] But these restrictions did not seriously limit the flow of immigration, and many legislators wanted greater controls on migration to America.

It was amid growing concern about immigration that Congress established the Dillingham Commission in 1907 to investigate immigration and make recommendations about policy. Named after its chairman Senator William Dillingham of Vermont, the Commission labored for four years and issued a report of 42 volumes of useful material. Most of the Dillingham Commission's volumes were devoted to economics, trying to determine the impact of mass immigration upon the American economy and American workers. The Commission asserted that the post-1890 immigrants were economically inferior to the older European types, and it wanted fewer unskilled newcomers to come to America. This pleased labor unions such as the American Federation of Labor, which had endorsed a literacy test since 1897. The Commissioners also examined the issue of pauperism. It gave little comfort to those arguing that immigrants were draining the public and private sectors in seeking charity, but it did not include a number of social services in its calculations, nor did it do a cost benefit analysis that characterizes the modern debate about immigrants and welfare.[65]

As for crime, the Commission reported, "No satisfactory evidence has yet been produced to show that immigration has resulted in an increase in crime disproportionate to the increase in adult population."[66] However, the Commission did assert that the children of immigrants were more apt to be criminals than were the children of native-born Americans and that immigration had contributed to the changes "in

the character of crime in America."[67] In particular it singled out violence and prostitution, and claimed that Italians were especially connected to the rise in criminal violence.[68] These charges were hardly
sufficient to form the basis for immigration restriction, but they raised
again an old theme of the association of immigration and criminality.

At bottom its bias formed the basis of its conclusions that peoples
of southern and eastern Europe were inferior to those of northern and
western Europe, and hence should be restricted. The ban on Asians also
should be maintained said the Commission's majority. The Commissioners final recommendation was for a literacy test, such as that proposed by the Immigration Restriction League.[69]

The Dillingham Commission prompted defenses of the new immigration from scholars, such as Isaac Hourwich, who rebutted its
conclusions about the economic impact of immigration and attacked
its recommendations in *Immigration and Labor*, published in 1912.[70]
Hourwich also dealt with crime and pauperism. He argued that the
new immigration differed from the old mainly in numbers not quality, that it did not harm the United States economically, and that the
Dillingham Commission's conclusions were based on prejudice not
hard facts. He concluded, "It is to be hoped that the sound reason of
the American people will prevail, and that, after intelligent discussion,
they will reject the panacea of restriction as they have the greenback
and free-silver cure-alls."[71]

Congress ignored such pleas, however, and finally passed a literacy
test on the eve of America's entry into World War I. President Wood-
row Wilson, vetoed the bill, but Congress overrode the President and
it became law.[72] Now newcomers would have to be literate in order
to pass through Ellis Island.

Immigration dropped substantially, but this was mainly due to the
interruption of commerce caused by the outbreak of World War I in
August, 1914. Immigration had fallen steadily since that date; hence
the precise impact of the test was unknown during the war. While the
war itself cut the immigrant trade, it also fostered increased pressure to
halt immigration and end potential disloyalty. Former President Theodore Roosevelt was particularly outspoken in favor of 100 percent
Americanism.[73] Hysteria broke loose on German Americans, and any
"hyphenated" Americans considered potentially disloyal. Roosevelt
put it, "We are convinced that today our most dangerous foe is the for-
eign-language press and every similar agency, such as the German-

American Alliance, which holds the alien to his former associations and through them to his former allegiance. We call upon all loyal and unadulterated Americans to man the trenches against the enemy within our gates."[74]

It seemed as if the war against Germany in Europe had degenerated into a "War against German America."[75] Germans, who had won the admiration of many other Americans because of German science, music, literature and intellectual achievements, now were viewed with hostility. German submarine warfare and atrocities in Belgium received much unfavorable coverage in American newspapers, and German Lutheran churches were viewed with suspicion if they used the German language and if their ministers refused to support the sale of war bonds. To dispel fears of disloyalty, many Lutheran churches switched to English and individual pastors proclaimed their loyalty to the United States and their support of the war effort.[76] Many German Americans Anglicized their names, bought liberty bonds and publicly denounced Germany. Some parochial schools stopped teaching the German language, and German-language publications switched to English.[77] Such professions of loyalty were not enough for Governor William L. Harding of Iowa. In May, 1918, he issued a proclamation "that prescribed English as the sole medium of instruction in public, private, and denominational schools and as the sole means of communication in public addresses and conversations in public places, on trains, and over the telephone. Persons who did not understand or speak the English language were instructed to conduct religious worship services in their homes."[78]

The fact that some foreign-born radicals opposed the nation's participation in World War I and intervention in Russia in 1917 did not help the cause of those resisting immigration restriction. After the war, some Americans feared that the Russian revolution would be exported to the United States; consequently many radical aliens were rounded up and deported.[79]

Like the Civil War, the Great War drastically curtailed immigration to America, but what would the future bring? It had been hoped by the leaders in the Americanization movement that they could mold foreigners into good Americans by teaching them civics, English and the values of American society. Settlement houses, schools and evening programs all aimed at these goals. Many proponents of Americanization became disillusioned, and the movement fell apart during and immediately after World War I and the national mood once again emphasized restriction. As Higham wrote, "Thus, while the movement for the redemption of the alien ebbed in 1920, the old drive for the rejection of the immigrant passed all previous bounds."[80] This rejection headed in the direction of drastic curtailment of immigration, a policy much beyond the bounds of old fashioned nativism.

The issue in the 1920s was how not whether to radically restrict immigration and complete 50 years of federal regulation. In 1921, when over 800,000 immigrants arrived, it appeared that the literacy test would not seriously interfere with migration to America. Moreover, there were rumors that millions more wanted to come to America. A Congressional committee told Congress that "between 2,000,000 and 8,000,000 persons in Germany alone wanted to come to the United States." And another committee claimed, "If there were in existence a ship that could hold 3,000,000 human beings, the 3,000,000 Jews of Poland would board it to escape to America."[81] Moreover, growing numbers of southern and eastern Europeans were literate, which meant that a test originally designed in the 1890s was insufficient as a deterrent in the 1920s.

After the war a revived Ku Klux Klan (KKK), which attacked Roman Catholics, claimed millions of members; part of its credo was immigration restriction. Writers joined Ross and Grant in warning against the "danger which Nordic America faced from Mediterraneans and Alpines."[82] Antisemitism received new life from Henry Ford's newspaper, *The Dearborn Independent*, which thundered against an alleged international Jewish plot to dominate the world.[83] In this climate the demand for cutting immigration from southern and eastern Europe became overwhelming.

The American Federation of Labor; patriotic societies; the newly formed American Legion; the Immigration Restriction League; the National Grange; the Junior Order, United American Mechanics; and intellectual racists and eugenicists were more respectable than the KKK, and they had more influence in Congress. They differed in their views, with some using racist arguments and the American Federation of Labor claiming, "If the products of our mills and factories are to be protected by a tariff on articles manufactured abroad, then by the same token, labor should be protected against an unreasonable competition from a stimulated and excessive immigration."[84] Business groups such as the National Association of Manufacturers and the U.S. Chamber of Commerce still wanted a supply of cheap labor, but even some business leaders were won over to immigration restriction.[85] Nor could friends of immigrants, such as social workers and the Immigrant Protective League of Chicago, stem the nativist tide.[86]

The inability of prior restrictions, including the literacy test, to halt mass immigration from southern and eastern Europe prompted Congress to find a new formula. It was found in the national origins quotas, which radically reduced immigration. In passing the acts of the 1920s Congress drew upon the expertise of eugenicists and others who believed that the peoples of northern and western Europe, called "Nordics" or "Anglo-Saxons" were superior. In 1920 the House Committee on Immigration and Naturalization had made Harry Laughlin, a prominent eugenicist, its "expert eugenics agent."[87] Representative Albert Johnson, one of his followers and an admirer of eugenic thinking, led the charge in Congress for reductions in immigration and favoritism for northern and western European nations.

The first quota law, that of 1921, set a total of about 360,000 for European nations. Each European nation received a quota of that figure based on its proportion of the foreign-born population in the 1910 census. This gave northern and western European nations slightly over half the visas.[88] The law was meant to be temporary, and although it cut European immigration substantially, restrictionists wanted the numbers reduced further, especially for southern and eastern European nations. Congress obliged and cut the total and pushed the year back to 1890, which worked to the disadvantage of those nations sending large numbers after that date.[89] This change, too, was temporary and finally another system, the national origins quotas, was put into effect in 1929. Congress fixed the total at approximately 150,000 with the national origins quotas giving each European country a proportion equal to its share of the white population according to the 1920 census. While basing the quotas on the total white population and not just the foreign born gave southern and eastern European nations a greater share than did basing them on the foreign-born population as of 1890, it still drastically cut their allotments from their virtual open immigration before World War I.[90]

Those who protested against the new system represented urban districts with high proportions of immigrants, immigrant organizations, immigrant aid societies, and spokesmen for business and agricultural interests.[91] But the pressure to reduce immigration was too strong for these groups to defeat it.[92]

No doubt fears of immigration's alleged adverse impact upon American workers played a role in the enactment of legislation in the 1920s. So did the belief that the United States was being overrun by radicals, the diseased, criminals and morally unfit immigrants and that too many Jews and Catholics were arriving. But the triumph of the national origins quotas coupled with Asian exclusion demonstrated that Washington wanted the nation's ethnic make up to remain as it was in 1920. Italians had averaged 158,000 annually in the early 20th century, but Italy now had a quota of only 5,802. Greece fared even worse, with an allotment of 307.[93]

There was no reason to believe that President Calvin Coolidge, reflecting the national mood, would not sign the law. He had written, "There are racial considerations too grave to be brushed aside for sentimental reasons. . . . The Nordics propagate themselves successfully. With other races, the outcome shows deterioration. . . . Quality of mind and body suggests that observance of ethnic law is as great a necessity to a nation as immigration law."[94] The President signed the act.

The door had been closed to Asians and severely limited for Europeans, but where would new low wage workers come from? Southern blacks migrating north helped to relieve labor shortages in northern cities, and in the Southwest the shortage of labor would be filled by leaving the Western Hemisphere untouched by national origin quotas. Congress pondered the issue of numerical quotas for the Western Hemisphere, but the legislators rejected them. Americans, especially in the Southwest, thought no better of Mexicans than they did of Italians or Russian and Polish Jews. Labor unions, patriotic groups, and eugenicists believed that Mexicans should be banned. Representative John Box of Texas regarded Mexicans as "illiterate, unclean, peon masses" who came from a "mixture of Mediterranean-blooded Spanish peasants with low-grade Indians who did not fight to extinction but submitted and multiplied as serfs." He wanted no part of Mexicans who created the "most insidious and general mixture of white, Indian, and negro blood stains ever produced in America."[95]

In the end Box was outvoted by those who worried about the impact of quotas upon American relations with her Latin neighbors and by persons who desired a ready supply of low cost workers that Mexico could supply.[96] Mexico received no quota and was only covered by the general restrictions, such as a head tax and bans on prostitutes, illiterates, and persons with infectious diseases. Even these provisions of the law had little impact. The border between the United States and Mexico was loosely supervised (there was no border patrol until 1924), and if they could not meet the immigration laws' requirements, Mexicans could cross, work and live in the United States illegally.[97]

The hunger for low wage Mexican laborers disappeared rapidly during the Great Depression that began in 1929. Faced with massive relief problems and long lines of unemployed workers, state and local governments sent these immigrants back to Mexico. Still others, faced with unemployment and the prospect of little or no relief, left on their own.[98]

That Mexican immigrants were unwanted in the 1930s was part of the general hostility to immigrants during that era. The State Department, with President Herbert Hoover's backing, issued instructions that the "likely to become a public charge" provision of the immigration restrictions be strictly enforced. In the early days of the Depression this enforcement was hardly necessary, for there were few jobs available for immigrants.[99] With the triumph of Nazism in Germany and that nation's spread throughout Europe, many Jews and other potential refugees looked to the United States for a haven. But neither Congress nor the public wanted to take in many persons fleeing persecution. Nor would President Franklin Roosevelt initiate or support action to aid refugees. Thus, during the 1930s only 528,000 immigrants managed to come to the United States. In the decade before World War I, twice that many had arrived in a single year on several occasions.[100]

The economy alone does not explain the opposition to immigration. Antisemitism was strong during the 1930s, and Jewish organizations were reluctant to agitate for the admission of Jewish refugees. With antisemitic groups such as the German-American Bund and the Christian Front making noise and the popular radio priest Father Francis Coughlin ranting against Jews, such reluctance is understandable. Even the small quotas enacted in the 1920s were too much for some members of Congress; they wanted the quotas reduced further.[101] They did not need to pass further cuts, for some quotas themselves remained unfilled.[102]

Those wanting to help German children escape were frustrated in Congress. Edith Rogers of Massachusetts and Robert Wagner of New York introduced a bill to bring 20,000 German children to the United States outside of the quotas. The hearings generated sympathy, but also revealed strong opposition to immigrants. John B. Trevor of the American Coalition of Patriotic Societies, who had played a key role in advising Congress in formulating the national origins system, vigorously opposed the bill, as did the American Legion and the Daughters of the American Revolution. One witness during the hearings declared, "I say if we are going to keep this country as it is and not lose our liberty in the future, we have to keep not only these children out of it but the whole damned Europe."[103] Moreover, one senator promised to filibuster it if the bill ever got out of committee. It never did.[104]

Conditions deteriorated during World War II. While the United States could not have halted the Holocaust, David Wyman has argued that several hundred thousand Jews could have been saved.[105] But the Roosevelt administration dragged its feet. The administration said that it did not want to divert resources from winning the war. The President was also aware of antisemitism, which peaked during these years, and did not wish to challenge the national mood. Racial and ethnic tensions were hardly ideal during the war; some 110,000 Japanese immigrants and their American-born citizen children found themselves interned in virtual concentration camps. They were, as historian Roger Daniels wrote, "Prisoners Without Trial."[106]

By the time of World War II, the United States had erected a tight system of immigration controls. After allowing the states to regulate immigration until 1875, the federal government entered the scene. Responding to the growing demands for restriction of immigration, Congress enacted a host of minor barriers, banned Asians and finally established the national origins quotas for Europeans, thus ending a century of virtually unrestricted immigration from Europe. The traditional need for workers was overwhelmed by the fears that too many criminals, diseased persons, paupers, and undesirable and unfit immigrants were entering from Asia and southern and eastern Europe. Only the acute need for cheap laborers kept Congress from barring Mexicans and others from Central and South America. The nation had decided upon a course that differed substantially from the virtual open door of a century before.

# 2

## The New Movement to Restrict Immigration

*"We are a nation of immigrants. But where do you draw the line? We have to stop being the 911 of the world."*
—Bette Hammond, President of STOPIT (Stop the Out-of-Control
Problems of Immigration Today, 1992).

IN A REMARKABLE TURNAROUND after World War II, the United States adopted new immigration policies to make possible a whole new wave of mass immigration. Foreign policy considerations combined with a booming economy, at least until the 1970s; ethnic lobbying and growing toleration in postwar America to bring out these changes. The process of reopening the door began cautiously in 1943 when, at the prodding of the Citizens Committee to Repeal the Chinese Exclusion acts, Congress gave China an annual immigration quota of 105. The law also permitted Chinese resident aliens to become naturalized American citizens. Legislation passed for other Asians in 1946 was also modest, permitting immigration annually of only 100 and naturalization rights for Indians and Filipinos.[1]

The problem for those reformers who wanted to accept European refugees after the war was the small national origins quotas for many countries, which were kept in check by the McCarran-Walter Immigration Act of 1952. Congress had to enact special legislation for displaced persons and refugees. The legislators admitted about 600,000 European refugees when they passed the Displaced Persons acts of 1948 and 1950 and the Refugee Relief Act of 1953. Three years later President Dwight Eisenhower established a precedent when he used the parole power to admit Hungarian refugees fleeing the abortive Hungarian Revolution of 1956.

Although Congress reaffirmed the national origins quotas in the McCarran-Walter Act, they were being bypassed by these special laws and decisions of presidents, and finally national origins quotas were replaced with a system of preferences when Congress passed the Immigration (Hart-Celler) Act of 1965. Family unification received the highest priority (74 percent of the visas) but those with special skills and refugees were also among the preference categories.

The Hart-Celler Act did not allow many places for refugees but Congress passed the Cuban Adjustment Act of 1966 to permit hundreds of thousands of Cubans to come to the United States. The Cuban exodus slowed after 1973, but a new crisis erupted in 1980. In an effort to win asylum, a Cuban bus driver drove his minibus through the gates of the Peruvian embassy in Havana. When Castro removed the police from the embassy, thousands of Cubans stormed it. These dissatisfied people demanded asylum, and Castro responded by saying that any Cubans who wanted to go to the United States could do so through the Cuban port of Mariel. Approximately 125,000 headed for Florida without prior clearance from American authorities.

Larger than Cubans in number were the Indochinese refugees. President Lyndon Johnson signed the new immigration act in 1965, the same year that he escalated the American presence in Vietnam. The war itself created hundreds of thousands of refugees in Vietnam and the American bombing of Laos and Cambodia drove thousands more from their homes. When the American-backed government in Saigon fell in 1975, it set in motion a flow of refugees to the United States. By the late 1990s the Indochinese population in America exceeded one million. In the middle of the Indochinese crisis, Congress adopted a new refugee policy, the Refugee Act of 1980.

Even when Congress attempted to tighten immigration policy, the result ended in increases. Such was the case with the Simpson-Rodino Act of 1986. Simpson-Rodino, formally the Immigration Reform and Control Act of 1986 (IRCA), was a compromise fashioned after years of debate about undocumented immigration. By the early 1980s pressure on Congress to "do something" about undocumented immigration was building, the result was passage of IRCA that gave an amnesty to almost three million illegal aliens. On the face of it, because IRCA outlawed the employment of undocumented workers (employers' sanctions), it might appear that it was a restrictive law; but Congress failed to provide for an effective system to keep out undocumented aliens. It thus turned out to be a rather generous amnesty without teeth for employers' sanctions.

The last major change in immigration policy, the Immigration Act of 1990, also increased immigration. Congressional immigration advocates, with the backing of the ethnic, religious, and nationality immigrant lobby, pushed to revise the system. They were assisted by an emerging group of economic interests, largely firms seeking high-tech immigrants. As passed, the act increased immigration 35 percent.

The impact of these new policies was dramatic. In the late 1940s immigration to the United States ran about 250,000 annually.[2] After 1950 the figures increased substantially, and this rapid growth is one of the keys to understanding the renewed restrictionism. Immigration averaged about 325,000 annually in the 1950s and ran about 600,000 in the 1980s. When the Immigration Act of 1990 went into effect, it, along with refugee admissions and the 2.7 million IRCA immigrants, pushed immigration to all time highs in the early 1990s. In 1991 over 1.8 million persons were recorded, the largest figure in America history. With IRCA visas taken care of, the figures dropped by the mid-1990s, but were nearly 900,000 in 1992 and 1993. They were just under 800,000 in 1994 and a little over 700,000 in 1995 and back up over 900,000 in 1996. The Immigration and Naturalization Service (INS) thought the numbers would grow again in the late 1990s.[3] Once again immigration to America was truly a large movement of peoples.

These figures are gross amounts. The United States government stopped keeping data on return migration in 1957. The careful work of Guillermina Jasso and Mark R. Rosenzweig estimated that emigration varied by nationality group, with persons from the Western Hemisphere more apt to return than Europeans and Asians. They suggest that emigration between 1961 and 1980 for some countries could have been as high as 40 percent. This is a large figure, but compared to the higher figures around the turn of the century, it is not out of line with that era's emigration.[4] A more popular number used during the 1990s debates about immigration is that about 200,000 persons emigrated from the United States each year, so that the net gain annually was about 700,000 if legal immigration was 900,000.

These figures do not include illegal immigration. Estimating the number of undocumented immigrants has proved to be controversial, with those wanting to halt the illegal flow usually employing high figures to dramatize the numbers. During the debates over illegal immigration, the commissioner of immigration, Leonard Chapman, claimed in 1976 that some twelve million such immigrants resided in America. Such a high number was absurd; the IRCA amnesty ten years later produced just under three million.[5] More realistically in 1996 the INS estimated that there were five million undocumented aliens in the United States and that their numbers were increasing about 275,000 annually.[6] Add these to net flow of legal migrants and one can see that talk of one million newcomers pouring into the United States annually during the 1990s is not fanciful.

A second key to understanding the resurgence of restrictionist sentiment is the fact that the country of origin changed substantially after 1970. White Europeans, who had dominated the historical patterns of immigration to the United States, came in much smaller numbers after the 1965 immigration act went into effect. By the 1980s Europeans made up only about 10 percent of the migrant stream. Traditional sending countries, Italy and Germany for example, accounted for only a small fraction of the new immigration. Indeed, when Congress included a new provision for "diversity" visas in 1990 immigration law, the legislators aimed to increase immigration from those lands sending relatively few immigrants after 1965. They had in mind white Europeans, and especially the Irish.[7] From the late 1970s the United Kingdom was the leading European source until the late 1980s and early 1990s, when new legislation and refugee flows made it possible for Polish, Irish, and Russian immigration to increase.

Mexican immigration, which had been growing since 1950, became the largest flow, although in some years after 1970 refugees from particular nations topped the Mexican figures. Behind Mexico as major sending countries stood China, Taiwan, Korea, the Philippines, Jamaica, India, the Dominican Republic, Vietnam, Cuba, Haiti, Iran, Cambodia and Laos. Asians accounted for over 40 percent of the new immigrants after 1980, with Mexico and the Caribbean nations accounting for most of the rest.[8] Immigration to America had become truly global with several cities of high immigration claiming newcomers from over dozens of nations. But most of the latest migrants were not white; they were people of color from the so-called third world nations, who were largely responsible for the changing demography of the United States.

Third, it is important to realize that about three-quarters of post-World War II immigrants have settled in six states: California, New York, Texas, New Jersey, Florida, and Illinois. Whatever impact immigration has on American society and the economy it is first felt in those areas. One cannot visit southern California without being aware of the new immigration. It is no surprise that California became the center of immigration debate, especially when its economy turned sour in the late 1980s and early 1990s.

As revealed in public opinion polls, when immigration increased and changed Americans reasserted their traditional ambivalence or hostility toward immigrants. It is, of course, risky to utilize such polls to gage the public's attitudes. For a starter, some were very crudely carried out, especially the first such polls. The questions asked varied and were often vague. Nor is it certain that the public was well informed about immigration, about their numbers, areas of settlement and impact upon the United States. A 1993 *New York Times*-CBS poll, for example, revealed that 68 percent believed that "most of the people who have moved to the United States in the last few years are here illegally," up from 49 percent in 1986.[9] Finally, restrictionist organizations have sponsored some of the polls, making their results suspect.

Even allowing for the limitations of polling, the consistency of responses is impressive. No poll after 1945 indicated a majority by those responding for an increase in immigration; all reported opposition to increases or at best ambivalence about newcomers. Pro-immigration support probably peaked in the 1960s, and after 1990 polls indicated increased opposition to immigration and a desire to cut the numbers.[10]

A Roper poll conducted in 1990 found that Americans were worried about their growing population and that about half polled thought the nation took in too many immigrants. Not many favored increases.[11] Three years later a Gallup poll found stronger opposition to the new immigration.[12] These results were consistent with *Business Week*/Harris survey of 1992 and *Newsweek*'s 1993 poll.[13] A *New York Times*-CBS poll taken in 1993 found that 61 percent wanted immigration to be decreased, a figure up from the Gallup poll. A *USA Today* poll taken about the same time discovered 65 percent wanted a decrease in immigration compared to only 6 percent favoring more immigrants. Results of polls taken in the next few years by several groups yielded similar findings.[14] Negative Population Growth (NPG), a group which favored sharp reductions in immigration, commissioned Roper to undertake a survey in December 1995. Roper found that 83 percent favored reductions and that 70 percent of 1,978 Americans polled wanted immigration to be no greater than 300,000 annually.[15] A national poll conducted by the *Wall Street Journal* and NBC/News, published in March 1996, revealed that 52 percent of those responding wanted to halt all immigration, illegal and legal, for five years.[16] Locally, the Field polls conducted in California, where the immigration issue was particularly controversial, showed increased sentiment against immigration during the 1990s.[17]

Even residents of New York City, a place generally sympathetic to large numbers of immigrants, indicated uneasiness in a 1993 poll. An Empire State Survey found that half of the residents agreed with the statement, "Immigration has made this city a worse place in which to live."[18]

The polls indicated that Americans were particularly opposed to large numbers of immigrants from the third world nations. In 1990 *Newsweek* found a desire to decrease immigration from Latin America and Asia, with a closer division about Africans. It should be noted that African immigration was very small in that year.[19] Three years later the same journal reported even stronger opposition to immigrants from Asia, Latin America, and especially the Middle East. Only 18 percent thought that it should be made easier for people to migrate from the Middle East while 61 percent thought it should be made more difficult.[20] *USA Today*, asking different questions, found growing opposition to Haitians, Iranians, Cubans, Mexicans, and Vietnamese. In contrast, the Irish, once a scorned group, were perceived of being of great benefit to the United States.[21] In a careful analysis of polls over many years, Tom Espenshade and Maryann Belanger concluded, "Latin America/Caribbean migrants in general, and Mexican migrants in particular, rank somewhere near the bottom in terms of how Americans view immigrants from different parts of the world."[22]

The polls also reveal strong opposition to illegal aliens, especially while Congress was debating IRCA and again in the 1990s when illegal immigration became a major issue in some states and Congress. Persons being polled were quick to agree that undocumented immigrants were harmful economically, but the same polls revealed that many believed that illegal aliens took jobs that Americans did not want. Respondents also favored tough governmental action to cope with them. These included tightening border restrictions, outlawing the employment of illegals and denying them governmental benefits. Nor was an amnesty popular.[23]

Early polls were crude and reveal little about the respondents. Yet they do indicate that the affluent and better educated were more favorably inclined to accept large numbers of immigrants.[24] Later polls give us similar clues about those groups opposing or favoring immigration. Highly educated and well-off respondents tended to be pro-immigration while those of less skill and lower income and education tended to be opposed. Politically conservative and older persons were also more apt to be against liberal immigration policies as were those living in the South and Midwest.[25] A detailed study by Thomas Espenshade and Katherine Hempstead, based on the *New York Times-CBS* poll of 1993, revealed somewhat similar results. That study also focused on the respondents' sense of alienation and isolationist sentiment toward foreign affairs.[26] A poll financed by the Pew Charitable Trusts and conducted with 1,975 adults in 1996, revealed something about the religious views of respondents. White Evangelical Protestants were found to be more opposed to immigrants than were other major religious groups.[27] The NPG-sponsored poll released about the same time found that persons describing themselves as strongly religious were more apt to want cuts in immigration.[28]

In polls broken down by ethnicity, white Americans appear to be more inclined to favor decreased immigration or believe that immigrants are a burden than were other groups.[29] In the 1995 NPG's Roper poll 77 percent of whites, the highest percent of any group, wanted immigration to be capped at 300,000 annually.[30]

In the 1994 California election Proposition 187 provided another test of attitudes of whites and others toward immigration. The belief that immigrants, especially illegal ones, are a drain on the taxpayer was the driving force behind Proposition 187. Proponents of 187 largely worked at the grass roots, operating at first on a low budget. Among the leaders were Barbara Coe, Ron Prince, and former INS employees Harold Ezell and the late Alan Nelson. Like other grassroots leaders, Coe, later head of the California Coalition for Immigration Reform, operated out of her living room. Nelson was the most experienced in matters of immigration as he was head of the INS during part of the Reagan years, but Ezell had been the western head of the INS. Proposition 187 aimed to bar illegal aliens from receiving welfare and educational benefits. It denied illegal aliens access to the state's public educational systems, nonemergency medical care, and cash benefits. Service providers were required to report suspected illegal aliens to California's attorney general and the INS.

In January 1994, it did not appear that 187 had a chance to pass because Save Our State (SOS), the organization pushing the measure, had only 100 days to gather 384,974 signatures. Although the SOS campaign was virtually ignored by the media, volunteers set up tables in front of supermarkets. Many of these were manned by members of Ross Perot's United We Stand America. Perot, twice defeated running as an independent for the presidency, did not oppose immigration, but many of United We Stand America members did. When it was clear that SOS could not gather the signatures required to put 187 on the ballot, conservatives donated money and the SOS group paid $150,000 to professional signature-gathers. Anti-immigration Assemblyman Rick Mountjoy, a hero in the eyes of SOS, gave $43,000. By the end of 100 days they "had collected some 600,000 names."[31]

Even with so many signatures 187 still had to face the test of voters. In early fall, its future was uncertain. It was opposed by most mainline ethnic, religious, and educational organizations in the state. It also drew the opposition of national figures such as Jesse Jackson and conservatives Jack Kemp and William Bennett. Rising anti-immigrant sentiment, a poor state economy, and Governor Pete Wilson's endorsement helped change the voters' mood. Wilson's support brought that of the Republican Party and made it a partisan issue.[32] To the delight of SOS it carried by a vote of 59 to 41. Immediately after the election, however, it was challenged in the courts. California federal Judge Mariana Pfaelzer ruled the provision denying an education to illegal aliens unconstitutional and blocked enforcement of Proposition 187.[33]

In the hotly contested battle over California's Proposition 187 whites strongly supported it. The Catholic Church in California came out against Proposition 187, but white Catholics voted 58 to 42 percent in favor, about the same figure as the state at large.[34] Asian Americans, in the one of the few tests available about their views on immigration, favored 187 by a 57 to 43 margin.[35] Latino voters, mostly

Mexican Americans, in California, offended by the rhetoric and provisions of Proposition 187, were the major group to vote against it. They were particularly outspoken in their opposition to this proposition; they perceived it—quite correctly—as being aimed not just at undocumented aliens but also at the Latino community generally.[36]

Immigration is an important issue especially for Mexican-Americans, or in the 1993 words of Peter Skerry, "Immigration has probably been the issue most visibly identified with Mexican Americans in recent years. It is arguable the most important issue facing Mexican Americans today."[37] At the same time, poll data indicate that Hispanic Americans were also uneasy about the increase in immigration. Several polls taken after 1970 revealed that they worried about immigrants, especially illegal ones, taking their jobs.[38] The 1983 poll by V. Lance Tarrance and Associates and Peter D. Hart Research Associates, commissioned by the restrictionist Federation for American Immigration Reform, turned up a Latino majority in favor of an amnesty, but also a majority concerned about illegal immigration and favoring employer sanctions.[39]

Another extensive poll was the Latino National Political Survey carried out in 1989 and 1990. Recognizing that "Hispanics" represented a number of groups, the survey looked at three of them: Mexicans, Puerto Ricans and Cubans. Immigration was only one of a number of key issues explored. Not unexpectedly, Mexicans and Cubans proved to be more pro-immigrant than were Puerto Ricans. Nonetheless, more than 65 percent of all three groups either "agreed" or "strongly agreed" that the nation was accepting too many immigrants.[40] The recent poll commissioned by NPG, found that 52 percent of the nation's Latinos wanted fewer immigrants, even though Hispanic organizations were making liberal immigration a major issue.[41]

Just why had this split occurred? It was not always so. Prior to the 1970s, Mexican-American leadership did not support liberal immigration. David Gutierrez's careful analysis dates the changed perspective of Mexican-American leaders and organizations beginning during the 1950s. Some were angry at the INS, especially its tactics during "Operation Wetback" in 1954, when hundreds of thousands of Mexican illegal immigrants were deported. Leaders began to blend the issue of rights for Mexican Americans with those of Mexican immigrants. Organizations still supported border controls, but they were beginning to shift their attitudes about immigrants.[42]

The rise of a new militancy and sense of identity among many young Americans of Mexican descent helped trigger the change. By the 1970s both old line and new organizations, in part responding to the militancy of the young Mexican Americans in what was called the Chicano movement, had placed immigration politics high on their list of priorities. As Gutierrez explains, "By the late 1970s most major Mexican American and Chicano activists and civil rights organizations had reversed their traditional positions and were actively supporting the civil and human rights of Mexican immigrants in the United States, a stance they maintained well into the 1980s."[43]

In 1977 a conference attended by 2000 Mexican Americans and representing their major organizations was held in San Antonio. The First National Chicano/Latino Conference on Immigration and Public Policy opposed tighter controls on undocumented immigration and linked the cause of Mexican Americans with Mexican immigrants.[44] Most organizations have retained this stance, even though, as Gutierrez notes, "if public opinion polls are any indication—and their reliability as a gauge of Latino-American opinion is hotly disputed—Americans of Mexican descent remain about as deeply divided on these issues as other Americans are."[45]

African-Americans' responses to polls and voting over 187 also indicated considerable opposition to, and ambivalence about, immigration. A 1990 Gallup poll revealed a substantial majority of African Americans favoring cuts in immigration.[46] Two years later the *Business Week*/Harris Poll turned up similar negative feelings toward immigrants and indicated that 73 percent of black Americans believed that employers would rather hire immigrants than African Americans.[47] Some researchers have found that Korean merchants would prefer to hire Hispanics over African Americans.[48] In spite of these frictions, Thomas Espenshade's and Katherine Hempstead's analysis of 1993 *New York Times*-CBS data did not find such opposition to immigration among blacks.[49] Just over half of black voters cast a yes ballot for 187 in 1994.[50] One year later the NPG-sponsored poll conducted in December 1995 revealed that nearly three quarters of blacks surveyed wanted fewer immigrants.[51]

African Americans had a tradition of opposing immigration, or at least a number of prominent black leaders did.[52] This position was generally somewhat reversed after 1970 when immigration began to increase. African-American political leaders generally supported a liberal immigration policy. During the debates over Proposition 187, Jesse Jackson urged black voters to reject it. In October Jackson told a black audience to remember that "today we're celebrating Columbus Day. Let's not forget when Columbus landed in America he was considered to be an illegal alien and undocumented worker." He assailed Proposition 187, and John Mack, the Los Angeles Urban League president, condemned it as racist.[53]

Jackson's approach was part of his Rainbow Coalition, an amalgam of peoples of color seeking justice in the United States. On the whole, the Black Caucus in Congress backed the Hispanic Caucus on immigration issues. During the congressional debate over IRCA, blacks worked with Hispanics to either modify or defeat the bill. Lawrence Fuchs notes, "On all other key votes on Simpson-Mazzoli in 1984, the Black Congressional Caucus hewed to the line with Mexican-American congressional leaders."[54] When passage of the final bill occurred in 1986, the Black Congressional delegation split, but so did the Hispanic Caucus.[55] When Jackson was running for President in 1984 he assailed the pending bill harshly, saying it was restrictionist and racist. He even marched to the border in July 1984 to demonstrate to black and Hispanic youth his opposition to employer sanctions.[56]

Critics of immigration, with a good deal of evidence, claim that blacks generally oppose immigration because they are harmed economically by the newcomers, but that black leaders in Congress prefer to work with Hispanics. In making this analysis the Midwest Coalition to Reform Immigration reported in 1996, "Moreover, none of the Black Congressional representatives in Illinois were willing to take on the issue. As one congressional aide told us, 'you are probably right [about the adverse economic impact of immigration upon blacks], but we won't take any stand that threatens to split our political unity with Hispanics.' "[57]

Of course blacks in Congress had other reasons to favor a generous immigration policy. For one thing, they knew that the reforms of 1965 made possible increases in black immigration from the West Indies, and that the Immigration Act of 1990 increased immigration from Africa. For another, black leaders took the lead in criticizing the federal government's policy, begun under President Ronald Reagan, of denying most Haitians refugee status and the policy of interdiction of Haitians and returning them to Haiti. Representative Charles Rangel of New York was quick to point to the government's favorable reception to

Cubans or Chinese students and its hostility toward Haitians. Rangel, who represented Harlem, wanted equal treatment for Haitians.[58]

Yet, in spite of these reasons for supporting generous immigration, some blacks took a contrary view in the late 1980s and 1990s. Following enactment of IRCA, the National Association for the Advancement of Colored People (NAACP) refused to join Latino groups in calling for a repeal of employers' sanctions. California NAACP chair Hazel Dukes said blacks were frustrated by jobs being given to persons "who can't speak English." In New York City, the Rev. Calvin Butts, who heads the prestigious Abyssinia Baptist Church, called for keeping immigrants out of the city because New York lacked the resources to serve them.[59] In 1996 Harvey C. Roberts, a black management consultant, wrote in a Florida African-American newspaper, "Few American Blacks here have not been aware of the harmful way immigration disproportionately floods our labor pools, our neighborhoods and our schools. . . . We American Blacks must once again be vigilant and again diligently mount an intense protest movement against high immigration."[60]

Many blacks in Florida believed that immigrants took their jobs or that blacks received unfavorable treatment by governmental authorities. Miami, the center of Cuban and later other Hispanic immigrants, was one of the main cities experiencing conflicts involving blacks and immigrants. Resentment against Cubans played a major role in the 1980 riot in that city.[61] Another riot there in 1989 pointed again to the hostility of African Americans toward immigrants. One bitter youth told the *Wall Street Journal*, "See that store? We burned the sucker. It was run by goddamn Latins."[62]

Moreover, Asian-run stores in black neighborhoods proved to be a source of considerable conflict. In New York City and elsewhere local black leaders instigated boycotts of Korean greengrocer store owners, asserting that they treated black customers rudely and would not hire black employees. In New York one of the boycotts ended in the destruction of the store and forced two others to close.[63] A 1995 poll by the *Houston Post* found considerable conflict between African Americans and Asians over stores in Houston's black neighborhoods.[64]

Nowhere were these conflicts more acute than in Los Angeles. In April 1992 when a nearby jury refused to convict white Los Angeles police officers of brutality against a black man, a beating witnessed on national television because it had been recorded by an observer, the city erupted. Several days of rioting and looting by African Americans and Latinos left many Korean stores destroyed. More than 2,000 stores (700 of which were owned by Koreans) were damaged or destroyed, resulting over $1 billion worth of damage. One year later only one quarter of them had reopened.[65]

Five years after the riot, sparked by both government and private aid, most stores had been rebuilt and repaired but many Korean store owners, whose businesses were not destroyed, nonetheless decided to move. Moreover, the Los Angeles Black-Korean Alliance, formed to improve relations between the two groups, broke up several months after the riots.[66] Because Hispanics were over half of those charged with rioting, the riots took on a multiethnic character. Yet there can be no doubt that many African Americans bitterly opposed some of the new immigrants.

Violence against Asian immigrants was by no means confined to blacks, and it was one of the disturbing signs of a growing uneasiness and hostility toward immigrants after 1980. One of the most prominent incidents occurred in Michigan when Vincent Chin was murdered in 1982. Chin was beaten to death with a baseball bat. His white attackers apparently believed he was Japanese and thus responsible for the hard times of the American automobile industry.[67] Other violence has been reported against Vietnamese and Cambodians and at places of worship.[68] The U.S. Civil Rights Commission said in February 1992 that although hate crimes are often not reported or not counted by many jurisdictions, an alarming number of such incidents had been recorded in recent years. Hopes for better data came with the enactment of the Hate Crimes Statistics Act, the result of which improved data collection beginning in 1991.

These signs of opposition to immigration took organized form after 1979. A variety of new groups called for the United States to take action to halt illegal immigration and substantially cut legal immigration. With support in Congress, they became a new lobby. Although similar to past organizational efforts to restrict immigration, the new anti-immigration lobby also used different arguments about immigration and its impact upon American society. The leading restrictionist group to emerge is the Federation for American Immigration Reform (FAIR), founded in 1979 and based in Washington, D.C.[69] Restrictionists organized other national groups after 1979, among them the American Immigration Control Foundation (AICF), formed in 1983.

In the early 1990s, a number of ad hoc or local groups appeared at the state level. Most prominent was SOS and Glenn Spencer's Voice of Citizens Together (VCT), both organized in California. Even the New York City area turned up a group: Tri-Immigration Moratorium (TRIM), organized in 1995. These organizations, some of which publish newsletters, do not have a uniform policy on immigration, and some are small in membership and not especially active.

Anti-immigration groups have taken direct action. They picketed federal governmental offices protesting their ineffectiveness in stemming immigration. They have also demonstrated outside of the Ford Foundation for its support of Hispanic organizations that support what they call "open borders." Activists proclaimed May 7–9, 1995, "Immigration Awareness Week," in Washington, D.C. In addition to rallying behind at that time presidential candidate Patrick Buchanan, who favored cutting immigration, they picketed the White House.[70]

Glenn Spencer, head of VCT, led a special caravan from California to New Hampshire, designed to reach the latter state just before the 1996 presidential primary. Called "Operation Paul Revere," the caravan, which consisted of several vehicles, aimed to publicize immigration issues along route, especially illegal immigration.[71]

One bizarre direct action took place several months later, in the spring of 1996. A group calling itself "U.S. Citizens Patrol" roamed through the San Diego airport trying to deter undocumented immigrants from using the facility. Their T-shirts with the letters "U.S. Citizens Patrol" in gold were no doubt designed to look official and persuade persons that they were an arm of the INS. The group's members denied that they harassed passengers but instead claimed that they asked airline ticketing employees to check all identification as required by the Federal Aviation Administration. The FBI said it had no complaints of law breaking, but a federal judge issued a temporary restraining order after a news conference called by Latinos led to a shouting match when members of the patrol appeared. The judge said the patrol would have to confine its activities outside the terminal because its inside actions were disrupting airport security. The INS added that it did not need the assistance of the U.S. Citizens Patrol.[72]

On July 4, 1996, demonstrators in favor of Proposition 187 marched outside of the federal building near University of California at Los Angeles (UCLA), where they found themselves confronted by the Progressive Labor Party and immigrant rights advocates opposed to 187.

Shouting led to violence as soda cans were thrown at the pro-187 pickets. Eventually the police were called to quell the violence but not before six people were injured and one treated at the UCLA Medical Center. An angry pro-187 supporter claimed, "One of the immigrant supporters was seen stomping on the American flag. I suspect that the flag stomper is also looking for the government that this flag represents to feed him, house him and take care of his medical needs."[73]

On election day in 1996, Barbara Coe, founder of the California Coalition for Immigration Reform, along with members of VCT, distributed fliers proclaiming "Only citizens can vote! Violators will be prosecuted!" While some governmental officials and immigrant-advocacy groups threatened her with legal action for "intimidating voters," her defenders insisted she compiled with the law and stayed 100 feet from the polling places. She was not indicted. The Mexican American Legal Defense and Educational Fund (MALDEF) claimed that its careful watching of Coe prevented her from intimidating prospective voters. Said one official, "We were watching very closely and had our people in Orange County patrolling to prevent any intimidation."[74]

Mostly the new groups aim at converting Americans and Congress to their cause. They publish books and pamphlets, run newspaper ads and conferences, and badger Congress to pass laws controlling illegal immigration and cutting the legal numbers. The titles of their sponsored works, *The Immigration Invasion, The Path to National Suicide: An Essay on Immigration and Multiculturalism*, or *The Immigration Time Bomb*, convey the sense of the dangers of immigration. Some writers, even if they are affiliated with the anti-immigration organizations, write on their own. Such was the case of Richard Lamm, former governor of Colorado, while on the board of directors of FAIR, spoke and wrote on his own. His major book, published in 1985, was co-authored with Gary Imhoff and entitled *The Immigration Time Bomb*.[75] The title of books published by main line publishing houses, such as Peter Brimelow's *Alien Nation: Common Sense About America's Immigration Disaster*, also warn of the dire consequences of American immigration policy.[76]

William Buckley's *The National Review*, the main voice of American conservatism, generally ignored immigration before the 1990s. But then it became outspoken in its criticisms of American policies, and it was joined by other conservative publications. One such journal is the Illinois-based Rockford Institute's monthly, *Chronicles: A Magazine of American Culture. The Social Contract*, published in Petoskey,

Michigan, and devoted to immigration issues, has a circulation of only 1,200, but it has been described as the "house organ" of the restrictionist movement. The emergence of new forces dedicated to cutting immigration does not mean that the pro-immigration lobby disappeared or gave in to the emerging anti-immigration sentiment. On the contrary, the pro-immigrant leaders ran well-organized campaigns to defend current policy. In recent years no groups have been more outspoken on immigration than the Hispanic ones, such as the National Council of La Raza and MALDEF. They want to maintain a generous policy and they see attacks upon Spanish-speaking immigrants as forms of bigotry or racism aimed at all Hispanics. A gathering of 450 Latinos in 1994 condemned the current immigration debate and declared, "In order to stop the immigrant bashing of our community, we must condemn the sensationalization of the immigration issue."[77] In October 1996, Hispanics staged their first major march on Washington. Among other things, the protesters wanted a new amnesty for illegal immigrants and no cuts in welfare benefits for those immigrants receiving them.[78]

Latino organizations have support from the ethnic, nationality and religions groups that became so important to the immigration cause after World War II. Thus, the National Council of Churches, the American Jewish Committee, and the Roman Catholic Church can be counted on to support a liberal policy. While older organizations remained active, new groups, alarmed by the rise in anti-immigration rhetoric, were formed. One such was the Asian-American Association, organized in 1996 by Marty Shih.[79] They also have the aid of civil liberties organizations and lawyers associations connected to immigration. Because of the economics involved, it is understandable that lawyers working with immigrants would want to see a generous policy. For the American Civil Liberties Union the issue was a national identity card favored by some restrictionists.

A number of these groups became affiliated with the National Immigration Forum, which was organized by Rick Swartz in 1982. It favors "the American tradition of welcoming newcomers" and aims to "dispel the myths that feed nativism and prejudice."[80] Under the leadership of Frank Sharry, its executive director in the 1990s, the Forum became effective in fighting against changes in legal immigration.

Books attacking immigration have generated rebuttals. In 1996 former journalist with National Public Radio Sanford Ungar, a professor at American University, published *Fresh Blood: The New American Immigrants.* While acknowledging problems with aspects of current policy, Ungar comes down squarely on the side of the pro-immigrant lobby. His book was heavily based on interviews with many newcomers, but he did survey some of the immigrant debate literature as well. Like so many defenses of immigration, he notes, "The United States is still a nation of immigrants, and by its very nature, it will always be one.... The principles and values involved in this concept are too basic, too fundamental to the soul of the country, to be thrown out for the sake of short-term political expedience or cyclical economic panic."[81] He ends his book apparently approving a quote from a hotel executive who helped many immigrants, saying, "There has never been any real basis for opposing immigration but racism, in one form or another. That is not what America is supposed to be about."[82]

Representing a variety of groups, individuals, and schools of thought, the new restrictionists nonetheless have found themselves united after 1980 in a growing debate about current immigration to America. They found plenty of things wrong, but their basic arguments centered on environmental concerns, the belief that the present immigration system was broken, the conviction that immigration was economically bad for the United States, and the fear that immigrants were seriously fragmenting American culture. Roy Beck's 1996 *The Case Against Immigration: The Moral, Economic, Social, and Environmental Reasons for Reducing Immigration Back to Traditional Levels* says it all.[83]

# 3

## Overpopulation, Immigration, the Environment, and the New Restrictionism

*"The litmus of immigration policy is the environment. . . . The resources of the environment are limited; minerals, soil, water, forests—all can be degraded through unwise use. Immigrants come to America hoping to increase their consumption of environmental resources. They soon succeed."*
—Garrett Hardin, *The Immigration Dilemma: Avoiding the Tragedy of the Commons*

THE FORMATION OF THE Federation for American Immigration Reform (FAIR) by environmentalists in 1979 marks the entrance of environmentalism into the modern immigration debate. Early restrictionist movements practically never touched upon the connections between the environment, population, and immigration. In 1914 A. Piatt Andrew, in defending the immigration of that day, noted that few newcomers went to the unsettled farming parts of America but rather that they went to overcrowded cities. "This is indeed a very serious phase of immigration with which our legislatures, Federal and State, must cope."[1] Yet, he did not discuss resources and the environment at all, and his solution to heavily populated cities was not immigration restriction but governmental plans to encourage the migrants to locate in uncongested areas.[2] If restrictionists in Andrew's day used population arguments, they said too many of the "wrong races" were coming to America. Such newcomers would overwhelm the allegedly superior peoples of northern and western Europe or lead to a racial amalgamation that they believed would be disastrous. For the most part, the debates immediately after World War II also avoided population issues.

It was during the 1960s that two books—Rachel Carson's *Silent Spring* (1962) and Paul Ehrlich's *The Population Bomb* (1968)—signaled a growing concern about the environmental degradation and population growth. Carson's best-selling *Silent Spring*, first excerpted in *The New Yorker*, pointed to the adverse affects of man-made pollution on the environment and the need for political action to control the negative impact of industrialization. However, she did not discuss immigration; rather her book was a warning about pesticides and other products harmful to the environment.

Environmentalism was not new in the 1960s; such groups as the hundred-year-old Sierra Club have existed since the late nineteenth century, and federal conservation policies date from about the same time, but environmental issues were not high on voters' minds right after World War II, or in 1962, when *Silent Spring* renewed interest in ecology. The first Earth Day, organized eight years later at the instigation of Senator Gaylord Nelson of Wisconsin, was not expected to be a major event, but it drew tens of thousands of participants across the nation. Since that time older environmental groups have gained in memberships, a variety of new organizations have appeared, and Congress has enacted bills to clear up the nation's rivers, land, and air.[3] The presidency of Ronald Reagan, an ardent proponent of economic growth and opponent of the environmentalists, caused membership in these organizations to continue to grow.[4] The major groups lost momentum somewhat in the early years of the Clinton administration, perhaps because many believed that Vice-President Albert Gore, who had a reputation as an environmentalist, would influence the administration to make pro-environmental decisions. This changed again with the 1994 elections.[5] After winning those November contests, Republicans quickly discovered that the public had not given them a mandate to eliminate popular environmental or conservation programs.

Growing organizational membership and the enactment of federal laws and regulations were clear signs that environmentalism was a popular issue. So were public opinion polls that indicated widespread support of the rules and regulations.[6] In California, the center of much anti-immigration sentiment, voters approved a 1985 proposition aimed at controlling toxic pollution by agricultural and chemical industries.[7]

Equally as important in triggering debate as Carson's *Silent Spring* was the publication of Paul Ehrlich's best-selling *The Population Bomb* in 1968. Allegedly written at the instigation of David Brower, longtime head of the Sierra Club, the book did not mention immigration. Rather, he warned of overpopulation in the world and about possible disastrous consequences in the near future. Eleven years later he published with Anne Ehrlich and Loy Bilderbak *The Golden Door: International Migration, Mexico, and the United States*, but this book did not recommend major immigration reductions.[8] Paul and his wife, Anne, have been wary about calling for huge cuts in immigration, although they have appeared on the boards of restrictionist groups. However, in a 1992 book devoted to discussions about immigration, population, and the environment, they wrote, "We can never have a sane immigration policy until we have a sane population policy.... our own view is that immigration adds important variety to our population and permits the United States to give refuge to people who really need it.... The immigration issue is extremely complex and ethically difficult, but it must be faced."[9]

Paul Ehrlich's concern about population received a brief acknowledgement in 1969 when President Richard Nixon established the Commission on Population Growth and the American Future, chaired by John D. Rockefeller. Rockefeller was a logical choice to head the commission, for he had already founded the Population Council to deal with population issues. The commission reported in 1972 about population goals for the United States, but said little about immigration, although it wanted the United States to adopt a policy to stabilize population. The commissioners wanted employers' sanctions to halt the flow of illegal immigration. Some commissioners wanted decreases in immigration as part of a population stabilization program; but the majority, pointing to humanitarian considerations and the contribution of immigrants to American society, favored the present level of immigration, which was about 400,000.[10] This report had no immediate impact on immigration debates; however, the U.S. government had already begun to participate in population programs in conjunction with other nations and the United Nations. These expanded after 1972, but were curtailed during the Reagan years when abortion was disputed. The *Population Bomb* and *Population Growth and the Amer-*

*ican Future* did trigger the formation of new groups, notably Zero Population Growth (ZPG), with a membership of about 40,000 in the mid-1990s. ZPG did not take a stand on immigration numbers, although it did favor action to stem illegal immigration. The organization said that "the United States should adopt an overall goal for immigration as part of its national population. This goal should be set in the context of a federal commitment to plan for demographic changes and to stop population growth."[11] Recognizing the shifting patterns of immigration, ZPG specifically insisted that immigrants and refugees "should be admitted equitably, without preference to race, national origin, color, religion, gender, or sexual preference."[12]

Immigration and population growth were not yet widely connected to environmentalism.[13] It was in 1977 that Gerda Bikales, later closely tied to FAIR and head of U.S. English, made the connection clear. Writing in *National Parks and Conservation Magazine* Bikales argued:

> Not so very long ago an article about United States immigration policy would have seemed out of place in a publication on environmental concerns; too social, surely, and outside the realm of interests of a readership dedicated to the preservation of the natural habitat.
>
> The continued degradation of the environment, a growing national awareness of the adverse effects of increased population pressures upon our natural resources and of the ensuing decline of the quality of life, the swelling stream of immigrants landing on our shores and crossing our borders, and an immigration policy incapable of coping with this invasion have changed our perspective during the past decade.[14]

Tony Smith, head of the National Parks and Conservation Association (NPCA), also wrote a piece about immigration and he too wanted his organization to take up the population issue. But in 1979, following a financial crisis in NPCA, Smith was ousted as president, and NPCA did not follow his advice.[15]

The reluctance of NPCA and ZPG to become involved in the growing immigration debate was echoed by the Sierra Club, which adopted a controversial pro-choice position and favored population stabilization, yet was unwilling to take a stand on immigration. It was this very reluctance led environmentalists to form FAIR, which has become the major force in the new restrictionist movement. While claiming only 70,000 members in 1996, FAIR runs a Los Angeles office in addition to its headquarters in Washington, D.C. It publishes a newsletter and sponsors studies about immigration. Moreover, FAIR's leaders, first Roger Connor and later Dan Stein, frequently appear in the media debating immigration and before congressional committees. Beginning in 1996, Dan Stein hosted a cable TV show discussing the issues surrounding immigration. FAIR also helped found the Center for Immigration Studies (CIS) in 1985. CIS's orientation is toward research. It sponsors many academic studies about immigration and population and provides information to those using the internet. Originally centered on environmental concerns, FAIR quickly branched out in its arguments about the need to limit immigration.

The founder and leader of FAIR in its early days was Dr. John Tanton, also the founder of U.S. English four years later (1983). Tanton has been a forceful presence in the immigration debates, a successful fundraiser and organizer, a writer, and the center of much controversy whether at FAIR or U.S. English. His critics have not been kind; he has been called a bigot and racist. One unnamed staffer of ZPG was particularly harsh. Tanton talks, he said "in very legitimate terms about protecting our borders and saving the nation's resources and so on. But the trouble is, after you've heard them, you want to go home and take a shower."[16] A one-time official in the Gerald Ford administration and later Spanish-language radio station official, Fernando Oaxaca, insisted that Tanton and his kind were "motivated by xenophobia and probably racism."[17]

Dr. Tanton's defenders, who praise him personally and politically, deny these charges and insist that Tanton is raising legitimate issues about the nation's future.[18] Richard Lamm commented in 1988 that Tanton is a "very concerned man who is asking questions that need to be asked. . . . That man is not a racist. Racism is our society is a motion for cloture. Accuse anybody of racism and it almost stops the debate."[19] The doctor himself answered, "I'm disturbed that people toss these words around so lightly. . . . Instead of debating the issues, they call you a racist."[20]

Whatever one calls Tanton there is no question about his dedication to environmentalism, conservation, and concern about population growth. He grew up on a farm in Michigan and became an environmentalist. He has been involved with Planned Parenthood, ZPG, the Sierra Club, the Audubon Society, and a number of local conservation projects in and around Petoskey, Michigan, where he practices medicine. From 1971 to 1974 he chaired the Sierra Club's Population Committee, and from 1975 to 1977 he was president of ZPG.[21] Tanton believes that the nation's environment cannot be saved unless the issue of population is faced; because a growing proportion of the American population increase is attributable to immigration, he concludes that immigration to the United States must be curtailed.[22] Only after ZPG refused to support immigration reduction did he form FAIR.

John Tanton was not the only environmentalist in the founding days of FAIR, or several other key restrictionist organizations, for that matter. FAIR's Thad Rowland had been active in Planned Parenthood, a member of a population committee, and a student of demography. He spent time in Mexico studying population before becoming one of the founding members.[23]

The first director of FAIR, Roger Conner, also found the path from population and the environment to immigration a direct one.[24] He had been working for several years in these fields when he met John Tanton at an Earth Day meeting. From this initial encounter the two became well acquainted and Tanton asked Conner to join FAIR as its first director when the organization was founded in 1979.[25]

William C. Paddock grew up in a small town in Iowa and in college became interested in agriculture and food supply issues. He also joined ZPG and was a founder of The Environmental Fund (1972), which he chaired during the 1980s.[26] Otis Graham Jr., the historian, also came to FAIR via his concern about land use, population, and the environment. Like so many others, he was influenced by Paul Ehrlich's *The Population Bomb*. Graham was perhaps the most liberal of the founding members and was especially sensitive about the charges of racism.[27]

The most politically conservative early leader and sometimes benefactor of FAIR was Sidney Swensrud. A successful businessman, he became chairman of the board of the Gulf Oil Corporation. He, too, grew up on a farm in Iowa. In addition to his business career, Swensrud became active in such groups as International Planned Parenthood and the Association for Voluntary Surgical Contraception before joining the board of FAIR.[28]

FAIR is not the only restrictionist group with its origins in population or environmental concerns. Both Population-Environment Balance and the Carrying Capacity Network (CCN), headquartered in Washington D.C., are rooted in these issues. Neither claimed particularly large memberships, perhaps only 17,000 for CCN and 7,000 for Balance in 1997. Balance, which also runs a California office, grew out of The Environment Fund (TEF). Initially TEF's focus was not immigration, but simply population and the environment. Its first newsletter to deal with immigration, appearing in 1981, discussed illegal immigration.[29] As immigration grew, TEF's concern with it expanded as well. In 1986 a TEF spinoff became a new organization, Population-Environment Balance, with a more direct focus on immigration. Balance's policy is "dedicated to public education of the adverse effects of continued population growth on the environment. . . . It advocates measures . . . that would encourage a responsible immigration policy for the U.S."[30] And it believes that "America's current immigration policy is a disaster."[31]

Balance does employ economic issues in its campaign against liberal immigration. For example, it insists that immigrants are taking jobs from American workers and that newcomers also use social services that cost the American taxpayer billions each year.[32] Yet, the thrust of its call for immigration reduction is based on its belief that the nation has too many people and that immigration is contributing nearly 40 percent of the American population growth. Overpopulation, in Balance's eyes, is placing excessive burdens on the nation's water supply, polluting the atmosphere, injuring the national parks and forests, and draining America's fuel supplies.[33]

From its beginning, Washington-based CCN also used economics to argue for immigration restriction. But, like Balance, CCN is mainly concerned with the interrelated "nature of environmental degradation, population growth, resource conservation, and quality of life issues." It maintains that 60 percent of current population growth in the United States is due to immigrants and their children, it sees resulting overpopulation as a major problem for the world and the United States, and it argues that immigration must be faced and substantially reduced.[34]

While ZPG expressed reluctance to tackle immigration, several other population groups were not. No group has been more outspoken than Negative Population Growth (NPG), originally located in Teaneck, New Jersey. NPG was founded by Donald Mann in 1972. Although it claims only about 18,000 members it has nonetheless been very outspoken on immigration and population issues. NPG sends letters to newspapers, prints and distributes short pamphlets and leaflets about the dangers of immigration, places ads in environmental groups' magazines, and in general has supplied members of Congress with a steady stream of arguments supporting decreases in the American population.[35]

Mann has also been on the advisory board of FAIR, and in turn his organization has been praised by FAIR's Dan Stein. In 1995 Sharon Stein, Dan's wife, became the Washington representative of NPG. Some environmental groups have rejected NPG's ads, and the organization has been criticized by ZPG for its harsh stand on population and immigration. Mann, for example, has urged that "we should give incentives to low-income people who agree to sterilization. We should make available free abortion to low-income people on demand. And companies should cut back or deny maternity leaves to women who have more than two children."[36] While such talk makes many environmental and population control advocates uneasy because of the early history of population movements' connection to eugenics and sterilization programs for the mentally ill and criminals, Mann replies that they are "afraid. They're too politically correct to talk about the real nitty-gritty issues."[37]

NPG's stress is on population and the environment, but the organization publicizes information about what it considers the adverse economic impact of immigration upon the United States. Moreover, Mann strongly sympathizes with those who see an adverse impact of immigration upon American culture. "Sometimes you feel like you're not in your own country," he has been quoted as saying, "on the golf course, I dare say that sometimes 70 to 80 percent of the people there are Asians."[38]

In California, Californians for Population Stabilization (CAPS) has been active for years in pushing for stronger environmental controls, policies to encourage smaller families and immigration restriction. Centered in Sacramento, CAPS was founded in the mid-1980s by members of a chapter of ZPG. Dissatisfied with ZPG's unwillingness to deal with immigration, the chapter's members broke away and established a new organization. CAPS has about 11,000 adherents, mainly from northern California. It centers its attention on environmental issues.[39] Thus, the organization argues that the presence of too many people in the United States is leading to degradation of the environment; and because immigration contributes a large share of population growth, it advocates a limit of only 100,000 to 200,000 newcomers annually. CAPS devotes most of its attention to California issues, and organized a Population Day at the state capitol in February 1996. On Population Day, CAPS called on its members to come to Sacramento to lobby their legislators about "out-of-control population growth," which is causing "water shortages, dwindling open space, increased pollution and congestion," among other things.[40] Joining CAPS members in talking to 60 legislative aides and 22 legislators were members of Balance, CCN, ZPG, and the Sierra Club.[41]

Yet, CAPS looks at the federal government and has joined with CCN and Balance in calling for an annual immigration limit of 100,000.[42] Moreover, CAPS sued Hewlett-Packard, unsuccessfully, for violating worker protection laws. CAPS claimed that the giant computer company was employing foreign-born computer programmers at salaries below the market. The executive director of CAPS said that employers were "skirting the law and depriving Americans of jobs."[43]

FAIR, CCN, Balance, NPG, CAPS, and many local environmental groups have not been able to convince ZPG to change its position. In 1994 California voters had to decide whether to approve of Proposition 187, which cut benefits for illegal aliens, including keeping such immigrant children out of the schools. As the campaign heated up, ZPG attacked 187 as "punitive, inhumane, and clearly unconstitutional."[44] Finally, as the immigration debate reached Congress in 1995, the organization issued a lengthy statement. Entitled "More Than Numbers: A ZPG approach to Immigration," it called for improved management to check illegal immigration but rejected pleas for supporting immigration reduction. It also wanted more research on the impact of immigration on the United States, the adoption of an overall population policy by the United States, placement of immigration in the context of a worldwide framework, and passage of a variety of measures to preserve the American environment and resources. In the end, it noted that the nation "has always been a nation of immigration, a legacy that has contributed to democratic principles and rich cultural diversity."[45]

It is significant that major national environmental groups, the Audubon Society, Friends of the Earth, the National Wildlife Federation, and the National Parks and Conservation Association, have not followed CCN, FAIR, or Balance in their call for immigration restriction. Obviously these organizations fear being targeted as racist. After all, Fernando Oaxaca claims that the people behind FAIR are a "bunch of crazies who came out of the environmental movement and think the environment is damaged by people, especially people different from themselves."[46] National organizations avoided the issue and concentrated on their individual concerns such as preserving bird sanctuaries or urging the government to protect the nation's parks and wilderness.[47] The Audubon Society has issued a vague a statement that demonstrates it dilemma: "Population growth cannot be isolated from factors such as poverty, lack of education and health care, unjust land tenure policies, and overconsumption of nature by the United States and other industrial countries. All of these factors must be addressed in our efforts to foster environmentally sustainable development at home and abroad."[48] The one group to take a stand on immigration was the Wilderness Society, which declared in 1996 that U.S. "birth rates and immigration rates need to be reduced."[49] Immigration per se was simply too controversial.[50]

On occasion they have signed joint statements with FAIR, but these have not endorsed immigration reduction. In 1991, for example, FAIR joined the National Wildlife Federation, the Wilderness Society, Planned Parenthood Federation of America, and other population groups to call upon the United States and "all the nations of the world" to make "an effective response to the issue of population growth a leading priority for this decade."[51] In 1991 FAIR along with sixty population and environmental organizations signed a *Priority Statement on Population*. It asked President George Bush to place population issues on the national agenda. The signers agreed that a "humane, sustainable future. . . . depends upon recognizing the common ground between population and the environment."[52]

But the issue remained a hot one, especially for the Sierra Club, the nation's most well-known ecology group.[53] With over 500,000 members and a budget of over $40 million in the mid-1990s, the club favored abortion rights and family planning, but resisted taking a stand on immigration.[54] As immigration grew, especially in California—the center of the club's activities—individual members urged that the club adopt an immigration policy. By 1990 several local chapters had formed committees on population, which were addressing immigration. One Sierra Club leader, Alan Weeden, a trustee of the Frank Weeden Foundation, provided the organization with funds for population work.[55] Weeden was a strong believer in the adverse connection between immigration and the environment. He wrote in a letter to the *New York Times*, "Continued high levels of immigration, now accounting for 30 to 50 percent of the country's population growth, carry a high environmental cost that cannot be sustained." Weeden added that it was hypocritical to favor both wilderness protection and high immigration.[56]

In 1991 the San Francisco Bay Chapter Population Subcommittee advocated net zero immigration (wherein the number arriving equaled the number leaving), but the chapter's executive committee did not endorse this stand. Instead, a Task Force on Immigration was set up, which did not report in favor of immigration restriction. Rather, it favored a dialogue on the issue.[57]

The Bay Area chapter's executive committee was responding to critics like Norman La Force, who wrote an angry letter to the club's national president. He told the club, "We can turn people away at our borders, but unless we change our consumption patterns we will still use up the world's resources at a disastrous rate. . . . I will not create eco-totalitarianism while I seek ecotopia. Nor should the Club."[58] The chair of the Bay Area's chapter's population committee resigned in protest when the chapter did not support his call for cutting immigration.[59]

That same year Frank Orem, who also was active in FAIR, became chair of the club's national population committee. Two years later, the national population committee put forth a four-point plan dealing with population and immigration.[60] Point four stated: "Net immigration to the United States and Canada (immigration minus emigration) should be reduced so that their levels are consistent with U.S. and Canada population policies."[61]

The statement was immediately challenged by the club's Ethnic and Cultural Diversity Task Force as racist. The task force believed that such positions were echoes of FAIR, which they regarded with disfavor. Diversity Task Force leader Vivian Li attacked the statement: "I cannot begin to describe the anger and rage of many club leaders and members over the proposed policies, particularly the section on immigration." She concluded, "Many members and leaders believe the policy is ill-conceived, insensitive and racist, and will greatly damage the club's ability to become a more diverse and inclusive organization."[62] The Diversity Task Force prevailed as the national Board of Directors refused to urge immigration restriction, a position repeated in 1996, when it issued the following resolution: "The Sierra Club, its entities, and those speaking in its name, will take no position on immigration levels or on policies governing immigration into the United States. The club remains committed to environmental rights and protections for all within our borders without discrimination based on immigration status."[63]

Still not satisfied with this position, several members in the Midwest began a petition drive to permit members to vote on the issue. They were joined by Bill Hill in Palo Alto and Ben Zuckerman at UCLA. A statement by Alan Kuper, Population-Environment Committee chair of the Ohio chapter, put it, "The purpose of this Petition Drive is to give the membership the opportunity to vote for a comprehensive, fundamentally environmental Population/ Consumption Policy consistent with Club tradition."[64] Kuper, an active environmentalist for years in Ohio, also decided to run for the national board of the Sierra Club. A key issue in his candidacy was immigration restriction as part of an overall population policy. The Sierra Club agreed to once again discuss the immigration issue in 1998.[65]

If restrictionists with an environmental focus have been unable to move their conservationist organizations, they nonetheless had outlets within the rising restrictionist movement. Many individual members of environmental groups, frustrated with these groups' unwillingness to tackle immigration, have joined CCN, FAIR, Balance, or local associations in the emerging restrictionist movement. John Tanton's name can be found as a founder of TEF, along with Garrett Hardin, who figures prominently in the immigration debates. Hardin was for years professor of Human Ecology at the University of California, Santa Barbara, where he authored a number of books and articles about ecology, biology, and ethics. His most famous essay was the "Tragedy of the Commons," published in 1968. The United States can only support so many people, he argues, and for the future of Americans we simply cannot take in large numbers of immigrants.[66]

Richard Lamm, former governor of Colorado, is another prominent figure in the new movement to limit immigration. As early as 1981 he told the readers of the *New York Times* Op Ed pages that we must cut immigration, although he did not use environmental or population arguments.[67] He did in *The Immigration Time Bomb*, co-authored with Gary Imhoff in 1985, and has done so since. In *High Country News* he argued in 1994 that Los Angeles's problems of "intolerable traffic, unhealthy smog, inadequate water, ethnic conflict all have their genesis in population. Acid rain, climate change, loss of ozone, disappearance of species, loss of habitat—whatever the issue, at its root is population."[68]

David Brower, long-time head of the Sierra Club, has served on the board of directors of NPG. Nick Ervin, conservation chairperson of the San Diego Sierra Club, noted in 1993 that one "sensitive component of the population issue domestically is immigration."[69] He concluded, "I firmly believe, nonetheless, that we do neither our homeland nor our planet (including its human members) a favor by acting as a continuing sponge from other lands."[70] Like so many environmentalists, Ervin cited the drain on American resources and, again like so many others, he claimed that because consumer-oriented Americans used such a high proportion of the planet's resources, a large American population was undesirable.[71] Edgar Wayburn, onetime president of the Sierra Club and well-known California conservationist, became a member of the board of advisers for CCN.[72]

Ric Oberlink was another frustrated Sierra Club member. In 1994 he wrote, "For over 20 years I have been proud to be a member of the Sierra Club. The Sierra Club has been a leader on almost every major environmental fight. . . . In recent years, I, and many other club members, have been disappointed in its unwillingness to confront the nation's number one environmental threat, population growth, and the immigration policy which causes it."[73] Oberlink channeled his concern about population into becoming the executive director of CAPS. When he resigned in December 1996, another environmentalist, Tom McMahon, became the new director. McMahon had worked with the U.S. Agency for International Development, handling population programs in Latin America, and had been a director for Population-Environment Balance.[74]

In early 1995 Balance help found the Coalition for United States Population Stabilization, which called for stabilization of the U.S. population by 2020 and limiting immigration to approximately 200,000 yearly.[75] The formation of this new umbrella group gave an opportunity for many local environmental organizations, located in states with strong conservationist movements or centers of immigration, to take a stand. Thus it included the Colorado Bird Observatory, Colorado Population Stabilization, and the Massachusetts Audubon Society as founding members. Other founding members were familiar names in the immigration restriction and environmental movements: Anne and Paul Ehrlich, CCN, NPG, Richard Lamm, David Brower, and the Weeden Foundation.[76]

Recognizing that the issue of immigration was becoming an controversial one within the conservation or environmental movement, the San Francisco Political Ecology Group (PEG) cosponsored a conference of groups in 1996 from both sides to "find common ground" and learn about other issues of mutual interest. Groups like PEG, the Sierra Club, and Greenpeace, which did not support immigration restriction, met with environmentalists who did.[77] Many wished to avoid the debate. Trish Sears said her Population Action International simply "doesn't partake of the U.S. immigration debate. Instead we look at global migration."[78] Others, like PEG's president, Brad Erickson, insisted that immigrants do not cause environmental problems. Rather, Erickson claimed, "many immigrant communities are unduly harmed by environmental hazards. They're disproportionately impacted by pesticides in the fields, and often live next to toxic dumps."[79]

While not resolving differences, the conference highlighted the dilemmas of environmentalists. They were often concerned with the nation's wilderness and its water supplies rather than urban toxic dumps and or the other environmental hazards faced by the poor in the nation's cities and immigrant neighborhoods.

FAIR attempted to meet this concern when it extended the environment argument in 1995, publishing *A Tale of Ten Cities: Immigration's Effect on the Family Environment in American Cities. A Tale of Ten Cities*, prepared by Leon Bouvier and Scipio Garling, matched cities of similar size with the crucial difference being the percentage of foreign-born. Using census and other data to compare the "family environment" the study focused on education, income, occupation, homelife, housing, cultural adaptation, crime, community and health: things "that contribute to a good environment for family life."[80] Not surprisingly, the authors concluded that cities with lower percentages of immigrants were superior places to live.[81]

FAIR, Balance, and CCN were not alone in the restrictionist movement in employing environmental concerns as a rationale for immigration restriction. The American Immigration Control Foundation (AICF), founded in 1983 and located in Monterey, Virginia, uses just about any issue to argue against immigration. Although illegal immigration, economics, multiculturalism seem to receive AICF's greatest attention, on occasion its newsletter features discussions that claim "immigration threatens resources."[82] AICF also publishes books that touch upon environmental issues, though it insists that the views of the authors are not necessarily those of AICF and its board of directors.[83]

*Social Contract*, published by John Tanton in Petoskey, Michigan, as could be expected, also argues that America must curb immigration for environmental reasons. Moreover, in a work written by Tanton and Wayne Lutton and published by Social Contract Press, the authors cite "Environment and Quality of Life" as one of the five major problems caused by immigration. In praising the advantages of small town or rural life (such as that found in Petoskey) and noting that many urbanites would like to live in such a pleasant environment, the authors write, "If reports can be believed, many urbanites would like to become ex-urbanites and enjoy some of these pleasures. We would like to keep that option open for them, but continued population growth, now substantially fueled by immigration, stands in the way."[84]

Others who contribute to the debate are freelance demographer and economist Meredith Burke and Lindsey Grant. Burke claims that the nation's farmlands are disappearing, that more cars on the roads have wiped out nearly "all potential air quality gains," and that population and immigration must be brought under control. Unless action is taken on these fronts "Demographic doom threatens us."[85] Lindsey Grant's *Juggernaut* used his environmental concerns to insist that America must reduce immigration.[86]

Both Peter Brimelow and Roy Beck, who have written the most sensational and arresting books published by mainline presses about the need to restrict immigration, concentrate on economics and social issues. Beck especially emphasizes economics, but he does believe that the nation needs to cut immigration in order to protect the environment and resources. Noting and praising the important work of the environmental movement in the last three decades, he insists that it has fallen short of its goals. One of the key reasons for this failure, he believes, is that America has too many people, which is heavily the fault of a liberal immigration policy. "Immigration," he writes, "has been a substantial cause of the negative environmental news that must be mixed among all the good. This is not because immigrants are environmentally bad people, but because they are people." He concludes by insisting that a replacement level immigration policy (when the number arriving equals the number leaving, or about 200,000 annually) would have been far better system than the current one; "instead the population is already about 265 million and headed to near 400 million by 2050. Virtually every aspect of U.S. environmental protection and quality—and the quality of life for America's human inhabitants—is changed because of that."[87]

Brimelow's attack on immigration rests only casually on environmental issues, but he too does state that immigration is bad for American resources. His case is vague and mostly limited to attaching the mainline environmental groups for not coming to grips with immigration.[88]

The most respected and prolific person to write about demography and its connection to immigration is population expert Leon Bouvier, who has been published by and associated with FAIR. He is widely quoted by anti-immigration organizations and individuals and enjoys a good deal of respect for his scholarly work. Bouvier was a demographic adviser to the Select Committee on Population of the U.S. House of Representatives and for the Select Commission on Immigration and Refugee Policy. He worked for the Population Reference Bureau until 1986 and taught at several universities during his career. His most recent publication, *How Many Americans? Population, Immigration, and the Environment*, was coauthored with Lindsey Grant and was sponsored by the Compton Foundation and the Frank Weeden Foundation and published by the Sierra Club.[89] Bouvier has been critical of the Census Bureau's projections of future U.S. population, and has offered various scenarios of his own. In 1994 he wrote that based on "current demographic trends, as best as they can be determined," the nation would have 397 million persons by the year 2050, a figure frequently cited by the anti-immigration lobby and now accepted by the Bureau of the Census.[90]

Bouvier and Grant worry about the nation's shrinking farmlands and pollution.[91] The cost of doing nothing is high they maintain.[92] They deny that it is racist to discuss immigration and consider its limitation. Bouvier freely admits there "are those who are driven by racism and xenophobia to oppose immigration." But in *Thirty Million Texans?* he asked, "Is it racist to show concern for the welfare of all minorities, whether African-American, Latino, or Asian? Is it racist to show concern for the environment and the state's infrastructure? Is its racist to want all Texas children to have the best schooling possible? Is it racist to desire a new all-encompassing culture where all groups can participate equally, but together rather than separately?"[93] Unlike some other advocates of immigration restriction, Bouvier has insisted that racial and ethnic considerations have no place in immigration policy; it is the number that counts.[94] We cannot continue to accept large numbers: "The nation simply has to adjust its immigration laws. Nothing could be further from the truth," he insists.[95] In the end "the message is clear." For Bouvier and Grant:

> A demographic future compatible with the requirements of the energy transition, the preservation of our farms and forest, clean atmosphere and water supplies, the forestalling of adverse climate change, and the restoration of a decent life for all, including our urban residents, will come about only if we act now. Fertility and immigration must be reduced.[96]

Yet resources alone will not be the only problem facing Americans in 2050. Bouvier points out that thousands of new schools will have to be built and teachers appointed who can deal with a growing school population of children lacking English. Moreover, there will be another 45 million automobiles on the road by the mid twentieth-first century. New jails and prisons will also be required and ways found to support a larger aging and retired population. In all, the future hardly looks bright to Bouvier, and the sooner the nation reduces both legal and illegal immigration, the better it will be for our children's future.[97]

The problem for the Sierra Club, for anti-immigrant environmentalist groups, and for writers like Bouvier was that most new immigrants were "persons of color"—Asians, Hispanics, and people from the non-Hispanic Caribbean. A call for immigration restriction appears to be a call to reduce the nonwhite population's growth, a de facto form of racism. Regardless of what politicians personally believe, it is no longer respectable to insist that some groups are inherently inferior or can never assimilate into American society. While the 1994 publication of Charles Murray's and Richard Herrnstein's badly flawed *Bell Curve* seems to reopen the old debates, it is still risky for politicians to take overtly racist positions.

For the mainline environmentalist groups the issue is particularly sensitive because their members are educated, middle and upper middle class whites whose concern is traditionally the natural environment. Already criticized by some nonwhites as being indifferent to the environmental concerns of the poor, largely located in the inner cities or on Indian reservations, liberal immigration restrictionists fear the accusation of racism. For some Sierra Club members even FAIR was anathema, and many oppose harsh measures to deal with immigration.[98] During the campaign for California's Proposition 187 to slash

benefits for undocumented immigrants, Sam Schucat, executive director of the California League of Conservation Voters, said that environmentalists opposed it. They believed, he said, that "we had to . . . [to
oppose it] just to make sure we were on the right side of history on
this one. . . . Environmentalists wanted to show that we are on the side
of people, not just endangered species."[99]

The population-environmental issue offers the possibility of avoiding the racist issue. By making the environment and overpopulation
the issues and not who is coming, anti-immigrant voices can say they
are not racists and at the same time can tie their crusade to a relatively popular issue. CCN took another step to head off the charge that
only white Americans want to cut immigration, when it organized the
Diversity Coalition for an Immigration Moratorium in October 1995.
Its director was San Franciscan Yeh Ling-Ling, a lawyer and an immigrant herself. Ling-Ling, of Chinese parents in Vietnam, came to the
United States from France in 1980 and worked for Population-Environment Balance before becoming head of the Diversity Coalition.
The Diversity Coalition, which insists that large-scale immigration is
harmful to the American environment, claims support from many minority organizations whose members represented over a half million.
Ling-Ling, a one-time member of the Sierra Club, insists, "In its very
diversity, the Coalition recognizes the many contributions that immigrants have made to our country." But she says the "problem is not
with immigrants as individuals, but with excessively high levels of immigration that run contrary to the best interests of both America and
of the immigrants themselves."[100]

The emergence of the environmental issue has reached Washington. A Cato Institute/National Immigration Forum sponsored study
written by University of Maryland economist Julian Simon, who had
discussed this issue in previous works, noted the environmental argument, but said:

> Natural resources and the environment are not at risk from immigra-
> tion. As population size and average income have increased in the
> United States, the supplies of natural resources and the cleanliness of
> the environment have improved rather than deteriorated. Immigra-
> tion increases the base of technical knowledge. That speeds the current
> positive trends in both greater availability of natural resources and
> cleaner air and water.[101]

To which FAIR retorted:

> Simon would be a minority of one if he truly believed that the supply of these resources is not being depleted, rapidly so in some cases. He would also have probably have little company if he truly believed that there is not a causal connection between the size of the U.S. population and resource consumption as well as with the quantity of solid waste that the population produces. It seems more likely that Simon is simply trying to use cost data to score a debating point, which unhelpfully obfuscates a real long-term concern over resources and the environment.[102]

The pro-immigration National Immigration Forum itself recognized the growing concern about population and the environment and issued a short report in 1997 arguing that immigrants are not harmful to the environment.[103]

When Congress established the U.S. Commission on Immigration Reform (CIR) in 1990 it instructed the commissioners to assess "the social, demographic and natural resources impact of immigration." In 1994 the commissioners said in the future they "will also compare natural resource utilization patterns of different groups of immigrants to native-born U.S. residents and to residents in their home countries."[104] In 1995 CIR published a volume by Ellen Percy Kraly, a geographer at Colgate University, on "U.S. Immigration and the Environment." After examining the work on this topic, Kraly said, "The direct or causal effects of U.S. immigration on the environment have not been established, however, through scientific study. Moreover, there are significant limitations in U.S. statistics on immigration and population for the study of environmental impacts."[105] Her recommendations concentrated on the need for future research.[106]

In the spring of 1995 CAPS members along with persons from CCN, Balance, and the Sierra Club attended a meeting of a subcommittee of the President's Council on Sustainable Development to urge the Council to take a stand on immigration reduction. Council participants replied that they would rely on the U.S. Commission on Immigration Reform to make recommendations about immigration.[107] The next year the full Council reaffirmed the goal of population stabilization, first announced the Rockefeller Commission on Population Growth, but it avoided dealing with immigration.[108]

As popular as environmentalism is, the President's Council statement brings to light the unwillingness of either Congress or the President to relate immigration to environmental concerns. Congress has held hearings on many aspects of immigration: crime, costs and benefits, asylum, family unification, and border patrol, but it has not probed the relationship between immigration and the environment. When the debated heated up in 1996 and Congress passed several major laws affecting immigration, population and environmental issues were not the center of the discussion. Legislators mainly discussed economic themes, welfare use by immigrants and the economic impact of immigration upon American society, and the meaning of family unification. They focused, too, on abuses within the system such as asylum procedures and above all on halting illegal immigration. In introducing a 1994 bill to curtail immigration, reinforce INS, and tighten the rules, Senator Harry Reid (D-Nev.) noted many reasons for his measure. One was that "our resources are being used up, and our environment is being significantly harmed by the rapidly growing population in the United States. . . . fully half of this population growth is a result of immigration."[109] His bill provided for a limit of 320,000 newcomers per year, but it got nowhere.

In the anti-immigration climate of 1996, proposals to deal with immigration faced a friendly Congress. But environmental arguments were unusual. In one of the moments touching upon population and the environment, Representative Anthony Beilenson (D-Calif.) declared, "In other words, much of what demographers consider our natural growth is actually the result of the large number of immigrants in our country—and the great majority of them have come here legally." The result? "Without a doubt, our ability in the future to provide the basic necessities of life, to insure adequate water and food supplies, to dispose of waste, to protect open spaces and agricultural land, to control waste and air pollution. . . . is certain to be tested in ways we cannot even imagine."[110]

Beilenson's remarks had little impact. Actually, the measure as finally passed in 1996 carried a provision that was a setback for environmentalists. In its ardor to build new fences and barriers along the border, Congress exempted environmental laws and rules in such projects. Though this was a relatively small issue, it represents further evidence that concerns about the environmental impact of immigration carried little weight in the Republican-dominated Congress.[111] Clearly environmentalism is popular, but as the debate in Congress indicates, its connection to immigration is another matter.[112]

Nor did it appear as if the public debate paid much attention to the connection between immigration, population, and the environment. In November 1996, *The Atlantic Monthly* carried two articles about the immigration debate, one by historian David Kennedy and the other by economist George Borjas. Neither discussed ecology. Commenting on this omission, Otis Graham of FAIR remarked in a letter to *The Atlantic Monthly*: "Neither Kennedy nor Borjas mentions the environmental and social consequences of today's immigration policy. . . . A third essay by a demographer-environmentalist would have deepened the analysis, and the alarm, by more than a third."[113]

The situation was ironic: the current movement to restrict immigration is heavily rooted in the population and environmental concerns growing out of the 1970s, but thus far the population and environmental issues surrounding immigration have rarely been debated in the political arena nor have the major environmental groups taken a stand on immigration. These arguments might be effective in attracting support, especially from liberals, but as the debate within the Sierra Club and the avoidance of the issue among other environmental organizations makes clear, liberals in these groups are reluctant to tackle immigration. As one disaffected member of the Sierra Club said, "They won't say the I-word. That may be politically correct, but it's not demographically correct or scientifically correct."[114]

No doubt the restrictionists' cause has been set back by the failure of worst case scenarios of Paul Ehrlich, among others, to come true. Most Americans are aware of many victories by environmentalists in cleaning the nation's rivers, lakes, and air. They are aware, too, that the price of gasoline for their cars does not seem to have grown in real dollars in the last thirty years. Such facts make it hard for environmental restrictionists to sell their message. Because of the difficulty in convincing Congress and the public of their case against immigration, the environmentalists in the restrictionist movement have turned to other issues in their call for cutting immigration.

# 4

## A Broken Immigration System

*"Our [immigration] system is broken and needs to be fixed."*
—Representative Anthony Deal (R-Ga.), March 19, 1996

THE NEW RESTRICTIONISTS found many things wrong with the American immigration system and the immigrants themselves besides their impact on the environment. These other perceived faults attracted critics who were not terribly worried about the environmental issue. For a starter, they strongly object to the power of the pro-immigration lobby, an "unlikely coalition of the far right and the far left, fueled by a coalition of big business and Hispanic pressure groups."[1] The theme of big business as the culprit is repeated by several key players in the anti-immigration coalition. William R. Hawkins's *Importing Revolution*, published by AICF, while blaming the Ford Foundation, Hispanic groups, civil liberties lawyers, and some cultural radicals for driving policy, nonetheless blamed agricultural employers for killing "all previous attempts at reform in the 1970s."[2] John Vinson, president of AICF, says that altruism alone does not account for liberal immigration policy. Politicians cater to voting blocs and business interests want "more cheap labor for their enterprises, even if this meant poorer wages and working conditions for Americans."[3] John Tanton and Wayne Lutton assured their readers, "Agribusiness will do anything to retain its immigrant labor force, short of paying fair wages and providing tolerable living and working conditions." But it was not agribusiness alone. "Big business has tended to be hostile to immigration reform. . . . The editors of *The Wall Street Journal* have long called for a constitutional amendment that would simply state, 'There shall be open borders.' "[4]

Besides seeing business as part of the "open borders" or "alienist" crowd, restrictionists indict a variety of politically active ethnic organizations, Latino ones particularly. William Hawkins's *Importing Revolution,* subtitled "Open Borders and the Radical Agenda," sees the hand of the Ford Foundation behind the Mexican American Legal Defense and Educational Fund (MALDEF). Ford's considerable funding of MALDEF convinces Hawkins that the Foundation itself has become a major advocate for immigration.[5] Hawkins also believes that leftist groups like the National Lawyers Guild are partly responsible for a liberal immigration policy, whose goal is a radically changed America.[6] More objective analysts agree that immigrant lawyers are part of the pro-immigration lobby, for the obvious reason that immigration is good for their business.

Roy Beck blames the failure of immigration reform in 1996 on the pro-immigration lobby. In an Op-Ed piece for the *New York Times,* Beck noted that business groups, religious and ethnic organizations, labor unions, taxpayer lobbyists, and even the Christian Coalition all united to defeat changes, which he argued, were supported by public opinion polls. "Congress has listened to lobbyists more than public opinion. If Americans want a different immigration policy, they may need to challenge their own religious, economic and political organizations," he concluded.[7]

The most sweeping assessment of all about the strength of the pro-immigration lobby was given by Chilton Williamson Jr. In the 1990s he writes, the "immigrationist coalition is huge." It consists of

> the national Democratic Party and the establishment wing of the Republican one; the business and agricultural lobbies (largely Republican); the ethnic organizations (mostly Democratic) and refugee agencies; the urban Democratic machines; welfare agencies and others serving the needs of immigrants (legal and illegal); most of the establishment and business press and all of the major television networks; numerous columnists; the academy; the federal bureaucracy and many

of the state and local bureaucracies; the liberal, radical, neo-conservative, and libertarian journals of opinion; and the bureaucratic super-
structure of organized religion.[8]

Few observers would deny the importance and effectiveness of the
groups in the pro-immigration camp. Frank Sharry, executive director
of the pro-immigration National Immigration Forum, noted of the
failure of attempts to cut immigration in 1996, "Those who seek to
preserve our country's 300-year-old tradition of welcoming immigrants have formed a unique coalition comprising conservatives, liberals and moderates alike who are concerned that the legislation goes
too far." He noted that the National Association of Manufacturers
agreed with unions on this issue and was joined by Intel and Microsoft
and a number of liberals connected to the National Immigration
Forum.[9] A writer for the *New York Times* reported that meetings of the
immigration advocates included liberal and conservative organizations
and leaders. Among them were the American Civil Liberties Union,
the National Council of La Raza, a Christian Fundamentalist group,
and the National Rifle Association.[10]

For the restrictionists, the "alienist" crusade has been extremely effective in radically changing immigration, with the main culprit being
the 1965 immigration act. IRCA and the Immigration Act of 1990
also came in for their share of the blame. Lawrence Auster's *The Path
to National Suicide* insists that the "browning of America" in the last
three decades was due to flawed political decisions, but there "seems
to be almost no awareness of the fact that this alteration of our society
is the result of, not of an act of God, but of Congress; not of some in-
violable provision in the Constitution, but of a law passed in 1965."[11]
Peter Brimelow also sees the 1965 law as the key. "U.S. immigration
policy was not transformed in 1965 without debate. There was a debate. It just bore no relationship to what subsequently happened."[12]
The president of AICF believes that the Hart-Celler Act has proven to
be a "recipe for disaster."[13]

The Immigration Act of 1965 was important in shifting some patterns of immigration, but it was not nearly as important as these critics say. They are correct that its consequences were not entirely fore-
seen, but they have exaggerated the outcome of the act.[14] Repeal of
national origins quotas in 1965 made possible a substantial increase in
Asian immigration, but there were limits. The Eastern Hemisphere's

allotment was only increased from 154,000 to 170,000, hardly a radical change. Each nation had a limit of 20,000, excluding immediate family members of U.S. citizens.[15] This turned out to be an underestimate as the quota exempt figure was running well over 200,000 by the late 1980s.

If the Hart-Celler Act changed immigration and increased it from the Eastern Hemisphere, the law was restrictive when it came to the Western Hemisphere. In October 1995, looking back thirty years when the Hart-Celler Act was passed, FAIR said that before 1965 "numerical limits on immigration kept the annual number of immigrants low."[16] Yet, before 1965 there were no limits for the Western Hemisphere. For the first time, Congress put a ceiling on that hemisphere of 120,000, excluding immediate family members of U.S. citizens. This was a crucial limitation. Canada and Mexico had become the leading nations for sending immigrants in the 1950s, and the Caribbean nations were sending larger numbers in the late 1950s and early 1960s. In the 1960s Mexico passed Canada as the leading source for immigration to the United States, except for a few years when Cuban refugees arrived in substantial numbers.

The total from the Western Hemisphere was about 120,000 annually when Congress acted. The legislators were in effect saying that too many people were coming from the Western Hemisphere, especially Latinos, and that the new ceiling would keep the numbers down. They were correct about keeping the numbers limited. There is a backlog today of over half a million Mexicans waiting for a visa to America. If pre-1965 rules still prevailed they would be able to come to the United States, no doubt with many others as well. Indeed, under the old rules, so many of the Mexicans and Central Americans who have come illegally in the last thirty years would have been able to arrive with visas.

Thus, the 1965 act has proven restrictive when it came to immigration from the Western Hemisphere. Congress removed the 100 limit on all former British colonies, but these newly independent nations had to compete with other nations in the Western Hemisphere because of the imposed ceiling. If they began to send more people to the United States, Mexico and other countries would be able to send fewer. In 1978 Congress gave the Western Hemisphere a preference system with a per country cap of 20,000, when it finally created a unified worldwide system.

There is vast irony in the 1965 immigration act. It was restrictive for the Western Hemisphere and liberalizing for most nations in the Eastern one, especially Asian countries that had very small (usually 100) quotas. It has been the Asian nations that have been able to utilize the Immigration Act of 1965 to come to America in substantial numbers, and excluding refugees, Asian immigration is now over ten times the figure for 1965. Yet most—but by no means all—of the attack on the new immigration is directed at Latinos and especially Mexicans, for whom the new law was more restrictive than previous policy. The issues of economics and assimilation mostly revolve around Hispanic immigrants. Americans, other than Asians themselves, are deeply ambivalent about Asians. Dependently upon the viewpoint, they are seen as bringing drugs and crime to America, as being inassimilable; or as being a "model minority"—high academic achievers and diligent workers. Some polls reveal almost as much opposition to Asian immigration as to Hispanic, but others sometimes signal less hostility to immigrants from Asia than from those south of the border or the Middle East.[17] A *USA Today* poll conducted in 1993 revealed that those responding were more likely to believe that Asians were hard workers and better students, and less apt to be criminals or end up on welfare than were immigrants from Latin America.[18]

The 1965 act was also connected to illegal immigration. Wayne Lutton, who has published a number of attacks on the new immigration, wrote in 1988 that Hart-Celler "resulted in a flood of Third World immigration, both legal and illegal. Today between 85 and 90 percent of legal immigration comes from the Third World. Those who cannot enter legally come in outside the laws, reflecting the indisputable Third World disdain for the rule of law."[19] Aside from the exaggerations in his statement, Lutton had a point about connecting the 1965 act to illegal immigration, but for reasons a good many critics did not understand. Because the 1965 act was restrictive toward Western Hemispheric immigration and because the Bracero program for temporary workers, mostly from Mexico, ended at the same time, Mexicans discovered that it was now more difficult to enter the United States legally. Hence, they came in without proper documentation. Later Central Americans discovered how hard it was to emigrate to the United States, they too decided to enter illegally. Thus in closing what Aristide Zolberg calls "the front door," American policy fostered "back door" illegal immigration. The only way to close the "back door" was to develop an effective plan to plug the nation's borders and to catch those who overstayed visitors's visas.

If the 1965 act did not envision major increases, how did immigration figures grow to the record highs of the 1990s? The immigration act of 1965 was changed; Congress and various presidents found it too restrictive for their purposes. Fleeing Cubans were first admitted by presidential parole and then by the Cuban Adjustment Act of 1966 that assumed that any Cuban was a refugee entitled to settle in the United States. The Indochinese population of the United States in the mid-1990s is over one million, although the original 1965 quota for Eastern Hemisphere refugees was only 10,200 annually. Yet after 1974, U.S. presidents, with congressional approval, permitted Indochinese to settle here, at levels much above the 10,200 annual figure. Congress increased the refugee "normal flow" to be 50,000 annually in the Refugee Act of 1980, but for the most part the administration has admitted twice that number.

Other changes in law were required to admit more immigrants. Many restrictionists accepted 1986 IRCA's amnesty because they thought, or hoped, that employers' sanctions and increased border patrols would stem the tide of illegal immigration from Mexico. What they and some others did not see is how ineffective the restrictions would be and how generous the amnesty was, admitting nearly three million persons.

Critics were certainly on target about the 1990 immigration act, which they viewed as specifically designed to catering to a variety of interests, business, ethnic, national, religious and legal. AICF put it, "Immigration control advocates generally view the 1990 immigration 're-form' act, which increased immigration by 40 percent, as a victory of selfish interest groups over the national interest and will of the people."[20] The Washington State Citizens for Immigration Control said the 1990 act was another "sneak attack on the American people."[21]

Making what the critics saw as bad policy was one issue, enforcement of the immigration laws was another. Here again, restrictionists blamed the "open borders crowd" for defeating adequate funding for the INS, for killing proposals for national identity cards for proper employers' sanctions enforcement, and for watering down plans to build effective barriers along the southern border of the United States.

FAIR and others had hoped that IRCA, with its trade-off of an amnesty for employers' sanctions, would be enough to stifle illegal immigration. But it quickly became obvious that IRCA was only a partial success. Apprehensions of illegals, mostly along the United States-Mexico border, were averaging over one million before IRCA was passed. Ten years later, when the debate over illegal immigration was heating up again, the General Accounting Office (GAO) noted, "Despite a brief drop in the estimated number of illegal entries to the United States after IRCA was enacted, the inflow of illegal aliens subsequently increased, so that the size of the illegal alien population is now estimated to have increased once more to pre-IRCA levels."[22] Some employers were fined—but not jailed—for violations of IRCA, but most observers, whether pro- or anti-immigration, believed that employers' sanctions were not effectively halting the employment of undocumented aliens. "Whatever else the IRCA legislation was supposed to do, it has quite clearly failed to control illegal immigration," declared Peter Brimelow.[23]

Congress authorized but did not appropriate funds for adequate border enforcement. Robert Goldsborough, president of American Immigration Control, caustically noted that authorizing but not appropriating was not new. He asked in 1994, "Will Congress allocate funds necessary for the increased Border Patrol, or will the politicians in Congress continue with their same old trick of *authorization without appropriation?*"[24]

FAIR and other groups urged a beefed-up Border Patrol, which included more agents, better fences and other physical deterrents along the border, and support for the INS's intensive efforts to halt illegal immigration from the south. John Tanton and Wayne Lutton said the nation needed "better barriers" and "patrols around the clock."[25] The INS did undertake several programs to plug the southern border, especially at El Paso and San Diego. At the latter site Operation Gatekeeper used new fencing, high intensity lights, and additional manpower.[26] The clampdown near San Diego was proclaimed a success after one year, but Operation Gatekeeper was alleged by some observers to simply force illegal border crossers to try somewhere else.[27] Moreover, reports circulated that INS supervisors falsified reports to make the operation look more successful.[28]

Under the supervision of Silvestre Reyes, chief of the El Paso section, the INS launched Operation Hold the Line, in September 1993. The INS used a high profile along the border in a 20-mile stretch around El Paso to deter undocumented aliens from trying to cross rather than apprehending them when they cross and then returning them to Mexico.[29] The Center for Immigration Studies (CIS) and AICF praised these efforts as demonstrating that the border "can be better controlled if the necessary personnel, infrastructure, and equipment are available."[30] Some advocates of tighter controls suggested that national guard units or perhaps even the United States army might be required if an effective job were to be done. The California Republican assembly even passed a bill authorizing the guard to protect California's southern border.[31]

These initiatives demonstrated that the anti-immigration message was beginning to be heard in Washington. The growing outcry about illegal immigration led to the 1994 passage of California's Proposition 187, which denied most social and economic benefits to illegal aliens. Congress and President Bill Clinton agreed on additional funding for the INS. In the Republican-dominated budget cutting Congress, it was one of the few agencies to benefit and its funding nearly doubled from 1994 to 1997. The additional funds permitted the INS to hire and train more border guards and reinforce fencing along the U.S.-Mexican border; an agency with 3,900 agents in 1993 by 1996 had 5,700.[32] The borders of California and Arizona received special treatment. Hispanic groups recognized the growing national hostility to illegal immigration. Raul Yzaguirre, president of the National Council of La Raza, said the improved fences were the most "effective, most humane method of reducing undocumented immigration" and conceded that the steps were good politics.[33]

Even if the border were secure, however, by the mid-1990s more than half of all undocumented aliens were estimated to enter with some type of temporary visa and then stay in the United States illegally.[34] CIS head David Simcox lamented that there was practically "no deterrence" to stop people from coming in and then overstaying; as late as 1995 the INS had no effective program to seek out and deport such illegal immigrants.[35] Even if they came with fake documents, the INS lacked personnel to do thorough checks.

The Commission on Immigration Reform, created by Congress in 1990, noted that the "a better system of verifying work authorization is central to effective enforcement sanctions."[36] But no sooner had IRCA been enacted than Hispanic groups called for the repeal of employers' sanctions. How, the restrictionists asked, would the United States eliminate undocumented aliens without these sanctions? Employers' sanctions needed to be refined, not repealed, said FAIR.[37] AICF noted that IRCA gave about three million people an amnesty, but did not provide for effective enforcement along the border or in the market place. AICF claimed that it knew this would happen and was "not among" the restrictionist groups supporting IRCA. Aliens would still come in and get jobs said *Border Watch* and that is what happened. IRCA has simply failed.[38]

FAIR's solution, and much of the anti-immigration lobby's too, was some type of "secure verification system." Because the social security card can be made "electronically verifiable" like a credit card or an ATM card, said FAIR "such a card could be utilized."[39] The INS did experiment with a telephone verification system based on a number of documents in order to cut down on fraud. It reported that the employers using its system on a voluntary basis were enthusiastic. As a result it expanded the program, but it was hardly national in scope.[40]

The question of employers' verification raised civil liberties issues, and it also focused attention on the widespread use of fraudulent documents—green cards, social security cards, drivers' licenses, and birth certificates among them. The new restrictionists urged that better methods be made to insure against fraud but Congress failed to come up with a workable scheme.

While not giving up the search for better identification, advocates of taking action against illegal immigration also focused on denying governmental programs for these aliens. Undocumented aliens were not eligible for most governmental programs, but because of fraudulent documents and the lack of cooperation between the INS and other federal, state and local agencies, some illegal aliens were able to utilize governmental programs, notably education and medical care. In California, Proposition 187, still hung up in the courts in 1997, was sold as a way to stem the invasion of illegal aliens, which, they argued, cost the taxpayer big money. The provision requiring service providers to turn over names to the INS was conceived as a way to rid the state of undocumented aliens while saving the state money.

Restrictionists also attacked the INS for being a poorly run and ineffective agency. In 1995 a detention center for illegal immigrants erupted into a melee. The center was a privately run one, which the INS did not carefully supervise. As a result, the inmates were treated poorly, sometimes beaten, given bad food and poor lighting. The inmates revolted and forced the INS to remove those being held there.[41]

A year later, when congressional representatives visited a center in Miami, INS officials removed some of the inmates to avoid the appearance of overcrowding and make the center look more presentable. Employees tipped Congress off about what had happened, and the deception was confirmed by a Justice Department investigation. This was another scandal the INS did not need.[42] So incensed was FAIR that its executive director, Dan Stein, called for the resignation of INS Commissioner Doris Meissner.[43]

While allegations of wrongdoing did not help INS's reputation, the beleaguered agency had to deal with complaints from pro-immigration advocates as well. Human rights groups like Americas' Watch reported that INS border agents abused illegal aliens.[44] Responding to the charges of human rights abuses, Congress investigated the allegations, though nothing significant resulted from these hearings. The INS denied any mistreatment of illegal aliens as a result of its efforts to tighten the border.[45] The issue of treatment of illegal aliens received national attention in April 1996 when sheriff deputies in California followed a truck that they believed was carrying illegal aliens. The truck stopped and most of undocumented aliens were apprehended, but two fled. When finally caught by the police officials they were beaten, but unbeknownst to the deputies the violence was captured on video. While many Californians were shocked at the brutality of the police, others found it galling that the Mexican consul was encouraging the victims to sue for damages. The *Fresno Bee* called it "Mexico Hypocrisy," and a rally supporting the two deputies, who had been suspended pending an investigation of the incident, bore a sign saying, "Put illegals away, not our deputies." A founder of SOS said "If our borders were secure, we wouldn't have these kinds of incidents."[46]

If the United States has lost control of its borders as the new critics complained, it was not only at the work place and along the boundary separating the United States and Mexico. Critics also saw the asylum and refugee policies as being another part of a broken system. This fault did not become manifest until a few years after FAIR was founded, but by the 1990s restrictionists agreed that something was dreadfully wrong with both the asylum system and refugee policy. The Cold War might have ended, but refugee crises continued, and opponents of immigration charged that refugee and asylum policies were simply another means of mass immigration. Brimelow put it, "The truth is that the 'refugee' and 'asylee' categories have become just another sort of expedited immigration program." Were Russians after 1987 or Cubans after 1980 really refugees, he asked? The answer: "Virtually all pretense that 'refugees' are fleeing war or persecution was abandoned in 1989, when Senator Frank Lautenberg (D-N.J.) succeeded in passing legislation requiring that all Jews from the territory of the Soviet Union, plus members of two small Christian minorities . . . should be presumed to be 'refugees' for the purpose of admittance to the United States." But the Cuban lobby had it best, according to Brimelow; the 1966 Cuban Adjustment Act effectively "guarantees that *any* Cuban reaching the United States can obtain legal immigrant status within a year."[47]

AICF maintained that the Lautenberg amendment condoned massive fraud. These were not real refugees, declared *Border Watch*. Some applicants were not even Jewish, but gained "fraudulent admission by claiming to have a remote Jewish ancestor." Pentecostal leaders have informed the INS, said the newsletter, that many of the people accepted as Pentecostals were "impostors."[48]

Critics of American refugee policy saw another loophole when Congress gave Chinese students caught here after the failure of the Democratic Movement in China the right to stay in the United States. Norman Matloff, another critic of American immigration policy, said, "In effect the students were given blanket political asylum, even though only a very small fraction of them would have qualified for asylum had they applied individually."[49] When Congress in 1990 gave Salvadorans the right to stay in the United States temporarily, CIS warned that "temporary protected status" might become another new migration channel. "Congress may have risked unforeseen consequences and opened a major new immigration spigot in the new act's creation of 'temporary protected status.' "[50]

The asylum issue became increasingly controversial in the 1980s when tens of thousands of persons reaching the United States without proper immigration documents requested asylum. Because the backlog grew to over 400,000 by 1994, the INS could not dispose of their cases quickly. The agency gave them working papers and scheduled a hearing later. Often the potential asylees did not show up for their hearing, and even if they did and were rejected, they were ordered to depart voluntarily. As one critic noted, "A growing number of would-be immigrants have attempted to exploit our porous borders and lax procedures either to extend a stay in the United States while their application is being considered or simply to gain legal entry to the country and then, illegally, disappear."[51] The INS simply did not have the manpower to cope with the asylum crisis.[52] Commenting on CBS's *60 Minutes* FAIR's Dan Stein said asylum fraud had reached epidemic proportions. "Every single person on the planet Earth knows, if he gets into this country, he can stay indefinitely by saying two magic words: political asylum. The word is out."[53] John Tanton and Wayne Lutton agreed and added that "International airports have become open doors into America. All arriving aliens need [to] do is say the magic words 'political asylum.' "[54]

Actually few pro-immigration leaders by the 1990s denied the existence of an asylum crisis. The backlog was simply too large to ignore.[55] They too wanted a better system, more immigration judges, and adequate INS facilities to house those awaiting hearings or appeals. Muzaffar Chishti of the pro-immigration National Immigration Forum admitted the situation was a "mess" and laced with fraud.[56]

President Bill Clinton agreed that mass asylum was undesirable, and in 1994 he took action to stem a mass migration to the United States from both Cuba and Haiti. Cubans might have been welcome from 1959 to the mid-1990s, but not after. When the numbers picked up again in 1994, President Clinton, not wanting to see a repeat of the 1980 Mariel episode when 125,000 Cubans reached the United States by boat without prior screening, announced that Cubans rescued at sea would not be allowed to enter the United States. Rather they would be granted safe haven at the American Guantanamo base in Cuba. Negotiations with the Cuban government brought a solution. Henceforth Cuba would halt people fleeing by boat. In turn the United States would open the door for those at the Guantanamo base and place Cuba under the normal immigration rules, which granted preference to those with close family ties in the United States.[57] In effect the Cuban Adjustment Act, which guaranteed that almost any Cuban reaching the United States would be considered a refugee, was being repealed by the President, much to the relief of important Floridian politicians, who did not want the burden of paying for new refugees.[58] However, Congress did not respond by repealing the act, in spite of Clinton's new policy, and some members along with Cuban Americans were critical of the President.[59]

The President's actions proved to be effective in cutting the numbers trying to leave Cuba on their own. The last of those interned at

Guantanamo were admitted in early 1996.[60] Few Cubans attempted to sail to the United States after the new plan went into effect, and for those that did, the Coast Guard caught them and returned them to Cuba, unless they were entitled to remain in the United States. Until October 1996, the Coast Guard reported that it had intercepted only 278 rafters in that year.[61]

In the case of Haiti, President Clinton's action was even more dramatic. Haitians had an even more difficult time gaining entrance to the United States. Unlike Cubans, Haitians, who were not fleeing a communist regime, had no special legislation to guarantee refugee status when they escaped to the United States. Instead Haitians had to win asylum on a individual basis, which was difficult, and only a few managed to do so. During the Reagan and Bush administrations, the Coast Guard was ordered to head off boats from Haiti and return their passengers to Haiti. Bush later ordered the boats to be taken to Guantanamo where the Haitians would be processed to see if they were entitled to asylum in the United States. During the 1992 presidential election campaign, candidate Clinton criticized this interdiction, but as President he continued the policy.[62]

Clinton sought through economic sanctions to force the military dictatorship that ruled Haiti to resign and to return the elected president, Jean-Bertrand Aristide, to office. When his policy failed, Clinton ordered the invasion of Haiti. The President told the nation that thousands of Haitians had been rescued at sea and that thousands were confined to the Guantanamo Naval Base, which was unsatisfactory. He made it clear that the goals of the invasion were to restore democracy and to end the refugee crisis. He said the United States had already spent $200 million to support Haitian refugees and more would flee unless conditions changed in Haiti. "Three hundred thousand more Haitians, 5 percent of their entire population, are in hiding in their own country. If we don't act, they could be the next wave of refugees at our door. We will continue to face the threat of mass exodus of refugees and its constant threat to stability in our region and control of our borders."[63]

Clinton's policy toward Cuba and Haiti might have won approval from the anti-immigration groups, but what of the many others entering and claiming asylum. Tighter rules were implemented at airports such as JFK in New York, no doubt in response to the growing number of persons arriving there and claiming asylum. The INS beefed hearing procedures and told asylum-seekers that they would have to wait six months before receiving a work permit. This did cause a drop in the number of persons requesting asylum at that point.[64]

Advocates for asylum seekers worried that the government might turn down appeals too quickly, or that potential asylees might find themselves imprisoned needlessly or that they would be denied work permits while their cases dragged on for months. Moreover, some immigrants' rights attorneys raised the potential of expanding the grounds for asylum. Should women who are treated as second-class citizens in their own lands, for example, African women subjected to genital mutilation, be granted asylum? A woman, after several years of pleading her case, did win asylum on that ground in 1996.[65] George High of CIS said extending asylum to women because of violence against them as women was stretching the limits of the Refugee Convention.[66]

What of Chinese who claimed asylum status because they disagreed with China's family policy of one child per family? Had not this policy led to forced sterilizations and abortions? Among a group of 300 illegal Chinese aliens who attempted to enter by boat, the *Golden Venture* that ran aground off Long Island in 1993, several insisted that they were entitled to asylum. A few did win asylum, but about one-third were deported and others found themselves still interned three years later.[67] In 1996 Congress passed a law making it possible for them to win asylum.

Should gays be granted asylum? They were not clearly specified in the law, and in fact were actually barred from entry prior to 1990. But, in 1994 Attorney General Janet Reno issued a directive saying that the law allows political asylum for foreign nationals if they were persecuted abroad because they were homosexuals. Not many such cases were decided for those claiming asylum on this ground; only 60 were granted in the next two years.[68]

Even more troubling to those who believed that the immigration system was out of control was that persons with AIDS might gain admission to the United States via the asylum route. Individuals with AIDS or who were HIV positive had been barred from entry but in 1995 the President's Advisory Council of HIV/AIDS hinted that such persons might be granted waivers and even asylum. A handful of such people had been granted waivers, but more outrageous to restrictionists was the fact that, before the Advisory Council's suggestion was made, an immigration judge in New York City did grant asylum to a

Togolese national who was HIV positive. Conservative talk shows hosts Rush Limbaugh and G. Gordon Liddy, among others, assailed this decision and the Council's advice. The Clinton administration quickly pointed out that the Council's position was only advisory and that the INS had rejected it. The ban still stood.[69]

To those who believed the asylum procedures were being abused, such cases simply proved the laxity of American immigration policy, Mark Krikorian of CIS explained a variety of pressure groups, "on the Left, feminists and homosexual-rights campaigners; on the Right, antiabortion activists—have been waging a battle to reshape the law so as to give sanctuary to their favored class of victims."[70]

Worse yet were terrorists immigrating to the United States and asking for asylum. Columnist David Gergen noted several notorious persons who had applied for asylum in order to stay in the United States. Mir Aimal Kansi of Pakistan, whose legal visa had expired, applied for political asylum and, while awaiting a decision, purchased an AK-47 and killed two Americans outside the CIA headquarters in Virginia. He then fled to Pakistan.[71] Of course, defenders of generous immigration did not want terrorists to be admitted either, but for the critics of current policy such cases were simply another example of a broken system.

Even more embarrassing for the INS was the case of Sheik Omar Abdel Rahman, who was charged with and convicted of plotting to blow up New York City's World Trade Center in 1993. Wanted in Egypt for involvement in the assassination of Anwar Sadat, he was on a "lookout list" making him ineligible to migrate to the United States, but he slipped through anyway.[72] Once in the United States the sheik moved his residence, changed his name, and received a green card from the INS office in Newark, New Jersey. The authorities caught up with him and revoked his status, but the sheik then applied for political asylum. The case was pending when the World Trade Center exploded.[73] To make matters worse, several others convicted along with the sheik were immigrants from the Middle East.[74]

The case of Sheik Omar Abdel Rahman was the most newsworthy, but to the restrictionists it was simply another example of how the broken American immigration system, with an inefficient and understaffed INS, was unable to cope with the flow of legal and illegal immigrants. This man was a terrorist, but thousands of others slipping in were involved in criminal activity, ranging from extortion to murder.

Peter Brimelow wrote that immigration might not be the major or only cause in the current crime wave, but it was a factor.[75] A number of books have brought to the public's attention a new wave of ethnic crime.[76] FAIR's Dan Stein told the National War College in 1994, "A series of jarring incidents in 1993 gave the public the unmistakable impression that immigrants are not all honest and hardworking. Some are here to commit crimes, while others are part of a growing number of international organized crime rings that specialize in everything from alien smuggling to computer and credit card fraud. Criminal aliens are over represented in the federal criminal justice system, and information about the nature of sophisticated international syndicates is creating resentment and anxiety among the general public."[77]

Perhaps the most prolonged account of immigrant criminals occurred in the case of the Mariel Cubans, who arrived in the spring of 1980. About 125,000 fled by boat to Florida from the Cuban port of Mariel, before President Jimmy Carter halted further sailings. The President acted amid rumors that Fidel Castro was dumping his criminals and mentally ill patients into the boats going to America. Those Cubans who were criminals, or who later ran afoul of the law, received extensive coverage when they rioted at the Atlanta federal prison and at a Louisiana immigration facility that they destroyed. After lengthy negotiations with the Cuban government, several hundred were sent back to Cuba.[78] CIS considered the entrance of the Mariel Cubans a fiasco, the effects of which "are still with us. . . . By 1987 more than 10,000 Marielitos had been sentenced for crimes committed in the U.S."[79]

Few alien criminals entered in such dramatic fashion as the Mariel Cubans, but for the new restrictionists it seemed as if the United States was being invaded by criminals of all sorts. Gang wars, violence, robberies, drug smuggling and dealing, and even murder were among the crimes committed by immigrants, legal or illegal. John Tanton and Wayne Lutton warned of some of the dangers: "Criminal activities committed by immigrant aliens in the U.S.A. have escalated dramatically." Worse yet, "Under current immigration laws and procedures, frighteningly large numbers of newcomers see crime as their avenue to the American dream. . . .The FBI warns that international crime and terrorist organizations have placed America under siege."[80] AICF agreed: "Gang violence and other gang-related criminal activities are growing problems in American cities. Many of the gang members are immigrants or the children of immigrants who have not assimilated to the basic standards of American society."[81]

Crime was seen as spreading to America's interior. FAIR reported in 1996, "Immigrant-Related Crime Wave Hits America's Heartland." In Sioux City, Iowa, where a growing number of Latinos had been employed by the meatpacking industry, crime was on the rise. This included the appearance of street gangs, shootings, and drugs. The mayor, said FAIR, wanted the INS to set up an office in Sioux City.[82]

Asian gangs were charged with kidnapping and forcing illegal aliens into virtual slavery working to pay huge amounts of money to the gangs.[83] Asian prostitutes were also held as indentures.[84] Moreover, the media featured stories of Colombian drug rings, replacing Asian control over drugs.[85] Drug smuggling itself was viewed as a major problem by Tanton and Lutton. Our border was simply too porous. "Until the federal government is willing to secure our border, there is little hope that the 'war on drugs' can be won, claimed one critic."[86]

So sensational had been the coverage of alien criminals that a 1996 study by William Kleinknect, *The New Ethnic Mobs: The Changing Face of Organized Crime in America*, insisted it was not a plea for immigration restriction. His work focused on the emerging Chinese, Russian, Vietnamese, Hispanic, and Jamaican syndicates in American cities. Kleinknect was aware that writing about immigrant criminality might give rise to a movement to restrict migration, a view he does not share. "I would also ask the reader not to mistake this work for an argument against immigration. My views are quite to the contrary. I see the last two decades of immigration as having been a windfall for urban America, breathing new life into neighborhoods that others had left behind. Most new immigrants came here to work and start businesses, not collect welfare."[87]

The pro-immigration lobby's defense of immigrants points to the nation's long list of distinguished immigrants and their contributions to American society. Perhaps with tongue in cheek, *Social Contract* put out an issue called "Infamous Immigrants." These were not the Albert Einsteins, but rather some unsavory aliens, including criminals. Author James Robb pointed to Mafia gangsters; Sirhan-Sirhan, the man who assassinated Robert Kennedy; Marielito criminals; Meyer Lansky, another gangster; Sheik Omar Abdel-Rahman, "the most bloody-Minded Immigrant of Them All"; and even a Nazi war criminal who came to America to help develop rockets.[88]

While drug and alien smuggling, forced prostitution, and gang warfare might have seemed the most sensational, almost as vexing to the restrictionists were the many other immigrant criminals convicted of lesser offenses but who managed to avoid being deported. Or if they were deported, they returned again through the nation's porous borders. In 1986 Senator Alfonse D'Amato of New York, asked GAO to report on INS's investigations of alien criminals in the New York City area. GAO reported, "There is insufficient data to fully measure the extent of the deportable criminal alien problem in the New York City area. There is little doubt, however, that not all of the criminal alien population is being investigated by INS. As a result, criminal aliens who should have been deported have remained in the country and have committed additional crimes."[89] Senator D'Amato was dismayed by the report, saying that if an alien commits a felony, "the chances are pretty good that he will not be deported."[90]

A decade later, a U.S. Senate report called attention to a similar situation: "America's immigration system is in disarray and criminal aliens . . . constitute a particularly vexing part of the problem. Criminal aliens occupy the intersection of two areas of great concern to the American people; crime and the control of our borders." The senators insisted that alien criminals were a growing threat to public safety, but although "criminal aliens who commit serious crimes are subject to deportation under current law, the deportation system is in such disarray that no one, including the Commissioner of the Immigration and Naturalization Service can even say with certainty how many criminal aliens are currently subject to the jurisdiction of our criminal justice system."[91] Many such criminals were not deported, and if they are they "often return to the U.S. in a matter of days or even hours."[92]

In a congressional hearing on criminal aliens, Representative Romano Mazzoli (D-Ky.) said that the problem was due to the fact that detention "facilities have not been able to keep up with the growing numbers of deportable aliens."[93] In September 1994 a story in the *New York Times* related just how a criminal alien could remain free. Jorge Luis Garaz Gorena was first deported to Mexico in 1974, but within one week he crossed the border illegally to reenter the United States. He was deported five more times over the next fifteen years, but always managed to return. In 1989, reported the *Times*, the INS lost track of him altogether. He was a thief, a burglar, and a heroin addict, but when the *Times* tracked him down he was free. He told the reporter, "After all the time that immigration wasted, I guess they finally just got tired of hassling me. I haven't heard from them for years."[94]

It was a story to chill the hearts of the anti-immigration lobby. In California, New York, Florida, New Jersey, and Texas, where so many immigrants—legal and illegal—settled, there was fear that dangerous criminals were being let loose simply because the INS lacked detention facilities or the manpower to ensure their deportation. Barbara Coe, one of the chief instigators of Proposition 187 and leader of the California Coalition for Immigration Reform, in running for the state assembly, declared in her campaign literature, "We are heartbroken when we learn of yet another brutal murder of an innocent victim, many of them children, at the hands of illegal aliens. . . . And most of all, we are outraged by those representatives who allow this activity to continue at the expense of the quality of life for us all and take little action to protect us from the illegal alien perpetrators of violent crime."[95]

The *Miami Herald* reported in 1995 that immigration was a hot issue in Florida. Staff reporter Lizette Alvarez said interviews across the state revealed that Floridians "bolt their doors to keep criminals from their home, then learn that illegal immigrants are taking up jail space."[96]

Some of the concern about alien felons was driven by economics, the belief that convicted criminals were being incarcerated by state and local governments and that the costs should be paid for by the federal government. States that had convicted and jailed illegal aliens sued the federal government for reimbursement, and politicians attacked the federal government and the INS for not doing its share; these protests, though getting nowhere in the courts, began to have some impact in the mid-1990s. The federal government moved to prosecute some alien criminals and to work more closely with state and local officials to deport convicted criminals. In July 1996, a Russian organized crime leader was convicted in New York City. The prosecutor said, "We're glad that an early attempt by the F.B.I. to strike at this group before they really spread out was successful."[97]

Frustrated Florida officials announced in 1994 that the state would become the first to deport illegal aliens who had been imprisoned for nonviolent offenses while residing in Florida. "The cost [of incarceration] is astounding," declared Governor Lawton Chiles. "What's worse, we have to release a state inmate for every criminal alien who enters our prisons."[98] Other states established similar programs.[99]

In 1995 the Clinton administration announced that 51,600 illegal aliens had been deported, up 15 percent from the previous year. And in 1996 the figure was 68,790, with nearly 100,000 deportations projected for 1997. The INS reported in 1997 that it deported a record number of aliens in the first three months of that year. Growing numbers of criminal aliens were among them.[100]

Immigrant crime was one worry, but so was immigrant health. "Epidemics and immigrants have suffered a lethal association in the public mind from the Irish in New York wrongly blamed for the cholera epidemic of 1832 and Chinese in San Francisco vilified for causing the bubonic plague in 1900, to Haitians in Miami stigmatized as AIDS carriers in the 1980s," historian Alan Kraut wrote in *Silent Travelers*.[101] Thus, like the connection of immigrants to crime, the linking of immigrants to disease has an old history. But the fear seems less today though the anti-immigration groups and leaders worry that the United States might become the hospital of the world. Immigrants carrying certain diseases are barred from the United States, though they can receive a waiver in some cases.

Still, *Border Watch* told its readers that, according to the *Los Angeles Times*, "waves of Third World immigrants . . . bring with them medical problems that have not been seen in the United States for generations." Tuberculosis is up, *Border Watch* reported, and so are other serious diseases. And worse of all, "failure to control illegal immigration allows people with any disease to enter American society."[102] While not dwelling on disease, Peter Brimelow wanted his readers to know that the increase of TB was connected to new immigrants, as was leprosy. And cholera and malaria "widespread in Latin America . . . have been reported in the United States recently." It was another worrisome aspect of immigration.[103] Their fears were not exactly unfounded, for epidemiologists agreed that the foreign-born did have higher rates of TB.[104]

If one issue caught the eye of those concerned about immigrants being carriers of diseases it was the AIDS crisis emerging in the late 1980s. When the United States Food and Drug Administration (FDA) recommended that Haitians be excluded from donating blood on the ground that many Haitians had tested positive for HIV, New York Haitians staged a protest. The FDA backed down and reversed its position.[105]

But what of those Haitians at Guantanamo who tested HIV positive or any other prospective immigrants with similar results? In 1987

Senator Jesse Helms introduced legislation that barred persons with the AIDS virus from emigration to the United States. It passed unanimously. Later the Center for Disease Control recommended that AIDS and some other diseases be removed from the list barring potential immigrants. Congress compiled when it passed the Immigration Act of 1990, giving the Department of Health and Human Services (HHS) the power to make the removal.[106]

INS wanted to keep the ban, but the secretary of HHS, Louis Sullivan, announced that he would take the controversial step of allowing infected persons into the United States. Sullivan said that admitting the small number of such persons who would probably come would not pose a serious health risk for the United States and that supporting him were public health leaders.[107] Conservatives in and out of Congress objected to Sullivan's suggestion and sent 40,000 letters of protest to Washington. The Bush administration backed down and kept the ban.[108]

When Bill Clinton became President, a new move was made to lift the ban on persons testing positive for HIV or having AIDS. Congress quickly responded. The Senate voted 76 to 23 and the House 356 to 58 to keep the ban in place.[109] Looking at the lopsided vote, President Clinton, still feeling the effects of his defeat on gays in the military, decided not to challenge Congress. When the issue was raised about this possibly being discriminatory against homosexuals, Senators denied it. One said, "This is a deadly disease. It is a communicable disease. It is spread by sexual contact. It is spread by IV drug users. Those are facts." He insisted that immigrants with AIDS would place a huge demand on health services and cost the American taxpayers.[110] Similar arguments were heard in the House of Representatives, where one debater remarked, "Because HIV is always fatal, the public health consequences of allowing HIV individuals to immigrate is of the highest order. We have never before permitted immigration of those who were infected in the middle of an epidemic. We should not start now."[111] Such positions were the same as that of Dan Stein of FAIR: "Our medical care, social-services net and free public education are a magnet for immigrants. We can't bring people here en masse for medical treatment."[112]

Barring persons with AIDS, as most commentators admitted, would have little effect on immigration to the United States. And if the INS and local and state authorities worked more carefully together to remove immigrant criminals, the total numbers being deported would not make much of a dent in the immigration flows. Exact figures are lacking, but at most aliens in American federal prisons comprised only one quarter of the incarcerated.

Cutting the flow of illegal immigration would have a greater impact on the numbers than dealing with criminals and alleged health risks. Restrictionists usually use high figures of illegal aliens electing each year to stay permanently in the United States. According to Peter Brimelow the INS catches about one million at the border each year, but he accepts the border patrol's estimate that for every one being caught, three were getting through. Thus three million illegal immigrants got to the United States annually, of whom, he says, 300,000–500,000 remain.[113] These high figures are clearly exaggerated to give the impression of an immigration invasion. The INS has estimated that there were five million undocumented persons in the United States in the mid-1990s and that they were increasing at a rate of 275,000 annually.[114]

INS figures nonetheless indicate that it was no easy task to halt illegal immigration, the source of so many immigration problems according to the restrictionist lobby. Yet, if a more efficient INS, tighter border controls and some type of counterfeit proof ID card became a reality, there remains the issue of legal immigration. The 1990 immigration act, in conjunction with refugee policy, permitted at least 800,000 persons to settle legally in the United States annually. The forces of restriction believed that the new legal immigrants arriving after 1970 were causing unacceptable economic and assimilationist problems that could not be ignored.

# 5

## Old Wine in New Bottles
### *The Economics Debate*

*"The first thing an immigrant should read after arriving on these shores is the help-wanted section of the newspaper, not an application for food stamps."*
—Letter to the *New York Times*, October 4, 1996.

*"The continual enlargement of the low-wage labor pool in the United States by immigration since the sixties is probably one of the reasons that wages have stagnated or declined at the bottom of the American class system."*
—Michael Lind, *The Next American Nation: The New Nationalism and the Fourth American Revolution*, 320.

RECENTLY, NO ISSUE about migration to America has been debated more than the economic one. Of course deciding whether immigrants are good or bad economically for Americans has a long history. What is new in recent years about the economic discussion of immigration is the rising sophistication of the arguments. Although the Dillingham Commission provided data and useful studies, most popular or political charges about the economic impact of immigration remained vague and were devoid of data or empirical studies. But after 1980 the debate has drawn in a number economists and sociologists who marshal statistical evidence to support their positions.

Two major issues have emerged from this debate. First is the controversy over the labor market impact of immigration, both illegal and legal. Second is the issue over whether immigrants are a drain on the American taxpayer because they use social welfare programs, such as Aid to Dependent Children (ADC), food stamps, and medical care, or attend the public schools. It is important to note, however, that even though the debates have become more scholarly, there remains an intensity of emotion that distorts the issues. Critics of immigration often look only at those studies that support their point of view, while defenders of liberal policies likewise depend upon selected evidence and studies. Thus, although there is a growing literature about the economics of immigration, it is most frequently used to attain political goals.

At times, immigration restrictionists arguing about labor market effects single out illegal or undocumented immigrants, but the thrust of their attack envelops all kinds of immigrants, legal and illegal. Restrictionists see the economic danger in the large number of immigrants and not simply their status in law. No one has written more about the adverse impact of immigration on the labor market than Vernon Briggs Jr., a labor economist at Cornell University. In a number of books, essays, testimony before congressional committees and material reprinted by the anti-immigration lobby, he has sketched a broad view of immigration's effects. Briggs sees the "original role of mass immigration," which he dates in several waves after 1830, as being consistent with the "development trends and labor force requirements of the United States."[1] Put simply, the United States needed large numbers of unskilled laborers, and immigrants furnished a considerable number of them. Thus, immigration prior to the 1920s was on the whole beneficial.

Once the United States substantially cut immigration in the 1920s employers were forced to turn to native-born laborers, including black Americans, who had largely been left out of the industrial process. Blacks began migrating to northern industrial areas seeking to fill the jobs that were once held by immigrants. "Black Americans, in particular but also other excluded or marginalized groups needed a chance to enter the work force and to develop their latent human resource abilities."[2]

To Briggs, what happened after World War II was a carelessly conceived renewed mass immigration policy. Like many other critics of immigration policy, Briggs believes that laws and decisions driven by political forces do not make economic sense. Partly as a "spillover effect of the civil rights movement," Congress passed the Immigration Act of 1965 and then subsequent laws to admit more immigrants and refugees. Unfortunately, says Briggs, "There was no thought at the time that many of the same urban labor markets where blacks were concentrated were about to receive a mass infusion of new immigrants—most of whom would themselves be from minority groups."[3]

At the bottom of the occupational structure, black Americans discovered rivals for less-skilled jobs. African Americans, says Briggs, bore the brunt of competition with the new immigrants. "Already having an abundance of unskilled or poorly educated adults, the last thing that the nation needs is to continue to allow unskilled and poorly educated persons to immigrate into the United States."[4] On another occasion Briggs has characterized United States immigration policy as a "revived instrument of institutional racism."[5]

Briggs's attack on the new mass immigration was based on history, an overall assessment of labor trends, and general theory. He did not examine local labor markets. However, his argument was picked up by others and he became an important person in the debate about the labor market impacts of immigration. One such other was *Forbes* editor Peter Brimelow, whose *Alien Nation* devotes several chapters to what he believes are the adverse economic consequences of immigration.[6] Equally as vociferous in arguing that the nation does not need a mass movement of incoming migrants is Roy Beck. In *Re-Charting America's Future*, published by the Social Contract Press in 1994, Beck attempts to refute the usual arguments for immigration.[7] Social Contract books are probably written for the converted or near-converted, but his *The Case Against Immigration* (Norton 1996) was no doubt aimed at a larger audience. Of the prominent writers within the restrictionist camp, Roy Beck is the most convincing. He deals with a variety of issues, but his core argument is based on economics. Unlike much of the material put out by the anti-immigration crusade, Beck's carefully crafted book is based on considerable research and knowledge of the debate among economists. He argues that America does not need large-scale immigration for economic growth and that it is simply not true that immigrants only take jobs that Americans will not do. "In many cases, so-called immigrant occupations already have Americans working alongside foreigners. There are plenty of unemployed Americans who might take those jobs if they began opening up

after a halt in immigration, especially if the work place culture once
again became American-and-English-speaking."[8]It is not simply poor
black Americans who bear the burden of immigration, according to
Beck. In Texas, for example, "Many established Mexican-Americans
have given up their attempts to work on the migratory route where
they face discrimination because they are citizens and where more recent immigrants continue to bid wages further downward."[9]

Most mainstream economists by no means share Beck's views, but
some do. In the field of the growing literature about the economics of
immigration, Harvard economist George Borjas is probably the leading authority. In his 1990 book, *Friends or Strangers: The Impact of Immigrants on the U.S. Economy* and other essays, Borjas has reviewed the
economic literature on this subject, noting that "until recently little
was known about the impact that immigrants have on the native-labor
market."[10] He says that the research done before 1990 indicates that
immigrants only have a small negative effect on the earnings of native-
born Americans. "The earnings of the typical native are barely affected by the entry of immigrants into the local labor market."[11]

Recently, however, Borjas has been more critical of U.S. policy. He
now believes that low-skill immigration might be contributing to a
new underclass and costing the American taxpayer. His underclass is
not necessarily of low-income native Americans, but of the immigrants themselves, many of whom do poorly in the American labor
market.[12] "Ethnic skill differentials disappear very slowly. It might take
four generations, or roughly 100 years."[13]

Borjas's concern about certain classes of immigrants not making it
in American society has been the subject for academic debate for a
number of years. Trying to settle the issue, the RAND Corporation's
Center for Research on Immigration Policy reported in 1996 that the
earnings of Mexicans did not catch up with native-born Americans;
indeed, they lost ground economically. Asians and Europeans on the
other hand, did well.[14] Whether this automatically leads to a permanent class of poorly educated immigrants stuck at the bottom of the
income pile is another matter, but such detailed findings alarmed
some observers.[15]

Since Borjas published *Friends or Strangers* new reports have appeared that have added to the controversy. Several studies had already
suggested that native-born Americans were leaving areas of high im-

migration when William Frey, of the University of Michigan, in articles based on the 1990 census, concluded that when large numbers of immigrants pour into an area, many native-born Americans leave, perhaps responding to a more competitive labor market.[16] Frey wrote, "Data show that out migration from immigrant magnets is most pronounced among less-educated, lower-income domestic migrants. They are the workers who most directly compete with the less-skilled immigrants moving into metros like Los Angeles and New York."[17] Still another careful study by David Jaeger examined the data for 50 metropolitan areas and found a significant negative impact of immigration on low-skilled (less than a high school education) native-born workers, accounting for half of the decline in real wages of native drop-outs.[18]

Not all of the work in this field has been by economists. Sociologist Roger Waldinger of the University of California at Los Angeles examined the hiring practices among a sample of Los Angeles restaurants and hotels. He found competition between black Americans and immigrants for these entry level jobs. Network hiring was extremely important for the employers he surveyed, and the end result worked to the disadvantage of African Americans.[19] Curiously, Waldinger, who has also done a study of New York City, does not think cuts in immigration will help blacks much.[20]

Another hotel and office building study produced a similar result: the displacement of blacks in Los Angeles hotels and offices by new Hispanic immigrants. Often cited as an example of how immigration hurts black Americans, the study noted that janitorial work was a good union job before employers turned to non-union firms supplying immigrants at half the union wages. Beginning in 1946, successful union drives brought a relatively high wage to many African Americans working as custodians in Los Angeles. When nonunion firms entered the field the union contractors lost out. In 1977, some 2,500 blacks were union members, but by 1985, under the assault of nonunion firms, their numbers had fallen to only 600. They were largely replaced by Hispanic immigrants who worked for lower wages.[21]

Richard Mines, author of the hotel study, also concluded that recent immigrants were pushing out blacks in the "frozen food industries in Watsonville, construction clean-up jobs in Orange County, and janitorial work in San José." Commentators have also pointed to other local largely unskilled jobs where blacks were losing out to immigrants.[22]

The debate about the economic impact of immigration upon low-income American workers has touched those whose primary concern is not about immigration. Michael Lind, an editor of the *New Republic*, believes that anxiety "about high levels of immigration . . . cannot in itself be dismissed as racism. A sober look at the numbers might be enough to make a restrictionist of the most humanitarian liberal."[23] Two critics on the Left concerned primarily with race relations, Martin Conroy and Stephen Steinberg, have made similar arguments.[24]

James S. Robb, writing in *Social Contract*, claims that as affirmative action programs have been extended to a wider circle; groups for which these programs were never intended to benefit have advanced much to the disadvantage of African Americans. Worse yet, he said, in passing IRCA Congress made it illegal to exclude immigrants from affirmative action programs.[25] He quotes Ricky Silverman, vice-chairman of the Equal Employment Opportunity Commission as saying that immigrant participation is "the ultimate nightmare of affirmative action. It is its Achilles' heel."[26]

Robb believes that universities and other institutions employ immigrant minorities and count them as statistics indicating the progress they were making in hiring minorities. And small business set-aside programs have also benefited immigrants, among them Asian Indians who run motels.[27] Although Robb is unsure whether U.S. minorities are "losing out" because of immigrants, the "clear winners, of course, were the non-citizens who came here looking for economic opportunity only to find themselves winners in the affirmative action lottery."[28]

Affirmative action preferences for immigrants were not major features in the debates, but a few critics picked up Robb's arguments. Roy Beck's *The Case Against Immigration* charges, "Ironically, programs of affirmative action—meant to compensate for centuries of legalized discrimination against blacks—now are being used by employers to avoid hiring blacks. This can happen because an immigrant who first set foot in the United States yesterday is considered to have exactly the same claim for redress as the descendants of slavery."[29]

It was not only the bottom of the American income structure that suffers from the new mass immigration, according to some critics. Norman Matloff, a professor of computer science at the University California at Davis, argues that foreign-born computer experts are finding jobs in Silicon Valley that American-born, educated workers could fill. "There are too many highly skilled workers for too few jobs.

In spite of the labor surplus, Silicon Valley employers continue to hire foreign nationals . . . the attraction is often a desire for a cheap, compliant labor force," says Matloff. He further suggests, "Sadly, the process is pitting Asian foreign nationals against Asian-Americans . . . [who have had] trouble finding work in the computer industry. Those who do manage to find positions . . . are often shunted into nontechnical job such as customer interface—while Asian foreign nationals are hired for the technical work." Matloff insists that hired foreigners are neither great innovators nor always well educated, but they are cheap. Matloff believes that existing regulations to help American workers were either not enforced or ineffective.[30]

Competition from skilled immigrants is not the only labor issue involving foreign labor. Several programs run by the U.S. government permit corporations to bring in temporary workers on H-1B visas for stays of up to six years. For example, American hospitals recruited nurses from abroad to fill vacancies, especially in large cities. Populists Donald Steele and James Steele noted in 1996 that temporary workers add up to a number greater than those coming under the occupational visas. "What all these numbers—permanent immigrants and alien workers here under jobs programs—add up to is this: Since 1990, at least 6 million foreign workers have been thrown into the competition for U.S. jobs."[31]

The dispute over the hiring of highly trained foreigners became especially contentious in California's Silicon Valley, home to many computer related companies. Intel and other firms insisted the experts they hired were needed for America and their firms to be competitive. Intel's president, Andrew S. Grove, said, "We need the best brains in this competitive battle." But Joel B. Snyder, chair of the Institute of Electrical and Electronics Engineers—USA, retorted, "They're not bringing in the best and the brightest. They're bringing in the cheapest."[32] Critics of immigration policy also said that Hewlett Packard used "body shops," contract-outfits that take on computer programming assignments and hire foreigners.[33]

As for educated blacks, Frank Morris Sr., former dean of Graduate Studies at Morgan State University, argues that American graduate schools educated alien students in preference to black Americans. "American universities are similar to the rest of American society and they continue to value non-American citizens over American minorities, especially African-American males."[34] Certainly the proportion of foreign-born graduate students in computer and some other sciences has gone up during the 1980s and 1990s, but whether this represented a deliberate policy of discrimination against black males is more open to question. Still, it was another charge about the adverse impact of immigration upon black Americans.[35]

Norman Matloff and others, while arguing that immigrants hurt both blue- and white-collar Americans, have also suggested that the contribution of immigrants in opening new businesses has not necessarily aided Americans. Some critics say that the new ethnic entrepreneurs do not necessarily hire American workers and in fact favor immigrants. Moreover, Matloff argued that the market for many of the new businesses was becoming saturated by the mid-1990s and that the current rates of "immigration are higher than the immigrant communities can stand." Too many immigrants equals too many out of work.[36]

Nor were agricultural workers overlooked in the debate about the impact on Americans. A Department of Labor study published in 1989 reported that while immigration was beneficial to the United States economically, in some sectors cheap Mexican labor adversely affected "wages [and] working conditions."[37] Philip Martin, professor of economics at the University of California at Davis, and Elizabeth Midgley agree that some local studies of agriculture indicate the flux of unskilled farm workers in California displaces Americans or lowers wages. A similar conclusion was reached by two other investigators studying unionization and labor conditions in California.[38]

Opponents of large-scale immigration are not the only ones critical of the American system. Indeed, others have also pointed to flaws in the American system, but without wanting cuts in the flow. Several economists, George Borjas and Barry Chiswick among them, have suggested that policy should place more emphasis on admitting those with skills to match the American labor market.[39] In part, the 1990 immigration act aimed to increase the economic-oriented visas, but the vast bulk of persons arriving still came under family unification and as refugees.

Yet it is difficult to see how Norman Matloff and others, who see competition in the skilled labor market as well as for the unskilled, would be satisfied with these recommendations. For those wanting sharp reductions in the total, shifting visas around and not making drastic cuts does not confront the basic problem of too many immigrants. A FAIR publication put it, "But highly skilled immigrants who earn high salaries pay proportionately high taxes, make few demands on taxpayer-funded services—except for schooling—and contribute to job growth. These immigrants are generally considered an asset to our society, although they too can have negative work force effects for Americans, when they arrive in large numbers."[40] For the restrictionists, these arguments are compelling; the 1990s are a wrong time to pursue a policy of renewed mass immigration.

Although originally rooted in the environmental movement, FAIR insists that immigration has adverse economic effects on the United States. When the National Immigration Forum and the CATO institute, both ardent proponents of liberal immigration, sponsored and published Julian Simon's *Immigration: The Demographic and Economic Facts* in 1995, it predictably declared that immigration was a positive good economically. FAIR responded almost immediately with two brief publications attacking Simon.[41]

No less insistent that immigration is harmful is AICF. Its newsletter *Border Watch* carries reports about the negative effects of mass immigration on American workers. A 1990 issue of *Border Watch* headlined, "Immigration Worsens U.S. Employment."[42] Like other critics of American policy, AICF insists, "American scientists, engineers, and other high-tech workers are having trouble finding jobs, in part because current immigration law has opened the gates for foreigners in these professions to enter and take employment."[43]

While Population-Environment Balance and the Carrying Capacity Network are both primarily environmental organizations, they too, attack large scale immigration on economic grounds. Virginia Abernethy wrote in CCN's *The Clearinghouse Bulletin*, "No administration or government program and no foreseeable private investment of the quantity needed, can expect to overcome unemployment in the face of up to 1.5 million legal and illegal immigrants every year."[44] Balance told its members, "Legal and illegal immigrants fill jobs that Americans need. They do not simply take migrant agricultural jobs which Americans allegedly do not want—over 80% work in non-agricultural areas and compete with Americans."[45]

Individual environmentalists and those primarily concerned with population also use economic language. Thus Richard Lamm and Gary Imhoff did so in the *Immigration Time Bomb* as did John Tanton and Wayne Lutton and demographer Leon Bouvier, who wrote in *Peaceful Invasions: Immigration and Changing America*, "Some programs to help the poor were undoubtedly misguided, but it is also true that competition from unskilled immigrants makes it harder for the American underclass to lift itself up by its bootstraps."[46]

The vast bulk of these groups and individuals arguing that immigrants hurt low-skilled American minorities are not minorities themselves. They no doubt believe what they say, but another advantage to their rhetoric is dealing with the race issue. By charging that low-income black and Hispanic Americans bear the brunt of the new mass immigration, they maintain that it is not racist to favor severe limits.

Restrictionists never say that the National Immigration Forum, the U.S. Committee for Refugees, and the dozens of other members of the pro-immigration lobby are racists, but this adverse economic impact turns the race card on its head. National policy is not driven by racism, but rather by indifference to the concerns of America's poor, corporate greed, and the lobbying of the pro-immigration network. The result is the same: a new racism. Immigration must be cut to aid blacks. Roy Beck suggests, "Until the number of black Americans in poverty drops significantly for several years, Congress should set the immigration level as close to zero as possible."[47] Aiding this line of thinking are ambivalence or explicit hostility to immigrants made by some African-American leaders. Dean Frank Morris typifies those in the black community opposed to immigration, and the Latino community is not united behind Hispanic organizations that overwhelmingly favor immigration.

The second major issue in the economics debate is the belief that immigrants are a burden on American taxpayers. No one is more important to making this case than Professor Donald Huddle, professor emeritus of economics at Rice University. In several studies he has centered on the welfare state, arguing that immigrants are using many social programs and that they are not paying their fair share of taxes. In 1993, in a study commissioned by CCN he alleged that illegal and legal immigrants cost the taxpayer $44 billion in 1992. About 12 billion were indirect costs due to the displacement of American workers by immigrants. His study included programs such as public education, Social Security, Medicaid, Supplemental Security Income (SSI), food stamps, and housing. The taxes the newcomers pay include federal income, Social Security, and state and local ones.[48] These figures add up on a year-by-year basis. He told readers of the *New York Times* Op-Ed page that "Curbing Illegal immigration could save $186 billion by

2002."[49] For the decade 1995–2004 he calculated the cost to American taxpayers at approximately $280 billion.[50] Professor Huddle also broke down the costs for several individual states, Texas and California among them, and updated his study after 1993. He pegged the cost at 65 billion for 1996.[51]

Huddle is not alone in his argument. New York State Senator Frank Padavan headed committees that issued reports on the impact of immigration policy on his state. *Our Teeming Shore* acknowledged the many benefits that immigrants were bringing to the State of New York, but said the taxes collected did not offset the costs of immigration. It urged Congress to fund the difference.[52] Two years later a second report calculated that immigrants cost the state at least $5 billion annually and again urged federal compensation.[53] Across the continent, a scathing Los Angeles County study of undocumented aliens argued that such immigrants were a burden and prompted a debate in the state assembly about the impact of immigration on California.[54] Hearings produced no legislation, but they highlighted the controversy over immigration in that state.[55] Many local officials in California agreed that immigration cost their communities too much.[56]

The problems of local communities were aggravated by the failure of Congress to fully implement IRCA. In passing the law, Congress had promised federal funding to aid localities with large numbers of amnestied immigrants. However, sufficient funds were not forthcoming, which only added to the problems of states such as California, the state claiming half of these newcomers. In 1992 a congressional conference committee stripped $812 million in "previously approved federal funding from health and education programs for newly legalized immigrants." Former Representative Edward R. Roybal of California explained, "I blame it on the fact that California is really the only state suffering the consequences of this."[57]

Just as the Los Angeles County study and others were challenged by defenders of immigration, so was the work of Huddle. Among others, the Urban Institute, located in Washington D.C., issued a report authored by Jeffrey Passell, Rebecca Clark, and Robert Warren. They attacked Huddle's conclusions, data, and methodology and turned his study on its head. Instead of immigration being a net loss, the authors claimed that immigrants generated an annual surplus of at least $25 billion. One issue that all agreed to, however, was that the burden of immigration fell on those states with high numbers of newcomers, whereas most taxes were collected by the federal government.[58] This fact no doubt explains why Los Angeles officials were upset. "Los Angeles County bears a disproportionately high cost for serving immigrants who are in this country as a result of Federal laws and/or policies and decisions, while most tax revenues collected from immigrants go to the Federal government."[59]

FAIR did note the differences in the two reports and pointed to the Center for Immigration Studies' work and challenged both Huddle and the Urban Institute. FAIR said that immigrants were a net deficit of $29 billion in the same year covered by the others.[60] Moreover, in 1995 FAIR pointed to a GAO report covering SSI and ADC that supported the negative assessment of immigration; for immigrants were more likely than the native born to be using these programs. Of course these were only two of many governmental welfare programs, and GAO did not deal with the many fault's of Huddle's work.[61]

For the most part, however, the anti-immigration lobby ignored the criticism of Huddle, whether from GAO, the Urban Institute or elsewhere. Huddle's reports, in spite of their inadequacies, became the gospel truth for anti-immigration players in the game. CCN sponsored his original study and was hardly going to refute it. Balance has used the Huddle study as has Negative Population Growth. Peter Brimelow noted that Huddle's work was under attack, but "at least it got the debate going—at last. And the debate needs to get going."[62] *The Immigration Invasion* and *The Immigration Time Bomb* also express the view that we have too many immigrants using welfare programs.[63]

The belief that immigrants use the American welfare system is firmly imbedded at the grass roots. The California Coalition for Immigration Reform told its readers that the United States was being invaded by illegal immigrants who cost (according to Huddle) the American taxpayers billions because of their use for "health care, education, and welfare benefits."[64] AICF has been adamant in insisting that immigrants abuse the welfare system, and *Border Watch* insists: "Immigration Costs Taxpayers Billions."[65] Norman Matloff analyzed census data concerning SSI and immigrant use and concluded, "Everyone knows that this is free money. The knowledge about this overseas has just mushroomed."[66] Moreover, GAO documented a growing use of SSI among immigrants.[67] In the words of Robert Rector of the Heritage Foundation, writing in *The Social Contract*, "The U.S. welfare system is rapidly becoming a deluxe retirement home for the elderly of other countries."[68]

The emergence of George Borjas, widely respected within the economics profession, in the immigration debate heartened foes of generous immigration. Borjas's recent research views the current flow of immigration with suspicion. In scholarly and political journals such as the *National Review* he has outlined trends about the economics of immigration. He finds that "increasing participation of immigrants in welfare programs" means immigrants "now receive a disproportionate share of cash benefits." His *National Review* article of March 1996 alleged: "it is not too much of an exaggeration to say that the welfare problem in California is on the verge of becoming an immigrant problem."[69] Particularly concerned about the low level of skills of so many recent immigrants, Borjas is dubious of the work of both Huddle and the Urban Institute, which "inevitably incorporate many hidden and questionable assumptions."[70]

Borjas, though advising Governor Pete Wilson of California on immigration issues, has not joined any of the anti-immigration groups, nor has he come out for radical cuts in legal immigration flows. He has, however, published several articles critical of immigration in the anti-immigration *National Review*. Borjas believes that immigration on balance benefits the United States, though not every group shares its benefits; some actually lose in the process. He has also warned that it would be better to reform the current policy now, because the "harmful effects of immigration will not go away simply because some people do not wish to see them." By postponing thoughtful policies, the long-run impact might prompt Americans to undertake a "seismic shift—one that, as in the twenties, may come close to shutting down the border and preventing Americans from enjoying the benefits that a well-designed immigration policy can bestow on the United States."[71]

Defenders of current immigration have insisted that one reason that immigrants might be using social services at such a high rate is due to refugees, who are entitled to special aid by the United States government. *Business Week* declared in 1994, "The high welfare use by refugees is a legacy of the cold war. . . . Because of the political popularity of anticommunism, refugees have been treated very well."[72] But Borjas said that new data indicate that welfare gap was not caused by refugees (and the elderly) alone. "The argument that the immigrant welfare problem is caused by refugees and the elderly is factually incorrect." He worried, "To what extent does a generous welfare state reduce the work incentives of current immigrants, and change the nature of the immigrant flow by influencing potential immigrants' decisions to come—and to stay?"[73]

The belief that immigrants, especially illegal ones, are a drain on the taxpayer was the driving force behind Proposition 187 in California's 1994 election, which passed only to be tied up the court battles. The November election victory of Proposition 187 nonetheless fueled movements in other states to pass similar provisions.[74] In Florida two groups rose to the challenge of meeting the costs of illegal immigration. Backed by polls showing residents favoring tough action, Florida imitators moved ahead to get the state to enact provisions like California's Prop 187. Save Our State, an Orlando-based group, put forth a constitutional amendment to deny schooling and other social services (except emergency medical care) to illegal aliens. Florida 187, backed by FAIR, went further, adding a provision that required governmental services to be provided only in English and required that public servants pass an English proficiency exam.[75] Worried that the section denying illegal children an education might be unconstitutional, backers of the Florida initiatives scaled down that section, but included other provisions requiring state agencies to report suspected illegals to the federal government.[76] The two groups failed to cooperate or to interest enough Florida voters to get their propositions on the ballot in time for the 1996 election.[77] When it was clear that they fell considerably short of the required number of signatures, they announced that they would try to have a measure ready for the 1998 election.[78]

Arizona proponents of 187 were also unsuccessful in getting their version, which was less stringent than California's, on the ballot for the 1996 election. Activists there noted several reasons why they could not obtain the necessary 112,000 signatures, including a late start, excessive heat, and a shortage of funds. It does appear that it was proving difficult to pass California-type 187s in other states.[79]

Denying illegal immigrants aid was not the only method of dealing with alleged high local costs of immigration. California and several other states requested aid from the government to offset the expenses of supporting illegal immigration, and they sued the government for funding. As one Texas Republican put the case, "Illegal immigration is a federal problem that is being borne by the state and local governments along our border. . .it is a federal issue." Even New York State, where anti-immigration sentiment was not so intense, joined the law cases.[80] But the suits were thrown out of court. Federal judges ruled that federal government was not obligated to reimburse the states for such expenses.[81] Not deterred, California went to court again in 1996, claiming that the federal government had allowed an "invasion" of illegal aliens and that it should reimburse California for their expenses, but this suit fared no better than the others. In 1997, two decisions by U.S. courts ruled that only Congress and the President can decide how to spend federal money for immigration issues.[82]

Yet, anti-immigration voices were beginning to be heard in Congress. In 1995 Congress began to vote funds to help states pay for the expenses of jailing criminal immigrants. The next year California received $270 million, the lion's share of the largesse. This was four times the amount voted the previous year, and for the first time Congress permitted some of the funds to be allocated to counties.[83] In doling out the funds, Justice Department official Chris Rizzuto remarked, "We understand that the states, particularly the big states, have a problem and to the degree the federal government can help . . . this is something that can be done."[84]

Because immigration, both legal and illegal, was a matter determined by the Congress and the President, propositions like California's 187 might not be enforceable and may turn out to be largely symbolic. Thus, the anti-immigration lobby increasingly turned its attention to Washington, calling for substantial decreases in immigration. Flush with the victory of 187 and the Republican wins in November 1994, the new restrictionists had reason for optimism.

There were federal laws, dating from the nineteenth century, banning persons likely to become a public charge, and these had been used to deport Mexicans and keep out refugees during the 1930s. Between 1952 and 1990 about 10 percent of the applicants for visas were denied on this ground. As for those already here, they could be deported if they became a public charge, but in recent years only a handful of immigrants becoming public charges have been returned home. *Research Perspectives on Migration* reported that only twelve such cases were recorded from 1981 to 1990.[85] Unless the law was enforced other means would have to be found to keep immigrants from receiving federal benefits. Republicans were particularly eager to change the welfare programs, and during the 1992 presidential campaign candidate Bill Clinton joined the chorus of opponents and promised to "end welfare as we know it." While most of the debate centered around programs such as ADC for native-born Americans and not immigrants, the welfare reforms gave Congress an opportunity to change benefits for newcomers as well.

Agreement that the system was not working was one issue, finding a consensus on what should be done was another. In May 1994 a number of moderate and conservative Democrats signaled their willingness to cut programs for legal immigrants, but hearings in the summer of 1994 indicated that there was considerable disagreement between the two parties and that the politics would play a role in welfare reform. Republicans accused Clinton and the Democrats of being soft on welfare recipients, but Democratic liberals attacked Republicans as being insensitive to poor children.[86]

When the Republicans swept the 1994 elections, winning both houses of Congress, the momentum for change grew. No doubt the victory of Proposition 187 in California, even though it was stalled in the courts, added to the pressure for Congress to act. Proposition 187 had dealt with illegal aliens, but reformers, as they called themselves, wanted to curtail benefits for legal immigrants as well. After all, illegal immigrants were already ineligible for most federal benefits.

In 1995 the Republican-dominated Congress passed a bill, which the President vetoed, that cut some benefits for legal immigrants. Moreover, the debates indicated that broad support existed among legislators to make sponsors of immigrants responsible for their support.[87] The lawmakers were certainly aware that SSI benefits were going to elderly immigrants who had been in the United States for only a few years. Congress had been holding hearings on the cost of aid to immigrants and had asked GAO to report on this issue. In February 1995 GAO told the legislators that the number of immigrants applying for and receiving SSI benefits had increased markedly since 1983. Although GAO lacked precise data Social Security Administration figures suggest that "some immigrants apply for SSI benefits shortly after a deeming period would have expired. . . . that is, soon after the sponsor's promise of support would have expired."[88] Until 1994 such immigrants had been eligible for SSI payments after residing only three years in the United States. Then the figure was changed to five years.[89]

The congressional debates in 1995 and 1996 over welfare largely ignored the impact of the cuts on immigrants. Senator Edward Kennedy lamented, "For the first time in history, Congress will ban legal immigrants from most assistance programs. . . . Hundreds of thousands of legal immigrant children will be robbed of a safety net."[90] He was answered by Senator Bob Smith of New Hampshire:"I am pleased that this bill takes a number of steps toward ending the abuse of the welfare system by those legal immigrants who come to America, not to go work but to go on welfare."[91]

After vetoing two welfare bills, President Clinton signed a third in August 1996. Clinton indicated unhappiness with some of the new limits on benefits to immigrants and asked for changes:"I am deeply disappointed that the congressional leadership insisted on attaching to this extraordinarily important bill a provision that will hurt legal immigrants in America . . . I am convinced when we send legislation to Congress to correct it, it will be corrected."[92]

Many liberal Democrats deemed the bill too harsh not only on children and single women, but also on immigrants. They had hoped the President would agree and veto it. The new welfare program consisted of block grants to the states to manage, within limits, as they saw fit. As for immigrants, Republicans estimated that over a six-year period $18 billion would be saved by cutting or denying food stamps, SSI, cash welfare, and Medicaid to resident aliens who were not yet citizens. The bill also made the sponsors more responsible for the care of immigrants.[93]

The estimated savings were well below those of Don Huddle and many in the anti-immigration lobby, but not all benefits were to be cut or eliminated. Actually no one knew precisely how much tax money would be saved by the changes.[94] Because states had more authority under the new system, they might decide to be more generous than the federal guidelines. States would still have to decide whether to give immigrants health care and some other cash benefits. If a state believed it had an obligation to aid needy immigrants, it might find that its block grant insufficient. California expected to save $300 million annually by eliminating its extra payments to SSI recipients, but on the other hand the state was giving nothing to counties to help pay for general assistance.[95] It might decide to do so.

There was also the possibility of court cases that would effect immigrants' benefits. All of these possibilities, according to Huddle, made the impact of the bill unclear. "The legislation provides for exceptions.

The courts may further weaken the law's effect. Additionally, federal cuts in entitlements for immigrants could shift much of the burden to states and local communities."[96]

The welfare bill had passed when unemployment and inflation were low and economic growth solid. What kind of pressure would California or other states feel to aid counties during a recession? In Texas, another state with large numbers of immigrants, Governor George Bush said he opposed plans to cut off benefits for elderly and disabled resident aliens. "We ought to take care of these people in the state of Texas," he said.[97] However, he did not recommend specific changes. In Florida disabled immigrants, "some paralyzed or suffering from Alzheimer's disease" gathered to protest the requirement that they must be citizens in order to get medical benefits. Surrounded by these unfortunate people, Representative Ileana Ros-Lehtinen said, "At some moments, they know where they're standing. At other times, some of them don't even know their own names."[98]

As expected, the new law prompted considerable anxiety as local officials attempted to put it into effect. Would immigrants without adequate documentation of their work patterns (they needed to have worked for ten years to be eligible for welfare) be denied benefits? Would nursing homes actually throw out elderly disabled immigrants?[99] Such confusions prompted Congress to delay implementation of the food stamp revision until April 1997 and prompted Republicans, especially governors, to suggest some changes were in order. As part of the congressional-presidential deal to balance the budget by 2002, congressional Republicans agreed to restore benefits to elderly and disabled immigrants who had arrived before August 22, 1996.[100]

The cost factor was also unknown due to the fact that legal immigrants had another way to obtain benefits: become citizens. Following passage of Proposition 187 and the rise in anti-immigrant sentiment, many eligible aliens decided to become U.S. citizens. As citizens they would be entitled to benefits they lost as immigrants; consequently there was rush to naturalize. "When 187 passed, it sparked a lot of concerns all over the country," said Maria Jimenez, of the American Friends Service Committee. In 1990 270,000 persons were naturalized, but it grew rapidly, topping one million in 1996 with predictions going as high as 1.8 million for 1997.[101] Mexicans, who had relatively low rates of applying, began to request citizenship in growing numbers.[102] Alameda County (Calif.) political leaders decided to allocate

$100,000 to aid its immigrants receiving federal benefits in seeking to become citizens. Better to have them become citizens and become eligible for SSI, food stamps, and other programs, the officials reasoned. Otherwise, noted one official, "There will be big trouble because there is no way any county can continue to provide for current recipients and add those coming off the federal dole."[103] The official was pointing to the fact that once removed from federal welfare, local governments would have to pick up the tab for those in need. The situation was ironic. States had been unsuccessfully suing the federal government for funds to cover the cost of serving or incarcerating immigrants, legal or illegal. Now Congress, instead of answering their pleas, had simply added to the economic burden of those communities that believed it was necessary to assist immigrants. It was not what Governor Pete Wilson of California had in mind for immigration reform.

Some low-wage businesses were also alerted to the new law. Several million American workers had wages so low that they were eligible for some federal government programs. For example, a family of three making only $17,000 annually was eligible for food stamps. Marriott, rather than raising wages, embarked upon a program to help its immigrant employees become U.S. citizens and retain their eligibility for welfare programs.[104]

The new restrictionists were not entirely satisfied with the prospects of millions of resident aliens rushing to obtain American citizenship. John Vinson, president of AICF, told readers that the INS was cheapening citizenship, which in turn would lead to additional immigration because the new citizens could bring in quota exempt immigrants. Moreover, he insisted that these new citizens would be ready-made new voters for the immigration lobby. Finally, he suggested that many of these new citizens would "have little understanding or appreciation of America."[105]

Journalist Georgie Anne Geyer added another concern about the citizenship campaigns. She believed that citizenship was becoming less meaningful. She lamented the fact that the naturalization test had become easier over the years and swearing-in ceremonies were conducted in languages other than English.[106] She partly blamed multiculturalism for making the tests a little more than a joke. "All can become 'citizens' with little study and often without even reasonable English proficiency, without knowing much about the history (and thus, the meaning) of the society they are joining, and without having to make most of the traditional commitments to it. So, of course, they remain what they were when they approached America: strangers."[107] Her fears were echoed by several Republicans who thought that the INS system of permitting voluntary agencies to help in the process too often led to careless naturalization.[108]

Even more alarming to the critics of the sharp increase in naturalization were reports that alien criminals were being naturalized. The Washington State Citizens for Immigration Control told its members, "Reports coming from around the country indicate that, in their blind haste to naturalize as many aliens as possible before election day, hundreds, even thousands, of criminals have become citizens and are now out of reach of deportation."[109] Alarmed Republicans charged that naturalization procedures were sloppy and that as many as 100,000 criminals had illegally become citizens.[110] The INS and the FBI did admit that some criminals, including felons, might have been hastily naturalized in the huge rush for citizenship. The Clinton administration announced new procedures for naturalization, and in May 1997 the INS declared it would seek to strip 5,000 persons of their newly acquired citizenship. However, House Republicans were not entirely satisfied with INS's progress in reforming the system for naturalization.[111]

There was also a political concern about these new citizen voters. An Op-Ed writer for the *New York Times* made a guess about the political outcome when he said that "attacks on immigrants hurt the Republicans" and make President Clinton look like "the immigrants' champions."[112] Frank del Olmo, a writer for the *Los Angeles Times*, put it, "It doesn't take a political science degree to figure out that many of these new voters are likely to vote for Democrats rather than Republicans."[113] That newspaper discovered in a poll that new citizens of Latin American ancestry favored the Democratic party by a margin of more than eight in ten.[114] In the 1996 election, the newly naturalized immigrants voted for the Democratic party of Bill Clinton. Hispanic voters turned in greater than usual majorities for the president.[115] In Orange County (Calif.), Loretta Sanchez even defeated Congressman Robert Dornan, no friend of minorities. Even Cubans in Florida gave enough of their usual Republican votes to Clinton to help him carry the state.[116] Moreover, the Democrats did very well among Asian-American voters. "What it all boils down to is this: when the number of new citizens becomes too large the whole process breaks down and runs the danger of becoming politicized," declared the newsletter of the Midwest Coalition to Reform Immigration. The answer: "reduce the annual quota of immigrants to a manageable number."[117]

These economic issues and worries about a diluted citizenship process certainly prompted the anti-immigration forces to call again for immigration cuts. They added them to the list of concerns upon which they built their case. In addition, the fear of a weakened commitment to American society by newly naturalized citizens was closely related to a belief by some restrictionists that American society was in danger of social fragmentation.

# 6

## Why Can't They Be Like Us?
### *The Assimilationist Issue*

*"If the American people truly want to change their historic European rooted civilization into a Latin Caribbean-Asian 'multi-culture,' then let them de bate and approve that proposition through an informed political process. . . . And if Americans do not want their society to change in such a revolutionary manner, then let them revise their immigration laws accordingly."*
—Lawrence Auster, *The Path to National Suicide: As Essay on Immigration and Multiculturalism* (1990), 8–9.

THE MAINSTREAM ANTI-IMMIGRATION movement of the past twenty years has largely avoided both the racist rhetoric and the religious intolerance of the past. Of course, the radical right neo-Nazi organizations favor immigration restrictions. The Southern Poverty Law Center noted that White Aryan Resistance leader Tom Metzger, of Fallbrook, California, publishes cartoons about "dirty Mexicans" and the Asian invasion. He also accused Jews of flooding the United States with immigrants who will eventually bankrupt the nation. And some Klansmen have volunteered their services to police the United States–Mexican border. Other such hate groups have also assailed immigrants.[1] The radical right journal *The New America* devoted its February 19, 1996, issue to immigration. Condemning the new immigration, *The New America* saw a conspiracy of groups demanding "open doors" to weaken American security and bring terrorism and revolution to the United States.[2] Yet it is significant that, while perhaps encouraging violence against immigrants, these groups play no significant role in the immigration battles in Congress or in the public discussions.

Immigration debates reflect the fact that anti–Catholicism and antisemitism have steadily become weaker in American society since the end of World War II. In a wide number of areas of American life, these forms of bigotry are no longer acceptable. Antisemitism played a role in the nation's resistance to the taking in Jewish refugees during the Great Depression and a role in shaping the first Displaced Persons Act. But in the 1970s things were different. Congress said that the Soviet Union should not be granted most favored nation trade status unless the Soviets were willing to permit Jews to emigrate. After the collapse of communism in the Soviet Union in 1989, Congress passed the Lautenberg Amendment that assumed that any Soviet Jews (and a number of Pentecostal groups) were automatically refugees, thus permitting 40,000 or so Russian Jews to migrate annually to the United States.

If the presence of Jewish and Catholic immigrants cause little anxiety, the increase of Muslims coming to America has prompted uneasiness. The American Arab Discrimination Committee (AADC) cites a number of violent incidents that have been recorded against mosques and individual Arab immigrants, Muslim or not. The Federal Bureau of Investigation hate crimes report for 1993 revealed only 15 offenses against Muslims, considerably less than the number of antisemitic and anti-Catholic incidents; but Muslim leaders insist that the vast majority of incidents were not reported.[3] During the Gulf War in 1991, AADC documented 119 incidents of violence against Arab Americans. Among the episodes noted in recent years were the burning of a mosque in Yuba, California; another torching in Springfield, Illinois; and an arson attack in Brooklyn, New York.[4] During Ramadan in 1997, two New York City mosques received threats, although no bombs were discovered.[5]

Public opinion polls have also indicated strong opposition to immigrants from the Middle East, but this might be more a reaction to terrorism or Arabs generally than to religion. In popular culture the nation had been used to seeing Arabs in a negative light.[6] The convicted organizer of the 1993 bomb plot against the World Trade Center was an Islamic cleric, and this spectacular act of terrorism linked Islam and Arabs with violence. As an official of the American Muslim Council put it, "If anything devastated the efforts of American Muslims to show the good face of Islam, it was the World Trade Center."[7]

Before the facts were known, some Americans were quick to blame the 1995 Oklahoma City bombing on an Islamic terrorist. The Council on American-Islamic Relations issued a special report on anti-Muslim stereotyping and harassment following the destruction of Oklahoma City's Murrah Federal Building. A variety of disturbing incidents were reported, and false rumors placed the blame on Muslim extremists.[8] There was some truth to Professor John E. Woods statement, "Almost immediately after the collapse of communism, Islam emerged as the new evil force in the world."[9]

Yet mention of religious issues is extremely rare among those debating immigration. AICF in one small note in its newsletter did raise the issue of assimilation: "Some observers question how well large numbers of Moslems can assimilate into a society which is largely Christian and Western in culture and orientation. They foresee tensions, misunderstanding, and clashes."[10] John Tanton and Wayne Lutton did point to the increase of Muslims in the United States, but what "this bodes for United States domestic affairs and foreign policy remains to be seen."[11]

Rather than singling out the religious views or the race of the new immigrants, restrictionists argue that the latest newcomers pose a danger for America because they believe that these immigrants will not assimilate easily into mainstream American culture. No group expresses more concern about assimilation than AICF. Founded four years later than FAIR, AICF was organized by Palmer Stacy, a lawyer who worked in the early 1980s for Senator John Porter East, a conservative from North Carolina.[12] Stacy wrote in 1985 that the United States was being invaded by immigrants and if "we do not act now to reverse this invasion, the America we know and love will be destroyed, never to reappear."[13] Located in Monterey, Virginia, AICF's newsletter *Border Watch* prints nasty cartoons and warns about multiculturalism and immigration's threat to American society. AICF's books, with titles such as *The Path to National Suicide* and *America Balkanized*, echo these themes.[14]

Lawrence Auster's *The Path to National Suicide*, for example, raises the question of whether America's cultural core is being changed by the new immigration. He believes the nation's European American common heritage is now under attack.

> It is only since the 1960s, with the great increase in the numbers of people from non-European backgrounds, that the battle cry of cultural relativism has become ideologically dominant. In demanding that non-European cultures, as cultures, be given the same importance as the European-American national culture, the multiculturalists are declaring that the non-European groups are unable or unwilling to assimilate as European immigrants have in the past, and that for the sake of these nonassimilating groups American society must be radically transformed.[15]

In short, the "combined forces of open immigration and multiculturalism constitute a mortal threat to American civilization."[16] Because any society has the moral right to preserve its identity "we have the right to open up this issue and re-evaluate our immigration law without fear of the crippling charge of racism. If our answer is no [to limiting immigration], then we shall simply continue on our present path to national suicide."[17]

Of individuals published by major houses, Peter Brimelow is clearly the most outspoken about culture and racial issues. He begins his *Alien Nation* with a curious sentence: "There is a sense in which current immigration policy is Adolf Hitler's posthumous revenge on America." He notes incorrectly that the United States elite emerged from the war determined to erase all taints of racism or xenophobia and subsequently changed the immigration laws to trigger "a renewed mass immigration, so huge and so systematically different from anything that had gone before as to transform—and ultimately, perhaps, even to destroy—the one unquestioned victor of World War II: the American nation, as it had evolved by the middle of the twentieth century."[18]

Peter Brimelow's conviction that mass immigration is a disaster, economically, politically, and culturally, makes him worry about the future life of his son Alexander in an America undergoing so much demographic change. We are reminded of Alexander, for whom *Alien Nation* is dedicated and who is featured on the back cover, more than once. He wants Alexander to grow up with white people around. "It is simply common sense that Americans have a legitimate interest in their country's racial balance. It is common sense that they have a right to insist that their government stop shifting it. Indeed, it seems to me that they have a right to insist that it be shifted back [to a point when whites were 90 percent of the population]."[19] But unless the "immigration disaster" is halted, this will not happen.

Singled out by conservative critics are the new Mexican immigrants. The growing Mexican-American population in the Southwest and along the U.S.-Mexican border is giving rise to "MexAmerica," an area of a large number of Latinos. Restrictionists are responding to the this rapid population growth and the Aztlan movement pushed by Chicanos. During the 1960s young Mexican-American activists took on the name Chicano, once a derogatory word, to symbolize their pride and solidarity against "a history of racial oppression and discrimination at the hands of Anglo Americans."[20] Some endorsed the Aztlan movement, which came from a conference of young militants held in Denver in 1969. Aztlan represented the spiritual and territorial home of people the United States conquered in the Mexican-American War. These activists, who considered themselves the descendants of the Aztecs, desired a nationalist home in the American Southwest. Rejecting Anglo culture and power, some Chicanos demanded control over their community schools, businesses, and even financial institutions "located in areas of high Chicano concentration."[21] The movement was far more symbolic than secessionist. Events demonstrated that it had only a small following, but it did represent a separatist challenge to the integrationist and assimilationist philosophy of older Mexican-American groups such as the League of United Latin American Citizens.

For Glenn Spencer, head of Voice of Citizens Together, a virtual war existed between the United States and Mexico, with the latter invading America. "Mexico *has* declared war on the United States. It is purposefully sending drugs into our nation to destroy us. It is sending its people to occupy our land. It is involved in 'Reconquista,' the retaking of the American Southwest."[22] He even sees the attack in racial terms: "The United States is being invaded by Mexico. Mexican gangs roam our streets. Mexican drugs destroy our children. Mexican politicians threaten White Americans with extinction."[23]

Less extreme, Brent Nelson maintains that the Aztlan partisans are contributing to the establishment of radical Chicano studies departments in colleges and universities. He believes the movement to be basically irredentist but if combined with other separatist movements in MexAmerica it could lead to the "worst-case" scenario. "The Southwest could become quasi-independent city-states and new states, each of which would claim for itself a kind of *imperium imperio*, while not disdaining to receive more than its share of the federal revenue." He concludes, "It is not inconceivable that a day may dawn on the U.S. when a curious reversal will have taken place in which States' Rights, from having been the last resort of reactionaries, will have become the favored strategy of revolutionaries."[24]

AICF's *Border Watch* has reported that these "extremist" groups were receiving public funds on college campuses and were a growing force.[25] AICF also warned that if Mexico permitted dual citizenship then naturalized Mexicans in the United States would give Mexico more political clout.[26] Worse yet if the "alienists" had their way, immigrants would have the right to vote and would use the ballot against those trying to control immigration.[27] Conservative columnist Samuel Francis told *Border Watch* readers that Hispanic extremists "call for violence and insurrection and . . . for the disintegration of the country."[28] AICF president John Vinson warned of the danger of too much Mexican immigration. "It is a matter of historical fact that the Melting Pot has not worked well across racial lines and deep cultural divisions. Though American whites, blacks, and Indians have lived together for centuries, only in recent decades have they forged bonds of common citizenship."[29]

Not all conservative commentators on multiculturalism are anti-immigration nor do they worry about the large-scale Mexican immigration into the Southwest. Indeed, they see the new immigrants as having conservative values. Dinesh D'Souza's *Illiberal Education* focuses on feminism, gay rights, political correctness, and Afro-centricism and contains only a page on immigration, commenting a "large majority of the people of color who emigrant to this country today, including those from Asia and the Caribbean, are Christian; or they are Muslim or Buddhist or Hindu, and, like the Catholics and Protestants, they hold tight to very traditional values."[30] Francis Fukuyama, writing for the neo-conservative *Commentary*, makes a similar point: "Those who fear Third World immigration as a threat to Anglo-American cultural values do not seem to have noticed what the real sources of cultural breakdown have been. . . . The real danger is not that the elites will become corrupted by the habits and practices of Third World immigrants, but rather than the immigrants will become corrupted by them."[31]

FAIR, CCN, and Balance, founded by environmentalists, also emphasize cultural or assimilationist issues, but their tone is less strident than AICF and they pay less attention to this particular issue. The same is true of anti-immigration critics such as Roy Beck, Leon Bouvier, and John Tanton. Beck's emphasis on economic factors masks his worry that too much diversity can lead to ethnic conflict.[32] Leon Bouvier is cautious about discussing multiculturalism or the implications of a diverse immigration flow but raises questions about the current trends and wants limitations on immigration. He opposes racial discrimination, which he still sees as a major problem in American society, but he asserts, "There can be no room for cultural separatism or for irredentist or secessionist movements on the part of newcomers."[33]

Gary Imhoff and Richard Lamm do not go as far as a Lawrence Auster, but they too nonetheless worry about the nation's growing diversity and its potential fragmentation.[34] John Tanton and Wayne Lutton's *The Immigration Invasion* also argues that the new immigration is leading to fragmentation, this time in the form of new distributions of power, bilingual education and ballots, and ethnic rights. They conclude, "The most fundamental change is the arrival, day by day, year by year, of very large numbers of immigrants who do not share our language or cultural values. As their numbers grow, so does their political influence and power, which they use in an attempt to derail any legislative movement to reduce immigration to a more manageable quantity."[35]

Restrictionists of all strips use history as a guide. They argue that the immigration restriction movements of the past gave America "pauses for digestion," which allowed immigrants to assimilate. No pause was more important than that beginning in the 1920s when Congress passed the national origin quotas. Some even acknowledge that the turn-of-the-century mass immigration benefited the American economy and that the descendants of those white Europeans had become useful and loyal Americans. One did not have to have English ancestors to become a "true American."[36]

Leon Bouvier, one of the more thoughtful of those wanting limits on the flow of newcomers, explained, "By the 1980s, the melting pot had worked quite well for immigrants from southern and eastern Europe, structurally as well as culturally.... In addition to different groups acting increasingly alike, a new population is in the process of forming—the 'unhyphenated Americans.' " This was the result, he told his readers, that the melting pot was working at the marriage altar. He noted, too, that the descendants of the turn of the century immigrants were taking their places among the corporate elite, in major universities, in politics and nearly all phases of American society.[37]

In comparing the earlier waves of immigration to today's flow, Bouvier noted that some objections to today's newcomers were similar to the assaults of the past. Of course many of current migrants came, as did those of yesteryear, to find freedom in America or achieve a better economic life, but there were differences. The American economy was not the same today as it was in 1900 and the main sources of origin of current immigrants were now Latin America, the Caribbean, and Asia, not Europe. When the earlier immigration movement ended in the 1920, "restrictive legislation, the Depression, and war all combined to drastically lower the levels of immigration. These factors contributed to the acculturation and social elevation of the new immigrants and their descendants. The shutting off of the immigration flow made it difficult for ethnic cultures to be maintained. As a result the newcomers were better able to adapt to their new homeland."[38] But today's migration seems "to be unending," and raised the possibility that "future cultural adaptation could easily regress into the more negative forms of cultural separatism."[39]

Restrictionists concurred that a "breathing space" of low or no immigration is once again required. John Tanton, dean of modern restrictionists, informs his audience: "We believe that all the facts presented in this book provide ample evidence of the need for a hiatus, a breather, a 'seventh immigration stretch' to assimilate the newcomers, to try to resolve the problems that have been created, and to consider what immigration policy we want for the future."[40]

One of the most popular solutions was a five-year moratorium on immigration, to give the nation the breather it needed. Hence restrictionists approved the bill introduced by Representative Bob Stump (R-Ariz.), which would have limited immigration to 200,000 yearly until at least the year 2000, but some wanted even fewer immigrants.[41] The figure of 200,000 was a popular one, based on the estimates that 200,000 persons left the United States each year. If only 200,000 arrived, the net gain of population through immigration would be zero. However, groups like NPG, which wanted the nation's population to decrease substantially, favored practically no migration.[42]

Avoiding the strident and unsettling language of AICF has not spared FAIR, and some others, from being condemned as racists. After all, the bulk of new immigrants are people of color; cutting their numbers helps maintain the current ethnic makeup of the American people. John Vinson of AICF, Peter Brimelow, and FAIR deny they are racists. Vinson says, "It is not racist or mean-spirited to face reality. To the contrary, the best way to preserve peace and goodwill among Americans is to know the limits of diversity."[43] For FAIR charges of racism proved to be particularly controversial because of at least one source of funding. The historian Otis Graham wanted FAIR to emphasize economic or other issues that might attract political liberals or moderates; he opposed taking money from the Pioneer Fund. Founded in 1937 by eugenist Harry H. Laughlin, who helped persuade Congress in the 1920s that southern and eastern Europeans were inferior peoples, the Pioneer Fund's early projects were tinged with racism. Its monies backed some of the research that Charles Murray and Richard Herrnstein drew upon for their controversial *The Bell Curve*.[44]

From 1982 to 1989, over Graham's opposition, FAIR received $680,000 from the Pioneer Fund to help finance some of its activities. The Fund denied sponsoring eugenics research, but it did not delete the word "white" from its charter until 1985.[45] While some critics have accused FAIR of being tainted by accepting money from the Pioneer Fund, FAIR has insisted that the Fund's views do not in any way affect its policies and that the Pioneer Fund's contributions have decreased in recent years, amounting to only 3 percent of its budget by the mid-1990s.[46] It should be noted that the Pioneer Fund has also financed projects at several well-known universities, such as the University of Pennsylvania, the University of Minnesota, and the University of Florence.[47]

A second issue surrounding FAIR, AICF, and John Tanton's Social Contract Press is the reissuing of Jean Raspail's *The Camp of the Saints*. Raspail's book was originally published in France in 1973, but it sounds as if E. A. Ross wrote it at the turn of the century. Scribner's marketed an English edition two years later, subsidized by Cordelia Scaife May, a Mellon heiress. It eventually went out of print. In 1995 it was reissued by the anti-immigration lobby, again subsidized by May, who has funded restrictionist organizations. It was republished and distributed by AICF and the Social Contract Press, which noted that the book was controversial but they were "honored" to bring it back into print, just as the immigration debate was heating up.[48] Both groups pushed the book as did FAIR, which commented, "When *The Camp of the Saints* was published in 1973, it became a critical revelation of what our future might be if the pressures behind mass migration are not controlled."[49]

Why was it so controversial? It is a parable or symbolic book dealing with two camps, the West and the Third World. The book is the story of the Third World's invasion of the West's camp. *Saints* tells about a flotilla of ships loaded with poor and wretched people from India who are sailing for southern France, hoping that they can take advantage of the West's inability to regulate immigration and settle there as migrants. Such a fleet in an age of high illegal immigration might strike a familiar tone. In June 1993 the freighter *Golden Venture* ran aground, not off the coast of France, but off of Rockaway Beach in New York City. *Golden Venture* was packed with 300 undocumented aliens, who had paid thousands of dollars to get to America illegally. Some were drowned trying to get ashore, while those who did make it were taken into custody to await their fate when they filed an asylum claim. Was not this as *Saints* had envisioned? Not quite.

Raspail's flotilla of people were not exactly poor illegal migrants eager to find a better life in the West. It was a vanguard of one million refugees, paving the way for a Third World invasion of the West. These were violent, depraved people, scarcely with any recognized characteristic of humankind. The filthy boats themselves became a Western vision of the worst slums of Calcutta. The fleet had simply brought with it the death rate of the Ganges, or even worse. Although not expressed in strictly racial terms, Raspail thoroughly demonized these Third World peoples. He is not sympathetic with the West either, for France and other Western nations (the camp of the saints) were seen as too willing in good faith and conscience to take in refugees, regardless of how subhuman they are. Misguided Protestant and Catholic church groups sent supplies while the ships were on route.

The *Camp of the Saints* was ironic. The Indians of Raspail were hardly the Asian Indians emigrating to the United States in recent years. Indian immigrants are among the best educated and most successful of today's immigrants. They are frequently physicians, engineers, computer experts, economists, and entrepreneurs, a virtual "brain drain" from India.

Apart from the irony, there remains the issue of racism or demonization of third world people. Because of the sensitive nature of the immigration debate about the issue of racism and because several groups have been charged with being tinged with racism for taking funds from the Pioneer Fund, one would think that they would avoid recommending or being associated with such an incredible book. By supporting *The Camp of the Saints* current restrictionists weaken their case when they insist that they are not racists.

An immigration "lull" to allow the nation to "digest" the latest newcomers was only part of the battle for a common American civilization. For the large numbers of new migrants already here Americanization was needed to avoid cultural fragmentation. One method of achieving unity was making English the official language, for language was a thread that held Americans together, the argument goes. As Bouvier put it, "This is not to deny the rights of various groups to encourage the use of their respective languages in the home. Nevertheless, English is the 'glue' that helps keep American culture vibrant and dynamic."[50]

Various groups wanting immigration cuts also support English-only or official English propositions. The Washington State Citizens for Immigration Control informed its members that they should give the English-as-the-official-language initiative pending in that state "our maximum support."[51] AICF told its members in September 1995 that English was being threatened as "common tongue." It noted that proposals were being made in Congress to make English the official language. "Immigration reform supporters generally support these recommendations," said AICF. "But they believe the best way to protect English is reducing immigration."[52]

Three political scientists studying Proposition 187 in California noted the close connection between it and a proposition declaring English to the be the state's official language: "There was a substantial overlap between the vote for the English-only and Proposition 187 initiatives." The overlap with the English-only voters suggests that there was strong element of "cultural nativism in the Prop 187 vote."[53] It is important to note that not all supporters of U.S. English's main goal favor immigration restriction. Official English has the support of many people, such as Newt Gingrich, who are not supporters of immigration cuts.[54]

The struggle over language, like the debate over immigration, is not new. Benjamin Franklin's well-known attack on German speakers in Pennsylvania was only the first salvo of those who distrusted immigrants who wanted to retain their own native language and refused to speak

English. Congress joined the crusade for Americanization in 1906 when it made knowledge of English a prerequisite for naturalization. World War I patriotism dictated the stamping out of foreign languages, and especially German, the tongue of the leading Central Power; the German language never fully recovered as a foreign language in the United States. In 1915, 25 percent of high school students were studying German, but by the early 1920s fewer than 1 percent were.[55]

In 1919 Nebraska outlawed all instruction in foreign languages except for teaching them as foreign languages in high schools, and a year later declared that English was its official language.[56] When Robert T. Meyer, teaching the fifth grade in a school run by the Zion Lutheran Church, gave instruction in German he was arrested and subsequently convicted. Although the Nebraska Supreme Court upheld his conviction, the United States Supreme Court found the law to be unconstitutional.[57]

Illinois passed an English-only law in 1969, but the first important political battle over language in the era of new mass immigration occurred in Miami, the center of the Cuban migration during the 1960s. Responding to that migration, in 1973 the Metro-Dade County Board of County Commissioners declared that Dade County was bilingual and bicultural. But after the Mariel Cubans poured into Miami in 1980, a Dade County's citizen initiative proclaimed the county's official language to be English and defined governmental areas where only English was to be used. The vote indicated the divided feelings of Dade's residents about the Cuban presence.[58] In 1993 Dade County officially repealed its English-only ordinance, but Florida voters rebuffed the county when they declared Florida to be an official English state.[59]

For Senator S. I. Hayakawa of California, state victories were important, but he and his followers wanted the United States Constitution amended to make English the nation's official language. Hayakawa first introduced his English Language Amendment (ELA) in 1981. Congress did hold hearings but there was little chance of passage at that time; the proposals never got out of committee. Latino and some other ethnic groups attacked the ELA. Representative Stephen Solarz of New York City said that it was unwise and unnecessary. English was our primary language, he noted, and the ELA might cause harm to a number of federal programs by prohibiting them from using foreign languages in order to reach into ethnic communities.[60] Changing the constitution by amendment was time-consuming and problematic. During the debates on early drafts of IRCA, Senator Hayakawa put forth an amendment to the bill saying it was the sense of Congress that English is the official language of the United States. It passed by a vote of 78 to 21 in the Senate, but was not included in the final act.[61]

John Tanton, founder of FAIR, also believed that English should be the official language of the United States. When FAIR resisted appeals to emphasize cultural separatism as an issue, Tanton founded U.S. English in 1983, with Senator S. I. Hayakawa as nominal head.[62] He recruited Gerda Bikales, a refugee from Nazi Germany, from FAIR to become the organization's executive director.[63] U.S. English's goal was the ratification of an amendment making English the official language of the United States, an end to bilingual ballots, curtailment of bilingual education, and strengthening English-language assimilation.[64] U.S. English insists that its members only wanted English to be the official governmental language. Such a policy does not include emergency services nor would in any "way restrict an individual's use of any language." Mauro E. Mujica, later president of U.S. English and an architect from Chile who was himself bilingual, insisted that "it's completely insane" to print IRS forms and drivers' licenses tests in languages other than English. We should be helping people acquire English, not avoid it, he concluded.[65]

The official English movement was also aided by the efforts of English First. Formed three years after U.S. English by Larry Pratt, a former Virginia state representative and the president of Gun Owners of America, English First was smaller than U.S. English, but Pratt was able to raise $7 million within a few years. English First's early tone was more strident than U.S. English, which was reflection of the right-wing politics of Larry Pratt.[66] Under executive director James Boulet Jr., in the mid-1990s, its tone moderated and it concentrated on getting Congress to act on the ELA.

U.S. English bankrolled several successful state campaigns. California in 1986, the same year that English First was founded, became the most important state to adopt an official English proposition (Proposition 63). San Francisco had been the center of a dispute over trilingual ballots (Spanish, Chinese, and English), and from this local issue there emerged a proposition to make English California's official tongue. During a heated campaign, the English-only forces were led by Stanley Diamond, a retired military officer and former aide to Senator Hayakawa, one of the founders of U.S. English. Latin and Asian organizations opposed Proposition 63, as did the Democratic Party and a number of prominent state leaders, but the campaign to place Proposition 63 on the ballot collected over one million signatures. When the balloting was completed Proposition 63 carried 73 percent of the vote.[67]

U.S. English successfully financed other several state campaigns to adopt English as the official language. The vote in Arizona was very close, perhaps because of a controversy involving Linda Chavez and a memo written by John Tanton. Chavez, a critic of affirmative action and bilingual education and Ronald Reagan's choice to head the Commission on Civil Rights, was asked to be chair of U.S. English, even though she claimed that she had made it clear that she did not approve of the proposal to make English the nation's official language by an amendment to the Constitution. According to James Crawford, as chair Chavez became alarmed at the source of funding for the organization. Tanton had gotten funds from Cordelia Scaife May, who had subsidized FAIR, Balance, and the distribution of Jean Raspail's *The Camp of Saints*, a book Chavez found "chilling" when she reviewed it in 1975. She felt it was a "cult" book, one she had not bargained for.[68] As she learned of funding sources, Chavez says she became disillusioned with U.S. English.[69]

Then came the Tanton memo, written for a study group called WITAN, composed of U.S. English, FAIR, and allied groups. It questioned the ability of Hispanics to assimilate and suggested that they might cause future ethnic conflict.[70] Tanton said he was only trying to raise points for discussion, but the memo was enough for Chavez, as well as for another well-known board member, Walter Cronkite. Chavez resigned as president of the organization, calling his memo "anti-Catholic and anti-Hispanic." Her resignation was followed by Tanton's as president of the board of directors.[71]

The flap nearly derailed U.S. English's Arizona's bid for English-only. After a heated campaign, the state's voters by a narrow vote approved the English-only constitutional provision.[72] The drive for English briefly lost momentum in the wake of the internal debate and resignations and U.S. English stumbled in its quest for English-only.[73] The organization recovered quickly, and the movement to make English the official U.S. language gained new steam. The movement certainly had wide public support, as indicated by the polls.[74] By 1996

U.S. English claimed 600,000 members and by that time 23 states had adopted resolutions or laws making English the official language of their states, but most of these victories came before 1990.[75]

What do these propositions mean? In California very little. The Los Angeles school board expanded its bilingual programs after passage of Proposition 63. In 1996 Supervisor Mabel Teng of San Francisco requested the city to provide translators, at a possible cost of $200 per hour, at the Board of Supervisors meetings. Teng found support, not surprisingly, from Martha Jimenez, the general counsel for the Mexican American Legal Defense and Educational Fund. Teng claimed the translators would give immigrants a chance to participate in the procedures of democracy. The director of communications for U.S. English retorted that the measure might be "well-intentioned, but it's heading in the entirely wrong direction. The City ought to put more money into hiring ESL (English-as-a-second language) teachers." Apparently no one thought the proposal would be illegal in the face of Proposition 63.[76]

At the state level officials continued to offer drivers' license examinations in a number of foreign languages. California Assemblyman (later state senator) Richard Mountjoy was a strong opponent of illegal and legal immigration and a proponent of official English. He introduced a measure in the state assembly to enforce Proposition 63, but it never got out of committee.[77]

Elsewhere, English-only propositions reaped similar results, becoming mostly symbolic gestures. They have led to a number of suits, claiming such provisions are discriminatory or in violation of free speech; one such case involving Arizona reached the Supreme Court. When a state employee, who insisted upon using Spanish in violation of the amendment, sued, the issue was joined. Kelly Yniguez claimed that the English-only provision violated her first amendment right under the U.S. Constitution. While she won initially, proponents of English-only appealed and the issue worked its way through the Arizona courts until the U.S. Supreme Court agreed to hear the case. In 1997 the court declared the case moot because the employee bringing the suit was no longer working for the state.[78] A frustrated English First 1997 newsletter lamented, "Official English laws have never been enforced, let alone enforced to excess."[79]

Because English-only propositions are seen by opponents as nativism, local communities were sometimes divided by the language issue. In Monterey Park, outside of Los Angeles, the community was racked by ethnic tensions and a fight over language.[80] Eighty percent white in 1960, the suburb began to receive an influx of Latinos and Asians. After 1970 so many Chinese immigrants found homes there that by 1980 Asians and whites were about equal in numbers; in 1990 Asians were about 60 percent of the population.[81] Many "old timers," as John Horton calls them, resisted the incoming Chinese. Conflicts over economic growth, neighborhood organizations, and political control erupted. Watching Chinese language signs for businesses proliferating, the "old timers," with help from U.S. English, managed to put an Official English referendum on the 1985 ballot, but it was ruled invalid by the City Attorney.[82] English-only advocates were encouraged, however, by the state's approval of Proposition 63, though this had no real impact on Monterey Park's economic and political life. The pro-official English candidates who won election in 1987 were determined to put teeth into the Proposition. When the library was offered a gift of 10,000 Chinese books, the mayor and city council blocked it from accepting the donation. When the library resisted, the council dissolved the library board. The mayor told the *Los Angeles Times*, "I don't think we need to cater too much to foreign languages. I think if people want a foreign language they can go purchase books on their own."[83] Eventually, however, the proponents of diversity replaced the English-only advocates as the suburb's leaders.[84]

In New Jersey white residents in seven towns objected to their growing Asian population and the proliferation of Asian-owned stores that carried signs for the customers only in foreign languages. The towns passed ordinances that said the signs must also be in English.[85] These victories for English-only were echoed in 41 counties and other towns and cities, but the English-only movement did not always achieve success. Mayor Rudolph Giuliani of New York City opposed such measures, and the city gave little indication that it disagreed with its mayor. In 1989 New York's Suffolk County English-only advocates lost their fight to pass an official English proposition.[86]

Stalled at the local level in the 1990s, English First took comfort from the Republican victory in the 1994 elections.[87] Then, Representative Toby Roth (R-Wisc.) reintroduced his Declaration of Official Language Act in the new Congress, and Senator Bob Dole, running for the presidency, injected official English into the national agenda when he endorsed ELA.[88]

The House added its approval of an official English proposal in 1996. In July of that year a House panel approved it by a strictly partisan vote, with Republicans favoring it and the Democrats opposing the measure.[89] When it reached the floor of the House the lawmakers split again along party lines. It passed by a vote of 259 to 169 after nearly six hours of debate. The bill would bar Social Security Administration clerks from helping a constituent in Vietnamese, ban election materials in Chinese, and stop the Internal Revenue Service from sending out forms in Spanish. The debate was familiar, with proponents saying language was the glue for American culture. One legislator put it, "We are trying to make sure that this Government conducts the language of its business in English, because that is the one unifying thing about America."[90] Democratic opponents said the measure was divisive, unnecessary, and that immigrants would be better served by providing more English language-classes.[91] The Senate took no action and was not likely to do so in the near future. Moreover, President Clinton promised a veto if it came up again.

The ironies of such debates are obvious to immigrant parents. The children of today's immigrants, like most of those in the past, are acquiring English at a rapid rate in the schools and from the mass media, particularly television. Adult immigrants were also attempting to learn English, and many were frustrated by the lack of English classes. Nearly everywhere there was a waiting list for such classes.[92]

Passage of such a sense of Congress resolution or bill would do little for these immigrants and their children, and it could be virtually meaningless and so, for that matter, would ELA. The key was what would the amendment include. English First wanted it to specifically bar bilingual ballots and bilingual education. U.S. English and many other official English proponents agreed that bilingual ballots were unnecessary and even counterproductive. Naturalization was supposed to include a knowledge of English, they argued; therefore, using bilingual ballots was a disincentive to learning English. Senator Alan Simpson, a leading proponent of cutting immigration, put it simply:

> We do not ask very much of a new immigrant to this country, but one thing we do expect of them is that they accept our system of government and our common language and a common flag. I refer to this as our public culture. What they wish to do in their private culture is nobody's business. . . . I fear that providing bilingual ballots to certain

groups in this country will not encourage the learning of English. . . .
We need to bring people into the mainstream of our society, and treating them specially, differently or separately, does not further that goal.[93]

Bilingual voting emerged as contentious issue during the 1970s.[94]
Congress passed the Voting Rights Act in 1965, and when the legislators renewed it in 1970 they banned literacy tests. By the mid-1970s
Mexican-American organizations were insisting upon federal action
to eliminate what they considered discrimination in voting and in
drawing political jurisdictions. Congress responded and created the
category "language minority."[95] Now bilingual ballots were required
by the amendments of 1975, provided a minority made up 5 percent
of a county.[96]

Originally passed because of pressure from groups like MALDEF
to support Spanish ballots, foreign language ballots expanded to en-
compass several languages other than Spanish. Proponents of official
English not only insisted that such ballots retarded Americanization
but they also claimed such ballots were expensive and not always ac-
curate.[97] English First considered bilingual voting a dangerous precedent that might lead to a "Quebec" in the United States. The organization pointed to fraud, misinterpretations, and great difficulties
translating some foreign languages for the ballots, such as that occurring in New York City involving Chinese-language translations. This
included confusing a "no" for a "yes."[98]

In 1983 San Francisco voters passed a proposition calling upon the
federal government to adopt policies of printing all election materials
in English.[99] California voters passed a similar initiative in 1984 by a
lopsided 72–28 margin, but these initiatives ran counter to federal law;
therefore they were not binding.[100]

Just as disliked by those who worried about the new immigration
and perhaps more controversial were bilingual educational programs.
Yet it should be noted that some attacks on bilingual education came
from the pens of commentators who rejected ELA or cuts in immigration. Historian Arthur Schlesinger was one such critic. To him "bilingualism has not worked out as planned: rather the contrary. . . . bilingual education retards rather than expedites the movement of
Hispanic children into the English-speaking world and that it pro-
motes segregation more than it does integration."[101]

While bilingual public schools, mostly in Spanish and German, were not unusual in the late nineteenth- and early twentieth-century America, the antiforeign hysteria of the World War I era prompted many to switch entirely to English. The modern system of bilingual schools began when the Cubans arrived in Miami during the 1960s. The success of these schools in teaching Cuban immigrants to acquire English quickly encouraged other communities in the Southwest and elsewhere to adopt variations of the Dade County ones, but none received federal support.[102]

Congress entered the field in 1968, when responding to the suggestion of Senator Ralph Yarborough (D-Texas), the legislators passed the Bilingual Education Act. Yarborough was acting on behalf of his Mexican-American constituents, and the initial federal funding and programs aimed at Spanish speakers.[103] The federal programs were expanded in 1974, and now involved the training of teachers as well as aid for schools generally.[104]

In that same year, the Supreme Court, in *Lau v. Nichols*, ruled in a case involving Chinese students in San Francisco that students must be given a meaningful education, one in which they could understand what was going on in the classroom. The court did not specify any one type of bilingual program. The 1974 act and the Supreme Court's decision occurred at the same time that immigration was growing from Third World nations.[105] Congress increased federal involvement and funding, but not without controversy, which grew after the election of Ronald Reagan in 1980.

William Bennett, Secretary of Education, began the Reagan administration's attack on bilingual education, saying that the overriding purpose "of bilingual education must be to enable children to become fluent in English as quickly as possible."[106] In criticizing transitional programs, which made up 75 percent of the federally funded ones, Bennett called for more flexibility in bilingual education.[107] Proponents of U.S. English, such as S. I. Hayakawa, also attacked bilingual programs for keeping students in them for more than two years and for not being effective in teaching English. These critics were distressed by the transitional programs that aimed at maintaining native languages while teaching English instead of emphasizing the rapid acquisition of English. They believed the federal government's role was rigid and was promoting the wrong approach to immigrants. They had some success in modifying the guidelines and trimming funds, but bilingual education remained.[108] English First was adamantly opposed to bilingual education, while U.S. English supported some forms of bilingualism.[109]

Other criticisms of bilingual education focused on the shortage of bilingual teachers and the inability of some teachers to speak English. Not a few critics believed that these programs were nothing more than a jobs program for Spanish speakers who often lacked proper credentials for effective classroom instruction. AICF's *Border Watch* praised critic's like Linda Chavez for pointing to the waste of taxpayer money on bilingual education.[110] One of the strongest attacks came from Rosalie Porter, a teacher who assailed the education bureaucracy of her state, Massachusetts.[111] She was not the only teacher to be suspicious of bilingual education. In 1987 the Los Angeles Teachers Union asked the school board to return to an English immersion approach for the education of those children who could not understand English well.[112]

Opponents of bilingual education said that it not only failed to teach English, but that it also promoted ethnic separatism, especially for Latinos. John Tanton and Wayne Lutton wrote about California bilingualism, "The educational results of this segregation by language have been disappointing, especially in learning English. Politically, however, the existence of a body of young people uncomfortable in English and alienated from the mainstream serves the politicians very well."[113] Gary Imhoff and Richard Lamm also attacked bilingual schools and saw separatism behind the supporters for them and claimed, with little documentation: "The startling fact is that many Hispanics who support bilingualism do not accept the predominance of English in the United States."[114]

The controversy over bilingualism was not resolved by studies as to its effectiveness, though they probably made proponents tighten their programs. In Los Angeles, for example, the Board of Education announced in 1996 that it would set aside funds to reward those schools for enabling students to pass English tests and move into the mainstream classroom. A report on the worth of New York City's program was not reinsuring to advocates of bilingual education.[115] But proponents of bilingualism believed that decisions like those in Los Angeles schools might make teachers and administrators ready to move the students too quickly.[116] Much like the debate over the economics of immigration, both proponents and opponents found published research to support their views.[117]

Public opinion remained divided, though Latino organizations were generally united in their support of these schools.[118] But Latino parents wanted first of all for their children to learn English; some even supported official English. In the 1986 California election on official English, 41 percent of Hispanic voters favored it.[119] Asian parents were much less likely to support bilingual classrooms and Asian organizations did not place a high priority on them.[120] Russian immigrant parents opposed such schools. As one New York educator put it, "the Russians. . . . want no part of bilingual education." One New York City school, composed predominantly of Russians and Chinese children, disbanded bilingual classes when the parents complained about them.[121]

The division among ethnic groups explains why so much of the controversy involved Spanish and the debate about assimilation of Hispanic immigrants into American society. As Imhoff and Lamm put it in 1985, "Political lobbying for bilingual education comes almost exclusively from the Hispanic community."[122] Of course bilingual schools also existed for Native Americans, but in view of who got here first, the critics would have found it embarrassing to be too hostile about Navaho bilingualism.

Controversy over bilingual education involving Latinos and, to a lesser extent, others would no doubt continue among educators, legislators, and others engaged in the debates over multiculturalism, English, and the new mass immigration. If they failed to change or eliminate bilingual ballots and education or make English the official language of the United States, restrictionists might intensify their efforts to radically cut immigration; they might see reduction as the only way to avoid the "fragmenting" of American society, a splintering they feared would lead to dire consequences.

# A New Immigration Policy
## *1994–1997?*

*"Your hopes of reining in uncontrolled immigration were dashed this spring—Congress gutted the long-anticipated Immigration Reform Bill . . . in the end, Congress sold out to the special interests."*
—From an Open Letter to the Citizens of the United States,
August 25, 1996, by Dan Stein, Executive Director of FAIR

THE GROWING MOVEMENT to restrict immigration pointed in one direction: congressional legislation and administration action to reduce immigration from its current level. After Congress enacted the 1990 immigration act increasing immigration some 35 percent, two of the major supporters of the goals of the restrictionists, senators Harry Reid (D-Nev.) and Richard Shelby (R-Ala.), proposed the Immigration and Stabilization Act of 1993, which set an overall ceiling of 300,000 a year on all types of immigration. Their proposal also included increased funding for the INS, tighter asylum procedures, and speedy deportation of alien criminals. Dan Stein of FAIR called it "a landmark piece of legislation" and pledged that FAIR would be "working hard in the coming months to try to pass S. 1351."[1] Senator Reid introduced his bill again the next year, claiming that after consulting with many different ethnic groups and experts, he believed his measure was a "realistic recognition that something must be done to reduce these escalating costs to ensure that our children and grand-children do not inherit a country in which no one would want to live."[2] In an article in the *Los Angeles Times*, Reid wrote that western-ers "have a real appreciation for dwindling natural resources . . . rarely do we consider the burdens that millions of new people place every year on our water supplies, air quality, parks, lakes, recreation areas, and public lands."[3] His defense of the bill was a virtual litany of the many wrongs the new restrictionists found with the law and the newcom-ers themselves. Representative James Bilbray (D-Nev.) cosponsored the measure in the House.

Alan Simpson, the key Republican senator on immigration matters, introduced a more modest bill. Simpson proposed reducing immigra-tion about 100,000, with small reductions in all family, occupational, and refugee categories. A more radical bill was that of Senator Bob Stump (R-Ariz.), which had 53 cosponsors from both parties. It would have slashed benefits for legal residents, provided for a tougher INS, and cut immigration drastically. While the system was being brought under tighter control, Stump wanted a moratorium on immigration.[4] Stump had been one of the heroes of the anti-immigration movement.

Given the makeup of Congress, then controlled by the Democrats, there was no chance these measures would become law. Neither the Democratic congressional leaders nor President Bill Clinton expressed interest in substantial changes.[5] Nevertheless, anti-immigration senti-ment, fed by a recession beginning in 1990, was on the rise in the early 1990s. Congress and the President were listening to those states that wanted financial aid for the costs of immigration, or at least funds to offset their costs of incarceration of illegal alien criminals. More money was voted for INS's budget and action was taken to speed up the deportation of alien criminals. Under the leadership of Vice-Pres-ident Al Gore and INS Commissioner Doris Meissner, the INS inau-gurated Citizenship USA to increase the number of resident aliens be-coming American citizens and to offset fears of a mass of indigestible immigrants aloof from American society.

The bombing of New York City's World Trade Center and the in-creasing number of Cuban and Haitian boat people being intercepted in the summer of 1994 added to the anxiety. The situation was made more complicated by the welfare debate, raising the question of how much welfare legal residents were entitled to. The Republican minor-ity wanted to eliminate most benefits for immigrants.

In the Fall 1994 elections the Republicans carried both houses of Congress and California voters ratified Proposition 187. Even though a judge enjoined 187 from being put into law, Republicans heard the message. But there were problems. The strong business wing of the Republican party saw immigrant labor, whether skilled or unskilled, as essential for the American economy. This wing was represented by Dick Armey in the House and Phil Gramm in the Senate. After giving a talk to a Washington think tank about immigration, Armey was asked about immigration reduction. He answered, "Should we reduce legal immigration? Well, I'm hard pressed to think of a single problem that would be solved by shutting off the supply of willing and eager new Americans. If anything . . . we should be thinking about increasing legal immigration."[6] House Speaker Newt Gingrich, after a December 1994 meeting with leaders of the National Restaurants Association, whose 25,000 members represented catering, fast-food establishments, and restaurant chains that employed many immigrants, remarked, "I am very pro legal immigration. I think legal immigration has given America many of its most dynamic and creative citizens, and I think that we would be a very, very self-destructive country if we sent negative signals on legal immigration."[7] What was one to make of arch-liberal Senator Ted Kennedy joining with conservative Republican Orin Hatch to urge repeal of the employer's sanctions provision of IRCA. Both senators thought that the sanctions led to discrimination against Hispanics and imposed unnecessary paperwork for employers.

The victorious Republican party of 1995 also contained conservatives who saw the new immigrants as recruits for its "pro-family" policies. Republican representatives Chris Smith and Mark Souder told readers of the *Washington Times* that Ronald Reagan was right when he said America was a "beacon of hope to those oppressed behind the Iron Curtain." Smith and Souder were pro-family conservative advocates and were "deeply suspicious of laws" that have had been unnecessarily harsh on families. They insisted that any cuts in family unification would be anti-family.[8] On balance, however, Republicans appeared more willing to cut immigration than were the Democrats.

Republicans were less divided about illegal immigration. Governor Pete Wilson, whose support of 187 was a major issue in his 1994 reelection, claimed to be reassured after talking with both Newt Gingrich and Bob Dole, Republican leaders in the House and Senate respectively, that Congress would act on illegal immigration. While neither Dole or Gingrich had discussed 187 in the fall campaign, they acknowledged to Wilson that immigration costs were a federal matter. Dole said on CBS's "Face the Nation" that Congress should not ask Texas, Florida, California, and others to pick up the financial burdens of illegal immigration if the federal government is "not willing to protect our borders."[9]

Not the least important part of the 1994 Republican victory was the removal of Senator Edward Kennedy from the chair of the Senate's Subcommittee on Immigration and Refugee Affairs. The Massachusetts senator opposed cuts in both legal immigration and benefits for resident aliens, and he was not especially interested in dealing with undocumented migration. Although Kennedy occasionally hinted that he might favor modest cuts in the legal numbers and measures to protect American workers, for the most part he was aggressively pro-immigration. While Alan Simpson, Kennedy's replacement, was no Bob Stump, he nonetheless advocated tighter controls over illegal immigration and supported cuts in the legal flow. Lamar Smith (Texas), who headed the International Law, Immigration, and Refugees Subcommittee in the House, was angered by undocumented immigration and supported modest reductions in legal migration.[10] If House Speaker Gingrich did not seem sympathetic to the cause of reduction, Senator Bob Dole, the Senate majority leader, was more so.

When the 104th Congress opened in January 1995, the mood was upbeat for the immigration reformers. Members offered a flood of new measures designed to deal with immigration. "Never before has this level of action been taken toward reforming immigration and never this early in a Congressional session. Immigration, thanks to the success of Proposition 187 and growing popular opinion as reflected in all major opinion polls, has Congress's attention," remarked Dan Stein.[11] President Bill Clinton, in his State of the Union address on January 24, declared that "in every place in this country [Americans] are rightly disturbed by the large number of illegal aliens entering our country." He pledged he would work with Congress to speed the deportation of illegals convicted for crimes. "It is wrong and ultimately self-defeating for a nation of immigrants to permit the kind of abuse of our immigration laws we have seen in recent years," said the President. He concluded, "we must do more to stop it."[12]

One Republican proposal aimed at modifying the birthright citizenship. This was an amendment to the Constitution that would restrict granting citizenship to persons born in the United States to those whose parents were American citizens or whose mothers were legal residents. Other Republicans supported an immigration moratorium for several years, an end to federal welfare benefits for aliens, tougher controls on document fraud and at the border, a crackdown on alien criminals, and modest cuts and refinements in existing policy. Because the two key players, Alan Simpson and Lamar Smith, held moderate views, radical changes were unlikely, but some new legislation appeared certain. One thing seemed assured: there would not be another amnesty like that of IRCA as a trade-off for tighter controls over illegal immigration. In addition, in view of the Republican desire to make fundamental changes in welfare and President Clinton's expressed desire to abolish "welfare as we know it," federal benefits for immigrants were a logical target for alteration if not elimination.

Reformers were buttressed by two important reports issued in June 1995. Speaker Gingrich, responding to Proposition's 187's approval, had appointed a bipartisan Task Force on Immigration Reform headed by Elton Gallegly, a Republican from California who wanted tough action on illegal immigration but was indifferent to cutting legal migration. Gallegly was hardly alone; the Task Force confined its recommendations to undocumented aliens. The majority concluded that IRCA "has failed," in its goal of stopping illegal immigration.[13] The representatives recommended tougher penalties for using fake documents and breaking the law on hiring of undocumented immigrants, prompt removal of illegals when discovered, more funds for the INS, reimbursement for states with incarcerated illegal aliens, pilot programs for worker verification, and tighter procedures for asylum cases. More controversial was a recommendation permitting states to deny education to illegal aliens and ending the birthright citizenship to the children of illegal aliens. The educational proposal was of course modeled on Proposition 187. Birthright denial would have required a constitutional amendment to nullify the Fourteenth Amendment's granting automatic citizenship to persons born in the United States and subject to the jurisdiction of the United States. Such a radical change was never seriously considered by Congress.[14]

The second major governmental report about immigration was that of the Commission on Immigration Reform (CIR), established by Congress in 1990. CIR was bipartisan, composed of an equal number of Democrats and Republicans and chaired by Barbara Jordan of

Texas. CIR's members included several scholars, such as Michael Teit-elbaum and Lawrence Fuchs, who were leaders in the field of immi-gration research and history, as well politicians such as Bruce Morri-son, a former congressman and main author of the Immigration Act of 1990. Generally liberal about immigration issues, these experts knew that American immigration policy contained many flaws and needed reform.

CIR's first report, published in 1994 and entitled *U.S. Immigration Policy: Restoring Credibility*, recognized the system's weaknesses. While praising the historic contribution of immigrants, "The Commission is mindful of the problems that also emanate from immigration. In particular, we believe that unlawful immigration is unacceptable."[15] After dealing with undocumented aliens the commissioners moved on to legal immigration; in June 1995, they urged pushing levels back to approximately where they were before the 1990 act.[16] Both the White House and Senator Bob Dole, the leading Republican candi-date to challenge Clinton in 1996, favored the proposed new limits.[17] In addition liberals such as Senators Diane Feinstein and Barbara Boxer endorsed tougher action to stem the tide of illegal immigra-tion to their state, California. Feinstein had suggested a national ID card for American workers.[18] Noting the nation's mood, Congress-man Lamar Smith said that a "consensus is emerging here. . . . The question is no longer whether legal immigration should be reformed but how it should be reformed."[19]

In spite of the rising anti-immigration tide, it was clearly going to be an uphill battle for the reformers to make major changes. The Gal-legly report had focused only on illegal immigration, and CIR's pro-posals were very modest. Both Lamar Smith and Alan Simpson, the two key players in the debate, were suggesting only modest cuts, not nearly enough to satisfy FAIR, AICF, CCN, or Balance and the likes of Peter Brimelow or Vernon Briggs. It appeared as if the consensus centered on illegal immigration not the legal numbers. While just about everyone criticized the impact of undocumented immigration, when individual proposals were put forward, they ran into staunch op-position. Feinstein's suggestions for national ID cards were character-ized as the beginning of a police state. Proposals for high and well-built fences along the border found opponents who believed them to be cruel and an affront to America's southern neighbor, Mexico. In-creased spending for the INS was rebuffed as too expensive.

Legislators had many suggestions but none had a ready package to present for a vote in 1995. Congress had too many other matters on its plate, and immigration was simply not the top priority. When Simpson's and Smith's bills were introduced they contained important differences. House Speaker Newt Gingrich's promise to get a bill to the floor of the House in 1995 could not be fulfilled. By the time that measures were working their way through subcommittees and committees, opponents of change had time to organize a brilliantly run campaign to block radical change. When Congress finally voted in September 1996 reformers were confronted with a stronger economy and extremely skillful opponents. In the end reformers had to settle for half a loaf, focusing on illegal immigration, terrorism, asylum, and only minor modifications in the rules for legal immigration.

The House, under Lamar Smith, moved first to deal with immigration. Smith did favor, and his committee agreed, to tackle both legal and illegal immigration in one bill as "both systems are broken."[20] Easy to agree upon were the tough proposals against undocumented immigration. Members also voted to have Congress reimburse states for medical charges caused by admitting and treating undocumented aliens. Legal immigration was to be reduced through trimming family unification and refugee admissions a bit; only minor cuts were approved for employment-based visas and temporary workers. Special additional spots were allocated to clear up the backlog of visas for immediate family members of resident aliens. Like the Jordan Commission, Smith's subcommittee wanted to eliminate the preference category for siblings of U.S. citizens.[21]

The House Judiciary Committee began to consider the Smith bill in September 1995. Most of Smith's proposals remained after the mark-up, but work was not completed quickly, and by then the opposition was beginning to lobby intensely. The National Immigration Forum began a series of meetings around the nation to alert the public, and in September 300 immigrants lobbied Congress not to cut family unification. Business and lawyers appeared to make sure that other cuts were not made. A New York lawyer representing companies such as I.B.M., Procter and Gamble, and Walt Disney cited worries about their freedom to hire foreign-born workers. "When Congressmen think of immigration," he declared, "they typically think of the Polish-American Alliance coming to beat them up. They never had any idea business was interested in immigration."[22] Actually, businesses had been interested in immigration for years. Attacking the Jordan Commission's suggestions, an attorney for Microsoft said, "The commission has missed the fact that to succeed in foreign markets, you need foreign personnel."[23] In October the House Judiciary Committee endorsed most of the Smith proposals, even as opposition rose.[24]

The bill introduced by Senator Simpson was a companion to Smith's, but cut immigration more drastically. A major difference was Simpson's wish to decrease employment-based visas from 140,000 to 90,000 whereas Smith's bill made only a token decrease.[25] Labor Secretary Robert Reich endorsed the Simpson approach, "Today, too many companies are reaping huge profits from exploiting foreign workers and laying off skilled American workers." Business officials thought differently. At a news conference called by the National Association of Manufacturers (NAM) to attack Simpson's bill, Jeff Joseph of NAM insisted, "This country is not producing the workers we need to be globally competitive."[26]

Simpson's measure did not reach the full Judiciary Committee until March 1996. By then the business pressure was overwhelming. After meeting with business leaders, Simpson agreed to drop proposed employment-based cuts and also a provision requiring companies to pay at least $10,000 per foreign worker hired into a fund to train American workers.[27] Simpson said he was tired of "trying to accommodate" the business community.[28]

However, the biggest blow for those wanting major reductions in legal immigration occurred when the Senate panel agreed to Senator Spencer Abraham's (R–Mich.) proposal to split legal and illegal immigration components into separate measures. Abraham denied he wanted to kill reform of legal immigration and insisted it was a "distinct and separate topic and ought to be dealt with that way." But the 12 to 6 vote to divide was clearly a sign that cutting legal immigration was unlikely.[29]

Between the retreat on occupational visas and the splitting of the bills, advocates of major restrictions were left with little hope that the Senate would support their goals. Mark Kirkorian, director of CIS, spoke for many of these advocates when he worried that the Senate would produce only "a very watered-down minor bill."[30] Senator Simpson did make one more futile attempt to reduce legal immigration when his much modified bill reached the floor of the Senate in April. The Wyoming Senator proposed a 10 percent reduction of family preferences to take place over the next five years, but he lost by a 80 to 20 vote.[31]

While the Senate Judiciary Committee was concentrating on illegal immigration, the House moved forward on the Smith bill that did not eliminate the legal immigration reductions. On March 21, representatives agreed to make the division thus bringing it in line with the Senate and also dooming any prospect of reducing legal immigration to the United States. Anthony Beilenson of California put it, "Supporters of eliminating the bill's reductions in legal immigration argue that legal and illegal immigration are separate and distinct issues, and therefore ought to be deal with in separate bills. . . . we all know that if these provisions are dropped now, the chances of the House acting on legal immigration reform this year are very slim indeed. . . . we are letting too many people into our country."[32]

The vote on the split was 238 to 183 and 333 to 87 on the final bill.[33] Dropping legal immigration now met with Clinton's approval because he had switched from supporting the Jordan Commission's cuts in regular immigration to opposing them. His Secretary of Labor, Robert Reich, continued to favor cuts in employment-based visas and special protections for American workers against competition from temporary foreign workers, but his view was no longer that of the administration.[34]

According to reports uncovered by the *Boston Globe*, Clinton switched his position as the result of a fund-raiser in which Asian Americans donated over one million dollars to the Democratic cause. John Huang, the Democratic National Committee vice chairman, told the President in a briefing memo that Asians were opposed to eliminating the sibling preference of the immigration law. "Brothers and sisters are considered part of the 'immediate family' in the Asian Pacific community," he said.[35] Besides, Huang told Clinton, many Asians were on the waiting list in this preference category for emigration to the United States. As late as March 13, Clinton had told the Speaker of the House that he favored killing this preference for legal immigrants. However, the President' views were different a week later. Special White House counsel Lanny Davis denied that the change was simply due to Asian-American pressure. Rather he cited "opposition across the spectrum." He referred to the pro-immigration forces, some Republicans and Democrats and groups from "the Roman Catholic Church . . . to the Microsoft Corp. as well as most of the high-tech industry."[36] "I never in my 18 years in Congress saw an issue that shifted so fast and so hard," observed Simpson.[37]

Reformers felt they had been dealt another blow by the administration when immigration statistics were released on March 28, just after the House vote but before the Senate deliberations. The INS reported that 720,461 newcomers had entered the United States in fiscal 1995, a 10 percent drop from the previous year. "This is a statement that the system can work," declared INS Commissioner Doris Meissner. "The United States can have moderate reductions in legal immigration, maintain a generous system for family unification, and still have room for growth in employment-based immigration." Meissner was referring to the fact that the employment-based visas were not fully utilized for that year.[38]

Yet, only one month later, after Simpson had failed in his modest cut in immigration, the INS acknowledged that 1995 was a bit of a fluke and that projected figures for the next year would be over 40 percent higher and still be over 850,000 in 1997. Those receiving an amnesty under IRCA would account for the big jump, for as newly naturalized citizens they were sponsoring immediate family members who could exceed the cap on immigration.[39] Restrictionists were angry. "We've all been duped," said Lamar Smith. "I take this as an intentional misrepresentation to the public and to Congress. And it's inexcusable." Spencer Abraham retorted, "The legislation before the Senate right now aims to crack down on people who break the rules, people who violate the laws, people who seek to come to this country without having proper documentation to take advantage of the benefits of America."[40] Subsequent figures revealed that the 1996 figure was 915,000, a substantial jump but only 23 percent and not 40 percent.[41]

Before Congress agreed upon a bill that President Clinton would sign, compromises were negotiated on asylum, INS procedures, border controls, and immigrant benefits. Congress wanted sponsors to have an income 200 percent of the poverty line to be able sponsor distant relatives and 140 percent of that level to bring over spouses and minor children. Clinton said the figures were too high, and eventually a figure of 125 percent to sponsor relatives was agreed to by both the President and Congress.[42]

Once the two houses had agreed to treat legal and illegal immigration separately, except for welfare and sponsorship issues, the key provision separating the House and the Senate was an amendment sponsored by Elton Gallegly to grant states the right to deny schooling to illegal immigrants. In an unusual speech supporting this section Newt Gingrich said, "This used to be the land of opportunity. Now it's the land of welfare."[43] His speech was denounced by Democrat John Bryant of Texas, "Shame on you, Mr. Speaker! This is a total failure of the leadership of the Speaker of the House."[44] Gallegly's supporters said the amendment merely extended the concept of denying illegal immigrants welfare, and the House approved it, 257 to 163, largely along partisan lines.[45]

Gallegly's provision, which might encourage a state's unconstitutional decision, pleased the supporters of 187, but faced the opposition in the Senate and from President Clinton. A White House spokesman said that the proponents of such a provision "seem to be suggesting that if (illegal immigrant children are) not in school, they'd be better off out on the streets participating in gang activities. . . . That's a nutty idea."[46] In the end Gallegly's proposal was dropped from the final bill when many Republicans in the Senate joined with Democrats to defeat it.[47]

The Illegal Immigration Reform and Immigrant Responsibility Act of 1996 easily passed both houses and was signed by the President in the last week of September. In addition to the provisions noted above, it contained additional support for the INS to enable it to double the border patrol force from 5,000 to 10,000 within four years.[48] Money was also voted for improved fences along the California-Mexico border. The act included more stringent provisions for aliens violating immigration laws and for expedited deportation of illegal aliens. More controversial was the creation of three pilot programs for testing electronic systems to verify an application of someone applying for work. One of these involved using Social Security numbers that could be read by a machine. The programs were voluntary for employers, to test how they might work. The anti-immigration lobby wanted more far-reaching procedures for determining eligibility to work, but Congress was wary of doing more lest it be accused of opening the door for the establishment of a national identity card.

Asylum procedures, another area of concern for both proponents and opponents of immigration reform, were slightly modified. The act required those seeking political asylum to file an application within one year of entering the United States. The anti-immigration movement argued that too many asking for asylum only did so when they were found to be illegally residing in America. Their claims, they said, were often frivolous attempts to avoid deportation and were not genuine.

Who won in 1996? The pro-immigration coalition desired to preserve the current rate of legal immigration and did so. While no cuts were made, the new monetary limits on sponsoring immigrants had a potential impact on some nations. Now, one had to have an income 125 percent of the poverty rate in order to bring in one's relatives, an increase from the old figure of the poverty level itself. Immigrants' rights groups and the INS said that more than 35 percent of the citizens waiting to sponsor newcomers would be unable to do so and that Mexicans and Central Americans in particular would have difficulty meeting the new guidelines. Whether this new figure would be really effective was not certain.[49] The same uncertainty applied to the new asylum procedures. The law attempted to reduce frivolous claims, although actual numbers could continue to climb if events abroad drove people to seek a haven in the United States. As a concession to conservatives, Congress explicitly allowed that up to 1,000 persons annually could be granted asylum if they were fleeing China's one child per family policy.

In July 1997 Attorney General Janet Reno also intervened in a dispute over new deportation rules effecting several hundred thousand Central American refugees who were in the United States on a temporary basis. Overruling the Board of Immigration Appeal, she suspended deportations for these persons, pending an investigation of the law's impact. This, too, was an example of the uncertainty of the 1996 law's effectiveness in tightening immigration rules.[50]

The new law projected major governmental tactics dealing with undocumented immigration. Increases in INS personnel will have an impact along the border dividing the United States and Mexico as will the new rules for deportation of those entering in violation of the law. Additional funds for deporting aliens convicted of felonies would no doubt increase the number of such deportations. Most illegal aliens come to America in search of work, not welfare. The GAO and the INS estimated that about half of all illegal aliens enter legally as visitors, students, and the like, and then stay when their visas expire.[51] More than a secure border will be required to end the employment of such illegal workers. The INS simply does not have the manpower to enforce employers' sanctions effectively or catch workers who are illegally employed. The anti-immigration lobby maintains that only a national identification system will halt undocumented aliens from gaining employment. The new pilot verification projects authorized by the new immigration act are voluntary, and even if they prove successful, Congress will face the task of expanding them and mandating some type of national identification card.

In all, it appears the pro-immigration lobby won the 1996 battle. Anti-immigration forces are comforted that no one seriously considered another amnesty as a trade-off for the new controls on illegal immigration. Moreover, a temporary worker program for agricultural interests was decisively beaten. But these seem marginal victories. If indeed, the problem is too many immigrants, then restrictionists were thoroughly defeated. Legal immigration is projected to run over 900,000 annually until the end of the 1990s; many others enter without visas, claim asylum, and can be paroled. Even if illegal immigration drops by half, over one million persons will annually migrate to the United States, a figure more than triple the goal of restrictionists' goal of 300,000 or less.

After the 1994 elections the prospects for immigration reform looked bright. What happened? In the first place, pro-immigration forces rallied their troops and persuaded Congress not to touch legal immigration. According to John Judis, Rick Swartz, a founder of the National Immigration Forum, ably coordinated a diverse coalition. He got the various businesses wanting to use immigrant labor to work together effectively in the fall of 1995 in order to wear Simpson down and eliminate cuts in employment-related visas. The Simpson proposals also bothered the Cato Institute and other free market or libertarian organizations, which traditionally favored liberal policy and the movement of labor across national boundaries. Swartz also forged a common ground that brought together opponents of governmental regulations such as the National Rifle Association and the American Civil Liberties Union.[52] Ethnic, religious, and nationality groups affected by changes in family unification naturally opposed changes, and even Ralph Reed's Christian Coalition told Congress that "scaling back the ability of Americans to reunite with their families will not improve national security, and could severely damage the American family."[53]

In view of the polls that indicated evangelic Christians were often opposed to immigration, the Christian Coalition's views might be surprising. But as Sara Diamond explains, "The Christian Right, representing a board evangelical subculture shared by millions, was focused on expanding its numbers, to win elections and to lobby on social issues. . . . The Christian Rights's game plan involved recruiting, not alienating, people of color, including immigrants."[54] While it might seem odd to see the Christian Coalition, MALDEF, the American Civil Liberties Union, and Microsoft working together on the same cause, the politics of immigration in 1995 and 1996 was mostly one of strange bedfellows, as it had often been in the past.

Few in either the pro- or anti-immigration camp disagree with this analysis. Frank Sharry, executive director of the National Immigration Forum, noted that an "odd mix" united to defeat proposed immigration legislation. "The controversy over the proposed immigration legislation pending in the Senate and House has fostered an unusual degree of cooperation among groups and individuals who are typically at odds." In particular he named NAM, Microsoft, Bill Gates, some trade unions, and Americans for Tax Reform as part of the coalition.[55]

FAIR agreed. In "An Open Letter to the Citizens of the United States of America," Dan Stein said, "WHAT WAS PASSED WAS NOT AN IMMIGRATION REFORM BILL. IT WAS A VICTORY FOR OPEN BORDER ADVOCATES." FAIR's ad, placed in the friendly *Washington Times*, also pointed to the work of Microsoft and the NAM, but other villains included MALDEF, the American Immigration Lawyers Association, and individuals such as Spencer Abraham, Dick Armey, and Phil Gramm.[56] While FAIR believed these organizations and individuals had "betrayed the American people," the National Immigration Forum hailed them: "Lady Liberty's torch must not be extinguished. America is certainly big enough, smart enough, and strong enough to continue to welcome law-abiding immigrants who are seeking opportunity and willing to contribute to our society."[57] CCN claimed the anti-immigration movement did its best to inform the public and influence Congress but, "In the end, under intense last-minute lobbying from the cheap-labor lobby on one extreme and open-border proponents on the other, the 104th Congress passed the buck on reducing legal immigration levels on to the 105th Congress convening in January."[58]

In the national debate of 1996, groups represented by the National Immigration Forum and its allies had an enormous advantage: their constituents had a direct connection to immigration and stood to lose if immigration were substantially reduced. They would have been hindered in hiring foreign nationals, in bringing in their relatives or in sponsoring refugees. For businesses traditionally suspicious of governmental regulation there was the additional bother of more forms to fill out if the regulations expanded. In contrast, the anti-immigration movement did not contain many groups and individuals who were directly affected by immigration. The line between immigration and the environment was unclear to Congress. Nor did the economic impacts of immigration seem so burdensome, except in a limited number of states and cities. The group probably most adversely effected by immigrants, low-wage and unskilled African Americans, was represented by members of Congress determined to work with the Hispanic Caucus, which saw immigration as vital to its interest.

In addition, the concentration of immigrants posed a problem for the restrictionist movement. The vast majority of the nation's latest immigrants settle in a half dozen states, which see the impact of immigration. Elsewhere it is not so obvious. While the polls indicated ambivalence and even growing opposition to large-scale immigration, politicians from many states can ignore these results because they are of very minor concern to their constituents. Montana, Nevada, Utah, Iowa, or Alabama voters place other issues on the front burner. It is difficult to see how to see how voting in favor of present levels of immigration will lose legislators either votes or office.

Economic conditions are critical in immigration debate. When the California economy was booming in the 1980s, little was heard about immigration. Only after the down turn did anti-immigration sentiment rise in that state. As things began to improve in the mid-1990s, the Golden State's mood against immigrants began to soften. Certainly Bob Dole, who tried to play upon immigration fears in the 1996 election, found it had little appeal among California voters. It is even possible that a 187-type measure would not have been approved in 1996 when new Hispanic and some Asians voters worked against those too vocal about cutting immigration.

Another factor making the task of the restrictionists more difficult is the emotional appeal of America's tradition of welcoming millions upon millions of newcomers, many of whom were poor or seeking religious or political freedom. Aiding such unfortunate people warms the hearts of Americans, from schoolchildren to members of Congress. Many Americans today have parents or grandparents who were immigrants, and the refrain, "we are a nation of immigrants," was constantly heard in Congress. One representative told his fellow representatives that America was "a nation of immigrants," and related how his grand-father had come from Norway when he was 16. "Like most immigrants, he sought a better life for himself and his family. . . . he was drafted, and served with distinction in the battle of the Argonne in World War I. And his story is only one of millions of immigrant stories of hope and opportunity, and of service to our Nation."[59]

Senator Arlen Spector of Pennsylvania was even more eloquent:

> When Senator Simpson came to talk to me recently about the immigration legislation that he has worked on judiciously . . . he noticed a grouping of photographs on the wall. . . . So I introduced him to my mother's father, Mordecai Shanin, who came from a small town on the Russian border when my mother was 5 and settled in St. Jo, Mo. And I reintroduced Senator Simpson to my father, Harry Specter, who was in his uniform, and I recounted that he emigrated from Ukraine, walking across Europe with barely a ruble in his pocket.

Spector added, "My sense is that America is a big, broad, growing country and that we do have room for immigrants."[60] Spector cherishes the myth that we are a "nation of immigrants." When one adds "families" to the powerful appeal of immigration, it creates a nearly unbeatable combination. Senator Abraham, himself the grandson of Lebanese immigrants, explained, "Families are the building blocks of our society. And an immigrant coming to America, working hard, and years later petitioning for his or her close family members is not creating a problem. He or she is simply carrying on the American experience. Perhaps none of us would be here if our parents or grandparents had not made a journey to this great nation."[61]

Yet the phrase "a nation of immigrants" does not answer the questions of how many and what kind of immigrants should be admitted to modern America. Peter Salins's *Assimilation American Style* is a case in point. Subtitled "An impassioned defense of immigration and assimilation as the foundation of American greatness and the American dream," Salin's book is impassioned, but a bit short on careful analysis. Fully aware that approximately one million persons annually are entering in the 1990s, he firmly believes that immigrants have "at all times been good for America."[62] His book advocates "allowing the largest possible number of new immigrants to come to the United States," but how does Congress determine "the largest possible number?"[63] Pro-immigration groups and individuals have effectively created the impression that *any* cuts in the current level immigration is a betrayal of our immigrant heritage. In the early 1980s, cutting below the then current 600,000 immigrants denies the immigrant heritage. But in the late 1990s the pro-immigration forces argue that dropping from one million back to 600,000 is unacceptable. In the late 1990s one favoring the limits of the 1980s might be accused of trying to build walls around America, of being a racist, or of wanting to end the heritage of being "a nation of immigrants."

It is difficult to estimate the importance of this emotional appeal. After all, it is nearly always better to appeal to altruism and enlightened principles than to crude economics. Was it simply rhetoric to use such appeals? Perhaps, but given the fact that immigration's impact is limited to only a minority of American states and cities, peoples from the other areas do not have to worry so much about economics; they can support noble traditions easily. This is especially the case when publicly expressed bigotry is no longer acceptable.

Dealing with illegal immigration is another matter altogether. Undocumented immigrants have no legal right to be in the United States, to take jobs (which possibly might otherwise be filled by American citizens and resident aliens) or use welfare. These aliens found few public defenders, although many politicians, for various reasons, were unwilling to take steps to try to stem the flow. When the pressure built to "do something" about immigration, illegal aliens were a natural target. And that is precisely what Congress did.

In the field of illegal immigration, restrictionists had some room for optimism. In January 1997, the INS announced that an additional 237 U.S. Border Patrol agents were heading to California, the center of so much debate about illegal immigration. INS Commissioner Doris Meissner noted that most would be used on the "front lines," along the border. The INS also announced that it was hiring 2,000 more employees and was updating its procedures. In dispatching the new patrol members, Meissner said, "The plan we laid out four years ago to build a firm, but fair, immigration policy is working. Our efforts have enabled us to strengthen control of our borders."[64]

But the question of benefits for legal immigrants remains unsolved. Clinton promised to seek changes in the restriction of benefits under the new welfare law, and he repeated his desire in his 1997 State of Union Address. Representative E. Clay Shaw, Jr., disagreed: "We're not going to be making any substantive changes to the welfare bill. . . . It's going to be far less than what the president is talking about. . . . Santa Claus is in retirement."[65] To which Michael Fix, of Washington's Urban Institute, answered:, "If you were a proponent of welfare reform, you would not want the first images coming back from the front to be the faces of this particularly vulnerable population losing their benefits." Better, he said, to "see the face of a healthy, able-bodied person leaving welfare and receiving their first paycheck."[66] Like other issues about immigration, welfare benefits will no doubt be debated in the future, in spite of agreement in 1997 between the President and Congress to restore some benefits for immigrants.[67]

The prospects for changing legal immigration appear slight to non-existent in the near future. First, public opinion might have shifted. A Knight-Ridder newspaper-sponsored poll released in 1997 revealed that as many Americans believed immigration to be good for the country as those who said t was bad. The results heartened pro-immigration leader Frank Sharry, who remarked, "in the early '90s we were in danger of losing our heads over this issue." But now he stated, the tide had turned. Moreover, most Americans expressed little concern about the demographic make up of the nation. Two thirds said they were not "at all worried" or "little worried" by the surging numbers of Asian and Hispanic immigrants or by the forecast that whites of European ancestry will eventually become an minority.[68]

Second, passage of the welfare and illegal immigration bills permits Congress to wait and assess their impact, so restrictionists face an uphill battle in Congress. In the 105th Congress immigration was a low-priority issue; Trent Lott (R–Miss.), the majority leader, told reporters, "I really don't see much prospect of more action in that area, at least not this year." [69] Lamar Smith, who led the House fight to cut immigration slightly, ruefully declared, "Unlike last year, I'm not planning to introduce a major bill any time soon." Smith was no doubt not eager for another fight like that occurring in 1996.[70]

Senator Alan Simpson retired and his subcommittee dealing with immigration is now chaired by Senator Spencer Abraham, a major villain of the play, in the eyes of restrictionists. Early in 1997 Spector spoke to Cypress Semiconductor Corporation, in the heart of Silicon Valley, whose executives had joined his fight against cuts in immigration. Abraham reassured his hosts by saying, "We addressed some real problems with immigration last year. Unfortunately, there were some who wanted to go a lot farther . . . and start building walls around our country." He pledged his influence would keep Congress from changing legal immigration.[71] Abraham had even opposed the pilot-verification projects and other ID card proposals as being unfair to business.[72] While FAIR followers picketed Abraham, they admitted, "It's going to be much, much more difficult to enact reforms if that wing of the Republican party dominates."[73] And Dan Stein added, "We've made no secret of our displeasure with Abraham."[74] How to turn that displeasure into a renewed campaign to curtail immigration loomed as a major barrier for FAIR and the restrictionist movement.

# Conclusions

THE 1996 ACTS dealing with illegal immigration and welfare were the latest laws forging an immigration policy. These measures tightened immigration controls and eliminated some benefits for immigrants, but they did not reduce the numbers permitted by prior legislation. They responded to the recent fears about immigration, and they also reveal that the historic ambivalence Americans have about immigration was alive and well. The original colonists wanted settlers, but they expressed little desire to see newcomers of other religions and nationalities; they preferred English Protestants settlers. They also worried about too many paupers and prisoners being dumped on American shores.

When the colonies achieved their independence, Congress was content to allow the states to regulate immigration until 1875. The states passed laws to keep out paupers and criminals and to regulate sailing vessels, but they deterred few from coming to America, and immigration grew rapidly after 1840. As it increased many Americans feared that too many criminals, paupers, and Roman Catholics were coming. However, no religious barriers were erected.

From 1875 on, Congress regulated immigration, and the federal government established processing centers for immigrants, the most famous being Ellis Island in New York City's harbor. Congress banned prostitutes and then persons likely to become a public charge, anarchists, polygamists, the insane, and criminal among others. For racist reasons, in 1882 the Chinese became the first group to be barred. Then the legislators banned other Asians: Japanese, Koreans, Indians, and Filipinos. After 1900 racism was increasing directed at southern and eastern Europeans, who were viewed as separate and inferior races. Religious intolerance, fears of radicalism, and economic worries also played a role in restrictionism. When a literacy test passed in 1917 failed to check mass immigration, Congress constructed national origins quotas that severely limited immigration from southern and eastern European nations. Virtually unlimited immigration from Europe came to an end. Enacted during the 1920s, the laws were tightly enforced and immigration sank to new lows during the Great Depression and World War II.

After 1943, the door for newcomers swung open once again. By the 1990s record numbers of people were migrating to America, chiefly from Third World nations. The latest immigrants, like the oldest, were viewed with growing suspicion. With the founding of FAIR in 1979 another movement developed to curtail immigration. FAIR and other such groups wanted to bar immigrants from governmental welfare programs and drastically cut both legal and illegal immigration, but they achieved only limited success in 1996. The 1996 legislation barred immigrants from some welfare programs, raised the income level required for sponsoring immigrants, imposed tighter procedures for asylum, increased the size of the INS, and put in place new regulations to curb illegal immigration. But those acts did not cut legal immigration. Although angered by their defeat, the restrictionists resolved to keep fighting to shrink the migratory flow. Dr. John Tanton, founder of FAIR, said in 1997 that he might run against Senator Spencer Abraham of Michigan, who had ably defended immigrants during the 1996 debates. Dr. Tanton indicated that the major issue in this possible campaign would be immigration.[1] FAIR along with other restrictionist groups announced in June 1997 that they were forming a new organization, Partners Against Illegal Immigration, to work together to check undocumented immigration.[2]

The battle over welfare benefits to immigrants, which many Republicans thought had ended with passage of the 1996 welfare act, was renewed in 1997 when the President and congressional Democrats and Republicans (pushed by Republican governors) agreed to restore some of the cuts for those who arrived before passage of the 1996 law. Unresolved were issues about immigrants arriving after; the parties did not agree to permit these latest newcomers to be eligible for benefits.[3] What the states would do to aid those dropped from federal programs was another unclear issue. In addition, immigrant advocates promised legal action to test sections of the Illegal Immigration Reform and Immigrant Responsibility Act of 1996.[4] Whether the new rules about the income levels needed for immigrant sponsorship would have a major impact was unknown in 1997.[5] Nor did the asylum question appear to be solved. CIR announced in June 1997 that it was recommending changes in the 1996 act's asylum procedures, which it deemed harsh. Restrictionists lamented CIR's report, but it was welcomed by the pro-immigrant Lawyers Committee for Human Rights.[6]

CIR was scheduled to make its final recommendations in 1997, and it requested the National Research Council to prepare a massive report on immigration. When the Council issued a preliminary draft entitled *The New Americans: Economic, Demography, and Fiscal Effects of Immigration*, in June 1997, its reception was predictable. The Council presented a generally favorable review of the economic and demographic effects of immigration, which pleased pro-immigration groups, but it did note some problems.[7] FAIR immediately stressed the negative aspects, claiming the report proved "that immigration at current levels is imposing enormous costs and fueling a variety of deeply troubling social and economic trends."[8] *Impact*, an anti-immigration newsletter devoted to the impact on African Americans, echoed FAIR.[9]

CCN issued a new two-volume *Carrying Capacity Briefing Book* in early 1997, with pieces advocating immigration reductions.[10] The *National Review* gave no indication that it would give up the immigration fight. In June 1997, the conservative journal carried several articles by Peter Brimelow, George Borjas, and Mark Krikorian among others, on immigration. Brimelow in particular warned of the perils of continued immigration to the Republican party.[11]

Attacks on immigration were not unanswered. In the first six months of 1997 four books were published either attacking restrictionists or defending immigration. Juan F. Perea's (ed.) *Immigrants Out! The New Nativism and the Anti-Immigrant Impulse in the United States* minced no words in its assault: "The essays in this book take an unflinching critical look at a series of contemporary political developments that may accurately be labeled nativist."[12] More sweeping was Joel Millman's *The Other Americans: How Immigrants Renew Our Coun-*

*try, Our Economy, and Our Values*, which virtually calls for an open immigration policy.[13]

Defenses of and attacks on immigration will no doubt continue. Immigrants make up slightly less than 10 percent of the American population in 1997, below the previous high of nearly 15 percent early in the twentieth century. Yet the foreign-born proportion has almost doubled since 1970, and immigration is running at record highs. Moreover, immigration is no longer predominately European. These large numbers and their changing sources make it extremely likely that restrictionist sentiments will find fertile ground. In addition, if the economy experiences another recession or sluggish growth, anti-immigrant sentiments could again find sympathetic audiences. If immigrants spread their settlements into more than a limited number of states then restrictionism might also have greater geographical appeal.

In recent years such dispersal has occurred when companies have hired foreign workers in places where few immigrants had lived. Storm Lake, Iowa, was one such town where they found employment in a food-processing establishment, and the arrival of newcomers caused tensions.[14] Wenatchee, Washington, was another city of new immigration; in this case of Latino immigrants. It is no accident that Washington State Citizens for Immigration Control was centered in Wenatchee.[15] Studies such as the National Research Council's will not end debate. It will continue, unfortunately, with much emotion and probably produce ad hoc policies, just as it has in the past.

# Notes

**Introduction**

1. *Congressional Quarterly*, Dec. 14, 1996, 3398.
2. *New York Times*, April 4, 1997.

**1. Toward Exclusion: American Immigration Policy Before World War I**

1. David Fischer, *Albion's Seed: Four British Folkways in America* (New York: Oxford University Press, 1989), 491–92.

2. Quoted in Frederick Binder and David M. Reimers, *All the Nations Under Heaven: An Ethnic and Racial History of New York City* (New York: Columbia University Press, 1995), 10.

3. Ibid., 8.

4. Leonard Dinnerstein, *Antisemitism in America* (New York: Oxford University Press, 1994), 3–12.

5. Lawrence Fuchs, *The American Kaleidoscope: Race, Ethnicity, and the Civic Culture* (Hanover: Wesleyan University Press, 1990), 9.

6. Morton Borden, *Jews, Turks, and Infidels* (Chapel Hill: University of North Carolina Press, 1984), 34.

7. See Sister Mary Augustina Ray, *American Opinion of Roman Catholicism in the Eighteenth Century* (New York: Columbia University Press, 1936).

8. Maldwyn Jones, *American Immigration* (Chicago: University of Chicago Press, 1960), 43.

9. Bernard Bailyn, *Voyagers to the West: A Passage in the Peopling of America on the Eve of the Revolution* (New York: Knopf, 1986), 295.

10. A. Roger Ekrich, *Bound for America: The Transportation of British Convicts to the Colonies, 1718–1770* (New York: Oxford University Press, 1987), 168.

11. Ibid., 137.

12. Ibid., 135.

13. Ibid., 138–39.

14. Jones, *American Immigration*, 44.

15. Ibid., 45.

16. Ibid., 48.

17. Ibid.

18. James H. Kettner, *The Development of American Citizenship, 1608–1870* (Chapel Hill: University of North Carolina Press, 1978), 74–76.

19. Jones, *American Immigration*, 60–61.

20. Matthew Spalding, "From Pluribus to Unum: Immigration and the Founding Fathers," *Policy Review*, Jan.-Mar., 1994, 35.

21. Ibid., 37–38.

22. Jones, *American Immigration*, 82–91; Kettner, *American Citizenship*, chapter 8.

23. Gerald L. Neuman, *Strangers to the Constitution: Immigrants, Borders, and Fundamental Law* (Princeton: Princeton University Press, 1996), 21–22.

24. Ibid., 25.

25. Ibid., 28.

26. Quoted in Tyler Anbinder, *Nativism and Slavery: The Northern Know Nothings and the Politics of the 1850s* (New York: Oxford University Press, 1992), 108.

27. Quoted in ibid., 109.

28. Jones, *American Immigration*, 148–50. The standard treatment of pre-Civil War anti-Catholicism is Ray Billington, *The Protestant Crusade, 1800–1860* (Chicago: Quadrangle Press, 1964).

29. Dale Knobel, *"America for the Americans": The Nativist Movement in the United States* (New York: Twayne, 1996), chapters 2–3.

30. Ibid., 105.

31. Ibid., chapters 2–3.

32. Anbinder, *Nativism and Slavery*, 121–22.

33. Gwendolyn Mink, *Old Labor and New Immigrants in American Political Development: Union, Party, and State, 1875–1920* (Ithaca: Cornell University Press, 1986), 82.

34. Ibid., 78.

35. Roger Daniels, *Asian America: Chinese and Japanese in the United States Since 1850* (Seattle: University of Washington Press, 1988), chapter 2.

36. John Higham, *Strangers in the Land: Patterns of American Nativism, 1860–1925* (New Brunswick: Rutgers University Press, 2d edition, 1988), 54–55.

37. Ibid., 80–87.

38. Ibid.

39. Dinnerstein, *Antisemitism in America*, chapter 3.

40. Higham, *Strangers in the Land*, 101–5.

41. Daniels, *Asian America*, 115–26.

42. Ibid., 151–52.

43. Ibid., 151.

44. Ibid., 145.

45. Ronald Takaki, *Strangers from a Different Shore: A History of Asian Americans* (Boston: Little, Brown, 1989), 296–97.

46. Joan Jensen, *Passage from India: Asian Indian Immigrants in North America* (New Haven: Yale University Press, 1988), 246–58.

47. Takaki, *Strangers from a Different Shore*, 326–35.

48. Higham, *Strangers in the Land*, 179–82.

49. Ibid.

50. Ibid., 181–84.

51. Quoted in Arthur Goren, *New York Jews and the Quest for Community: The Kehillah Experiment, 1908–1922* (New York: Columbia University Press, 1970), 25.

52. Ibid., 35.

53. Thomas Pitkin, *The Black Hand: A Chapter in Ethnic Crime* (Totowa, N.J.: Littlefield, Adams, 1977), 23–25.

54. Ibid., 25.

55. Ibid., 25–30.

56. See Higham, *Strangers in the Land*, chapter 6.

57. Ibid., 156–57.

58. U.S. Congress, Senate, *Statements and Recommendations Submitted by Societies and Organizations Interested in the Subject of Immigration*, Reports of the U.S. Commission on Immigration, S. Doc. 764, 61st Cong., 3d sess. (Washington D.C.: GPO, 1911), 107.

59. Ibid., 130.

60. Edward A. Ross, *The Old World and the New: The Significance of Past and Present Immigration to the American People* (New York: Century, 1914), 294.

61. Ibid., 287–88.

62. Higham, *Strangers in the Land*, 116–23. Higham believes that on balance Progressivism acted as a check on nativism at least before 1910.

63. Marion Bennett, *American Immigration Policies: A History* (Washington D.C.: Public Affairs Press, 1963), 23. For a list of diseases that would make immigrants ineligible for admission, see Alan Kraut, *Silent Travelers: Germs, Genes, and the "Immigrant Menace"* (New York: Basic Books, 1994), 273–76.

64. Bennett, *American Immigration Policies*, 24.

65. U.S. Commission on Immigration, Vol. 1, *Abstracts* (Washington D.C.: GPO, 1911), 36.

66. U.S. Commission on Immigration, *Immigration and Crime* (Washington D.C.: GPO, 1911), 1.

67. Ibid., 2.

68. Ibid.

69. Jeremiah W. Jenks and W. Jett Lauck, *The Immigration Problem: A Study of American Immigration Conditions and Needs* (London: Funk and Wagnalls, 1922), 410–11.

70. Isaac Hourwich, *Immigration and Labor: The Economic Aspects of European Immigration to the United States* (New York: Putnam, 1912). Hourwich's volume, like the Dillingham Commission, centered on economic issues.

71. Ibid., 499.

72. This was the fourth time that a President had vetoed the test.

73. Higham, *Strangers in the Land*, 194–222.

74. Quoted in James Crawford, ed., *Language Loyalties: A Source Book on the Official English Controversy* (Chicago: University of Chicago Press, 1992), 85.

75. William G. Ross, *Forging New Freedoms: Nativism, Education, and the Constitution, 1917–1927* (Lincoln: University of Nebraska Press, 1994), chapter 2.

76. Ibid., 39–41.

77. See Frederick Luebke, *Bonds of Loyalty: German Americans in World War I* (DeKalb: Northern Illinois University Press, 1974).

78. Ross, *Forging New Freedoms*, 44. This proclamation, which obviously limited free speech, was enforced with flexibility.

79. Higham, *Strangers in the Land*, 225–33.

80. Ibid., 263.

81. Bennett, *American Immigration Policies*, 40.

82. Higham, *Strangers in the Land*, 273–74.

83. Ibid., 283–86.

84. U.S. Congress, Senate, *Statements and Recommendations*, 373.

85. Michael C. LeMay, *From Open Door to Dutch Door: An Analysis of U.S. Immigration Policy Since 1820* (Westport, Conn.: Praeger, 1987), 77–81; Keith Fitzgerald, *The Face of a Nation: Immigration, the State, and the National Identity* (Stanford: Stanford University Press, 1966), 131.

86. See Higham, *Strangers in the Land*, chapter 11; Fitzgerald, *The Face of a Nation*, 132–44.

87. Kenneth M. Ludmerer, *Genetics and American Society: A Historical Appraisal* (Baltimore: Johns Hopkins University Press, 1972), 101.

88. Robert Divine, *American Immigration Policy, 1924–1952* (New Haven: Yale University Press, 1957), 5.

89. Ibid., 17; and Higham, *Strangers in the Land*, 316–24. See also Ludmerer, *Genetics*, 100–13.

90. Divine, *American Immigration Policy*, 17–18 and chapter 2.

91. Ibid., 104.

92. See also Mark Haller, *Eugenics: Hereditarian Attitudes in American Thought* (New Brunswick: Rutgers University Press, 1963), 152–57.

93. Elliott Robert Barkan, *And Still They Come: Immigrants and American Society, 1920 to the 1990s* (Wheeling, Ill.: Harlan Davidson, 1996), 14.

94. Ludmerer, *Genetics*, 104.

95. Divine, *American Immigration Policy*, 57.

96. Ibid., 52–68.

97. George Sanchez, *Becoming Mexican American: Ethnicity, Culture, and Identity in Chicano Los Angeles, 1900–1945* (New York: Oxford University Press, 1993), 56–62. About half of Mexicans arriving in the 1920s were estimated to be undocumented aliens.

98. Abraham Hoffman, *Unwanted Mexican Americans in the Great Depression: Repatriation Pressures, 1929–1939* (Tucson: University of Arizona Press, 1974); Sanchez, *Becoming Mexican American*, 210–217.

99. Divine, *American Immigration Policy*, 78–80.

100. Ibid., 78–91.

101. Ibid., 78–86.

102. For the struggle over immigration during the late 1930s see David Wyman, *Paper Walls: America and the Refugee Crisis, 1938–1941* (Amherst: University of Massachusetts Press, 1968).

103. Divine, *American Immigration Policy*, 101.

104. For Trevor's role in the 1920s see Higham, *Strangers in the Land*, 319–22. For the bill see Alan Kraut and Richard Breitman, *American Refugee Policy and European Jewry, 1933–1945* (Bloomington: Indiana University Press, 1987), 73–74; Wyman, *Paper Walls*, 75–79. For the thirties generally see Divine, *American Immigration Policy*, chapters 4–5.

105. See David Wyman, *The Abandonment of Jews: America and the Holocaust, 1941–1945* (New York: Knopf, 1984).

106. Roger Daniels, *Prisoners Without Trial: Japanese Americans in World War II* (New York: Hill and Wang, 1993).

## 2. The New Movement to Restrict Immigration

1. In 1952 all Asian nations were give quotas, usually 100 each, and their immigrants made eligible for naturalization. The discussion of postwar policy is largely based on David M. Reimers, *Still the Golden Door: The Third World Comes to America* (New York: Columbia University Press, 1992, 2d edition).

2. Figures are based on the annual reports of INS.

3. FAIR, *Immigration Report*, May 1996.

4. Guillermina Jasso and Mark R. Rosenzweig, *The New Chosen People: Immigrants in the United States* (New York: Russell Sage, 1990), 145.

5. Reimers, *Still the Golden Door*, 221.

6. *New York Times*, Feb. 8, 1997.

7. Reimers, *Still the Golden Door*, 259.

8. Figures are based on the annual reports of INS.

9. *New York Times*, June 27, 1993.

10. There are regional variations. Tom Espenshade found that New Jersey residents were generally more accepting of immigrants that were people from other states. Thomas J. Espenshade, ed., *Keys to Successful Immigration: Implications of the New Jersey Experience* (Washington D.C.: Urban Institute, 1997), 89–118.

11. Roper Organization, "American Attitudes Toward Immigration," June 1990.

12. Gallup Poll, *Public Opinion, 1993* (Wilmington, Del.: Scholarly Resources, 1994), 250–51.

13. *Business Week*, July 13, 1992, 119; *Newsweek*, Aug. 9, 1993, 25.

14. *New York Times*, June 26, 1993; *USA Today* July 14, 1993; and Federation for American Immigration Reform (FAIR), *Immigration Report*, July 1994.

15. *Washington Times*, March 5, 1996.

16. *Wall Street Journal*, March 26, 1996.

17. Elliott Barkan, "Immigrants and the California State of Mind: Assessing Public Opinion Regarding Immigrants and Ethnics, 1982–1995." Paper for the Pacific Coast Branch meeting of the American Historical Association, August 1995.

18. *New York Times*, Oct. 18, 1993.

19. *Newsweek*, Sept. 10, 1990, 48.

20. Ibid., Aug. 9, 1993, 25.

21. *USA Today*, July 14, 1993.

22. Tom Espenshade and Maryann Belanger, "U.S. Public Perceptions and Reactions to Mexican Migration," in Frank Bean et al., eds., *At the Crossroads: Mexican Migration and U.S. Policy* (Lanham, Md.: Rowman and Littlefield, 1997), 228.

23. Rita Simon and Susan Alexander, *Ambivalent Welcome: Print Media, Public Opinion, and Immigration* (Westport, Conn.: Praeger, 1993), 44–46; Roper Poll, June 1991, 20–31; Edwin Harwood, "American Public Opinion and U.S. Immigration Policy," *Annals of the American Academy of Political and Social Science*, September 1986, 205–207; Barkan, "Immigrants;" and *Washington Times*, March 5, 1996.

24. Simon and Alexander, *Ambivalent Welcome*, 34–40.

25. Barkan, "Immigrants," 18; Roper Poll, June 1991, 20–31; *Washington Times*, March 5, 1996.

26. Thomas Espenshade and Katherine Hempstead, "Contemporary American Attitudes Toward U.S. Immigration," Office of Population Research, Princeton University, March, 1995.

27. *New York Times*, Aug. 25, 1996.

28. FAIR, *Immigration Report*, March 1996; *Washington Times*, March 5, 1996.

29. *New York Times*, July 1, 1986

30. *Washington Times*, March 5, 1995.

31. Dale Maharidge, *The Coming White Minority: California's Eruptions and the Nation's Future* (New York: Times Books, 1996), 166–67.

32. *Migration News*, Dec. 1, 1994; *Los Angeles Times*, Oct. 29, 1994; Nov. 22, 1994.

33. It was still unenforced as of 1997. Pfaelzer's decision was based on a 1982 Supreme Court five to four ruling that Texas could not deny illegal immigrant children an education.

34. *Los Angeles Times*, Nov. 20, 1994.

35. *Migration News*, Dec. 1, 1994, 7.

36. See in particular Mike Davis, "The Social Origins of the Referendum," NACLA, *Report on the Americas*, November–December 1995, 24–28.

37. Peter Skerry, *Mexican Americans: The Ambivalent Minority* (New York: Free Press, 1993), 300.

38. *Wall Street Journal*, Oct. 21, 1986; *Washington Times*, May 5, 1994.

39. FAIR, *Hispanic and Black Attitudes Toward Immigration Policy* (Washington D.C., 1983).

40. Rudolfo O. de la Garza et al., *Latino Voices: Mexican, Puerto Rican, and Cuban Perspectives on American Politics* (Boulder: Westview Press, 1992), 100–101.

41. *Washington Times*, March 5, 1996; FAIR, *Immigration Report*, March 1996.

42. David Gutierrez, *Walls and Mirrors: Mexican Americans, Mexican Immigrants, and the Politics of Ethnicity* (Berkeley: University of California Press, 1995), 163–78.

43. Ibid., 180–81.

44. Ibid., 200–205.

45. Ibid., 215.

46. Simon and Alexander, *Ambivalent Welcome*, 40.

47. *Business Week*, July 13, 1992, 119; Nicolaus Mills, "Lifeboat Ethics and Immigration Fears," *Dissent*, Winter, 1996, 37–38. A *New York Times*-CBS poll conducted in 1986 revealed more ambivalence.

48. William Wilson, *When Work Disappears: The World of the New Urban Poor* (New York: Knopf, 1996), 190–192,

49. Espenshade and Hempstead, "Contemporary Attitudes," 14.

50. *Migration News*, Dec. 1, 1994, 3.

51. *Washington Times*, March 5, 1996.

52. For early views of African Americans, see Center for Immigration Studies, *"Cast Down Your Buckets Where You Are": Black Americans on Immigration* (Washington D.C.: CIS, 1996). For the black press, which was hostile or at best ambivalent about immigration, see Arnold Shankman, *Ambivalent Friends: Afro-Americans View the Immigrant* (Westport, Conn., Greenwood Press, 1982).

53. *Amsterdam News*, Oct. 15, 1994.

54. Lawrence Fuchs, "The Reactions of Black Americans to Immigration," in Virginia Yans-McLaughlin, ed., *Immigration Reconsidered* (New York: Oxford University Press, 1990), 304.

55. Ibid., 305.

56. Ibid., 304.

57. Midwest Coalition to Reform Immigration, *MCRI Immigration News*, Summer 1996.

58. *Amsterdam News*, June 12, 1993.

59. NACLA, Report on the Americas, *The Immigrant Backlash* (November/December 1995), 37.

60. *Miami Times*, July 11, 1996.

61. Alejandro Portes and Alex Stepick, *City on the Edge: The Transformation of Miami* (Berkeley: University of California Press, 1993), 38–50.

62. *Wall Street Journal*, Jan. 20, 1989.

63. Edward Chang, "Jewish and Korean Merchants in African-American Neighborhoods: A Comparative Perspective," in Edward Chang and Russell Leong, ed., *Los Angeles—Struggles Toward Multiethnic Community* (Seattle: University of Washington Press, 1994), 6; *Washington Post*, May 7, 1995; U.S. Civil Rights Commission, *Civil Rights Issues Facing Asian Americans during the 1990s* (Washington D.C.: GPO, 1992), 34–39.

64. *Houston Post*, March 20, 1995.

65. *New York Times*, May 2, 1993.

66. Ibid., Jan. 6, 1997; April 27, 1997.

67. U.S. Civil Rights Commission, *Civil Rights Issues*, 25–26.

68. Ibid., 31–32.

69. Oral histories, founders of FAIR, Office of FAIR.

70. *Border Watch*, July 1995.

71. *Los Angeles Times*, March 2, 1996.

72. *New York Times*, May 26, 1996.

73. *Sacramento Bee*, July 5, 1996; *Washington Times*, July 5, 1996.

74. *Washington Times*, Nov. 17, 1996.

75. Richard Lamm and Gary Imhoff, *The Immigration Time Bomb* (New York: Truman Talley Books, 1985).

76. Peter Brimelow, *Alien Nation: Common Sense About America's Immigration Disaster* (New York: Random House, 1995).

77. Statement, *El Plan de Riverside*, February 1994, 14.

78. *New Orleans Times Picayune*, Oct. 13, 1996.

79. *New York Times*, Jan. 3, 1996.

80. National Immigration Forum, *The Golden Door*, Winter 1996, 3.

81. Sanford J. Ungar, *Fresh Blood: The New American Immigrants* (New York: Simon and Schuster, 1996), 366.

82. Ibid., 373.

83. Roy Beck, *The Case Against Immigration: The Moral, Economic, Social, and Environmental Reasons for Reducing Immigration Back to Traditional Levels* (New York: Norton, 1996).

### 3. Overpopulation, Immigration, the Environment, and the New Restrictionism

1. A. Piatt Andrew, "The Crux of the Immigration Question," *North American Review*, June 1914, 878.

2. Ibid.

3. A brief account of the "green revolution," or environmental movement is Kirpatrick Sale, *The Green Revolution: The American Environmental Movement, 1962–1992* (New York: Hill and Wang, 1993).

4. Ibid., 49–55. See also Philip Shabecoff, *A Fierce Green Fire: The American Environmental Movement* (New York: Hill and Wang, 1993), 256–59.

5. Mark Dowie, *Losing Ground: American Environmentalism at the Close of the Twentieth Century* (Cambridge: Harvard University Press, 1995), 175–76.

6. Sale, *The Green Revolution*, 52.

7. Ibid., 58.

8. Paul R. Ehrlich et al., *The Golden Door: International Migration, Mexico, and the United States* (New York: Ballantine Books, 1979), 311–27.

9. Anne and Paul Ehrlich, "The Most Overpopulated Nation," in Lindsey Grant, ed., *Elephants in the Volkswagen, Facing Tough Questions About Our Over-crowded Country* (New York: W. H. Freeman, 1992), 130–31.

10. Commission on Population Growth and the American Future, *Population and the American Future* (Washington D.C.: GPO, 1972), 116–17.

11. ZPG, *Statement on U.S. Immigration Policy* (revised, 1994).

12. Ibid.

13. Nor were governmental officials especially interested, at least publicly, to relate immigration to the environment as late as the 1990s. See the account by Roy Beck on his interview with Environmental Protection Agency officials in Roy Beck, "Washington Notepad," *Social Contract* (Winter, 1993–1994), 131.

14. *National Parks and Conversation Magazine* (December 1977), 13–16.

15. John C. Miles, *Guardians of the Parks: A History of the National Parks and Conservation Association* (Washington D.C.: Taylor and Francis, 1995), 266–79.

16. *Los Angeles Times*, Oct. 20, 1986. See also James Crawford, *Hold Your Tongue:*

*Bilingualism and the Politics of "English Only"* (New York: Addison-Wesley, 1992), 151–63.

17. *Los Angeles Times*, Oct. 20, 1986.

18. Ibid.

19. *Washington Post*, Oct. 23, 1988.

20. *Los Angeles Times*, Oct. 20, 1986.

21. Oral History, Dr. John Tanton, 1989, Office of FAIR.

22. This discussion of Dr. John Tanton and FAIR is based on Crawford's excellent book, *Hold Your Tongue*, 151–63; interview with John Tanton, Feb. 11, 1997.

23. Oral History, Thad Rowland, 1991, Office of FAIR.

24. Oral History, Roger Conner, 1989, Office of FAIR.

25. Oral history, John Tanton; interview with John Tanton, Feb. 11, 1997.

26. Oral History, William Paddock, 1993, Office of FAIR.

27. Oral History, Otis Graham Jr., 1990, Office of FAIR. See also Crawford, *Hold Your Tongue*, 152–53.

28. Oral History, Sidney Swensrud, 1988–1989, Office of FAIR.

29. TEF, *The Other Side*, Spring 1981.

30. See the statement in Population-Environment Balance, *Balance Report*, August 1991.

31. Population-Environment Balance, fund raising statement, 1995.

32. See Population-Environment Balance, *Balance Report*, December 1994, May 1995.

33. Ibid., December 1993.

34. Monique Miller, "Is Immigration an Environmental Issue? CCN, *Clearinghouse Bulletin*, April 1992; April/May 1995.

35. *Bergen (County) Record*, August 5, 1996.

36. Ibid.

37. Ibid.

38. Ibid.

39. Interview with Betsy Ballash, legislative director of CAPS, Feb. 5, 1997. Recently CAPS has been drawing more members from southern California.

40. CAPS, *Newsletter*, winter, 1995–1996.

41. Ibid., Spring 1996.

42. Statement released by CCN, May 11, 1995.

43. *Sacramento Bee*, Oct. 8, 1993.

44. ZPG, *Statement in Response to California Ballot Initiative Proposition 187* (October 1994).

45. *The ZPG Reporter*, September/October 1996, 6. See also the letter of Executive Director Peter H. Kostmayer of ZPG criticizing cuts in immigration in *New York Times*, May 25, 1997.

46. *Los Angeles Times*, Oct. 20, 1986.

47. Karen Woods, "Condoms and Corporations: Perspectives and Action on Population Among Environmental Organizations." MA thesis: University of Montana, 1994.

48. Quoted Dowie, *Losing Ground*, 161.

49. Lindsey Grant, *Juggernaut: Growth of a Finite Planet* (Santa Ana: Seven Locks Press, 1996), 300, fn 233; CCN, *Focus* 7, no. 2 (1997): 47.

50. Telephone conservation with the director of the population committee of the Audubon Society, March 4, 1996.

51. Center for Immigration Studies, *Scope*, Summer 1991, 6.

52. FAIR, *Immigration Report*, June 1991.

53. *New York Times*, June 2, 1996.

54. Sierra Club, *Sierra Club Policy: Population*, November 1992; FAIR, *Immigration Report*, October 1989.

55. The Frank Weeden Foundation has supported other population groups and FAIR.

56. *New York Times*, May 13, 1996.

57. Hannah Creighton, "Not Thinking Globally: The Sierra Club Immigration Policy Wars," *Race, Poverty, and the Environment* (Summer 1993), 29.

58. *San Francisco Chronicle*, March 30, 1994.

59. Ibid.

60. Dowie, *Losing Ground*, 164.

61. Creighton, "Not Thinking Globally," 27.

62. Dowie, *Losing Ground*, 165.

63. Creighton, "Not Thinking Globally," 27; FAIR, *Immigration Trends*, June 1996.

64. Statement issued Aug. 5, 1996.

65. Campaign statement by Al Kuper, Feb. 5, 1997; CAPS, *Newsletter*, Winter 1996–1997.

66. Garrett Hardin, *The Immigration Dilemma: Avoiding the Tragedy of the Commons* (Washington D.C.: FAIR, 1995), 13–30.

67. *New York Times*, July 12, 1981.

68. *High Country News*, Sept. 5, 1994, 19.

69. Quoted in Nicolaus Mills, ed., *Arguing Immigration: Are New Immigrants a Wealth of Diversity . . . Or a Crushing Burden?* (New York: Touchstone, 1994), 91.

70. Quoted in ibid., 93.

71. Ibid., 92–93.

72. *San Francisco Chronicle*, Nov. 5, 1993.

73. CAPS, *Newsletter*, Winter 1994.

74. Ibid., Winter 1996–1997.

75. Coalition for United States Population Stabilization, *Statement of Principles*, 1995.

76. Statement issue by the Coalition for United States Population Stabilization, June 1996.

77. *E Magazine*, November/December 1996, 34–35.

78. Ibid., 35.

79. Ibid., 34.

80. FAIR, *A Tale of Ten Cities: Immigration's Effect on the Family Environment in American Cities* (Washington D.C.: FAIR, 1995), xvi.

81. Ibid.

82. AICF, *Border Watch*, August 1995.

83. See John Vinson, *Immigration Out of Control: The Interests Against America* (Monterey, Va.: AICF, 1992) and Palmer Stacy and Wayne Lutton, *The Immigration Time Bomb* (Monterey, Va.: AICF, 1985).

84. Wayne Lutton and John Tanton, *The Immigration Invasion* (Petoskey, Mich.: Social Contract Press, 1994), 92.

85. *Wall Street Journal,* April 1, 1993; *San Francisco Examiner,* July 25, 1994.

86. Grant, *Juggernaut,* 209–12 and 261–62.

87. Roy Beck, *The Case Against Immigration: The Moral, Economic, Social, and Environmental Reasons for Reducing U.S. Immigration Back to Traditional Levels* (New York: Norton, 1996), 31–34.

88. Peter Brimelow, *Alien Nation: Common Sense About America's Immigration Disaster* (New York: Random House, 1995), 187–90.

89. The sponsors note that the authors' views are not necessarily theirs.

90. Leon Bouvier and Lindsey Grant, *How Many Americans? Population, Immigration, and the Environment* (San Francisco: Sierra Club Books, 1994), 70.

91. Ibid., chapter 1.

92. Ibid., chapter 3.

93. Leon Bouvier and Dudley L. Poston, Jr., *Thirty Million Texans?* (Washington D.C.: CIS, 1993), 104.

94. Leon Bouvier, *Peaceful Invasions: Immigration and Changing America* (Lanham, Md.: University Press of America, 1992), 149.

95. Bouvier and Grant, *How Many Americans?,* 116.

96. Ibid., 123.

97. Ibid.

98. "A Place at the Table: A *Sierra* Roundtable on Race, Justice, and the Environment," *Sierra* (May/June, 1993); Linda Wong, "Why Communities of Color Fear the Population Debate," *Race, Poverty, and the Environment* (Summer 1993), 3–5; Dowie, *Losing Ground,* 165–66.

99. Quoted in John A. Baden and Douglas S. Noonan, "Migrating Species; Environmentalists Worry that Eco-Systems May Be Affected by Immigration," *The National Review,* June 16, 1997, 41.

100. *Los Angeles Times,* April 13, 1994; CCN *Network Bulletin,* January–February 1996; interview with Ling-Ling, April 18, 1997.

101. Julian Simon, *Immigration: The Demographic and Economic Facts* (Washington D.C.: National Immigration Forum, 1995), executive summary and 43–46.

102. FAIR, *Behind the Curtain: Julian Simon's Manipulation of Immigration Studies* (Washington D.C.: FAIR, 1996), 25.

103. National Immigration Forum, *Finding Common Ground: A Primer for Environment and Population Advocates Concerned About Immigration* (Washington D.C.: National Immigration Forum, 1997).

104. U.S. Commission on Immigration Reform, *U.S. Immigration Policy: Restoring Credibility* (Washington D.C.: GPO, 1994), 235–36.

105. Ellen Percy Kraly, *U.S. Immigration and the Environment: Scientific Research and Analytic Issues* (Washington D.C.: GPO, 1995), i.

106. Ibid., viii–x.

107. CAPS, *Newsletter,* Summer 1995.

108. Population-Environment Balance, Statement, December 1996.

109. *Congressional Record* (daily digest), March 10, 1994, S 2801.

110. Ibid., March 21, 1996, H 2594.

111. *Congressional Quarterly*, Sept. 28, 1996, 2759.

112. Polls about immigration have usually ignored population and environmental issues, but the detailed poll of Roper, commissioned by FAIR in 1990, revealed that a sizable proportion of respondents were uneasy about the connection between population growth and the environment. Roper, "American Attitudes on Immigration, 1990."

113. *The Atlantic Monthly*, March 1997, 11.

114. *San Francisco Chronicle*, March 30, 1994.

## 4. A Broken Immigration System

1. Gary Imhoff and Richard Lamm, *The Immigration Time Bomb: The Fragmenting of America* (New York: Truman Talley Books, 1985), 1–2.

2. William R. Hawkins, *Importing Revolution* (Monterey, Va.: AICF, 1994), 8.

3. John Vinson, *Immigration Out of Control: The Interests Against America* (Monterey, Va.: AICF, 1992), 5.

4. John Tanton and Wayne Lutton, *The Immigration Invasion* (Petoskey, Mich.: Social Contract Press, 1994), 141–42.

5. Hawkins, *Importing Revolution*, 10–14.

6. Ibid., chapters 7–8.

7. *New York Times*, April 30, 1996.

8. Chilton Williamson, Jr., *The Immigration Mystique* (New York: Basic Books, 1996), 9.

9. National Immigration Forum, *The Golden Door*, Winter 1996.

10. *New York Times*, Dec. 31, 1995.

11. Lawrence Auster, *The Path to National Suicide: An Essay on Immigration and Multiculturalism* (Monterey, Va.: AICF, 1990), 10–11.

12. Peter Brimelow, *Alien Nation: Common Sense About America's Immigration Disaster* (New York: Random House, 1995), 76.

13. Vinson, *Immigration Out of Control*, 7.

14. This discussion draws upon my *Still the Golden Door: The Third World Comes to America* (New York: Columbia University Press, 2d edition, 1992).

15. For an account of the 1965 act different from mine, see Gabriel Chin, "The Civil Rights Revolution Comes to Immigration Law: A New Look at the Immigration and Nationality Act of 1965, *North Carolina Law Review* (November 1996), 273–345. Either way, immigration from the Eastern Hemisphere was expected to increase only slightly.

16. FAIR, *Immigration Report*, October 1995.

17. Roper Poll, "American Attitudes Toward Immigration," 1990; *Newsweek*, Aug. 9, 1993; *USA Today*, July 14, 1993. It should be noted that some polls revealed little difference in America's views of immigrants.

18. *USA Today*, July 14, 1993.

19. Wayne Lutton, *The Myth of Open Borders: The American Tradition of Immigration Control* (Monterey, Va.: AICF, 1988), 47.

20. *Border Watch*, September 1993.

21. Washington State Citizens for Immigration Control, *News and Views*, April 1996.

22. GAO, *Illegal Aliens: National Net Cost Estimates Vary Widely* (Washington D.C.: GPO, 1995), 4.

23. Brimelow, *Alien Nation*, 35.

24. *Border Watch*, June 1994.

25. Tanton and Lutton, *The Immigration Invasion*, 157.

26. See GAO, *Border Control: Revised Strategy is Showing Some Positive Results* (Washington D.C.: GPO, 1995); *New York Times*, Oct. 6, 1994.

27. *New York Times*, Sept. 28, 1995; Nov. 26, 1995.

28. *Los Angeles Times*, July 6, 1996; *New York Times*, July 14, 1996.

29. CIR, *Illegal Mexican Migration and the United States/Mexico Border: The Effects of Operation Hold the Line on El Paso/Juarez* (Washington D.C.: GPO, 1994), 7.

30. Center for Immigration Studies, *Announcement*, May 31, 1995; *Border Watch*, November 1993.

31. Internet message, Feb. 1, 1996.

32. *New York Times*, Oct. 26, 1996.

33. Ibid., Jan. 13, 1996.

34. See GAO, *Illegal Immigration: INS Overstay Estimation Methods Need Improvement* (Washington D.C.: GPO, 1995).

35. *New York Times*, Jan. 3, 1995.

36. CIR, *U.S. Immigration Policy: Restoring Credibility* (Washington D.C.: GPO, 1994), xii.

37. FAIR, *Immigration Report*, May 1990.

38. *Border Watch*, December 1992.

39. FAIR, *Ten Steps to Ending Illegal Immigration*, March 1995.

40. U. S. Congress, House, *Worksite Enforcement of Employer Sanctions*, Hearing before the Subcommittee on Immigration and Claims of the Committee on the Judiciary, 104th Cong., 1st sess. (Washington D.C.: GPO, 1995), 5–6.

41. *New York Times*, July 7, 1996.

42. Ibid., June 29, 1996.

43. FAIR, *Immigration Report*, September 1966.

44. *Los Angeles Times*, April 7, 1995; Americas Watch, *Frontier Injustice*, May 13, 1993.

45. U.S. Congress, House, *Border Violence*, Hearing before the Subcommittee on International Law, Immigration, and Refugees of the Committee on the Judiciary, 103rd Cong., 1st. sess. (Washington D.C.: GPO, 1994); *Los Angeles Times*, April 7, 1995.

46. *New York Times*, May 6, 1996. In 1997 the county agreed to a $740,000 settlement with the immigrants. The two officers remained under suspension.

47. Brimelow, *Alien Nation*, 82. The Cuban Adjustment Act was effectively repealed by President Clinton in 1995.

48. *Border Watch*, January 1966.

49. See comments of Norman Matloff, internet, March 18, 1995.

50. CIS, *Scope*, Fall/Winter 1990/91, 4.

51. Mark Krikorian, "Who Deserves Asylum? *Commentary*, June 1966, 52.

52. *New York Times*, Dec. 3, 1994.

53. FAIR, *Immigration Report*, March/April 1993.

54. Tanton and Lutton, *The Immigration Invasion*, 122.

55. *New York Times*, Dec. 3, 1994. For various view points, see U.S. Congress, House, *Asylum and Inspections Reform*, Hearing before the Subcommittee on International Law, Immigration and Refugees of the Committee on the Judiciary, 103rd Cong., 1st sess. (Washington D.C.: GPO, 1993).

56. *New York Times*, April 25, 1993.

57. Ibid., May 25, 1995.

58. Kathleen Newland, "The Impact of U.S. Refugee Policies on Foreign Policy: A Case of the Tail Wagging the Dog" in Michael S. Teitelbaum and Myron Weiner, eds., *Threatened Peoples, Threatened Borders: World Migration and U.S. Policy* (New York: Norton, 1995), 196–98; *New York Times*, May 21, 1995.

59. U.S. Congress, House, *The Clinton Administration's Reversal of U.S. Immigration Policy Toward Cuba*, Hearing before the Subcommittee on the Western Hemisphere of the Committee on International Relations, 104th Cong., 1st sess. (Washington D.C.: GPO, 1995), 55. See also *New York Times*, May 3, 1995.

60. *New York Times*, Feb. 1, 1996.

61. Ibid., March 5, 1996; Dec. 25, 1996; *Miami Herald*, Sept. 20, 1996.

62. Newland, "The Impact of U.S. Refugee Policies on Foreign Policy," 198–200.

63. *New York Times*, Sept. 16, 1994.

64. Ibid., July 8, 1996.

65. Ibid., April 15, 1996.

66. CIS, *Immigration Review*, Spring 1993.

67. *New York Times*, Dec. 2, 1995; *Washington Times*, Dec. 17, 1996.

68. *Bergen (County) Record*, Nov. 27, 1996.

69. *Washington Times*, Oct. 22, 1996; Oct. 24, 1996; *New York Times*, Oct. 7, 1996.

70. Krikorian, "Who Deserves Asylum?" 53.

71. *U.S. News and World Report*, March 22, 1993, 59. In 1997 he was returned to the United States to face prosecution.

72. Ibid.

73. U.S. Congress, House, *World Trade Center Bombing: Terror Hits Home*, Hearing before the Subcommittee on Crime and Criminal Justice of the Committee on the Judiciary, 103rd Cong., 1st sess. (Washington D.C.: GPO, 1993), 53–4.

74. *New York Times*, Oct. 2, 1995.

75. Brimelow, *Alien Nation*, 182–83.

76. See for example, T. J. English, *Born to Kill: America's Most Notorious Vietnamese Gang and the Changing Face of Organized Crime* (New York: William Morrow, 1995); and Lydia Rosner, *The Soviet Way of Crime: Beating the System in the Soviet Union and the USA* (South Hadley, Mass.: Bergin & Garvey, 1986).

77. Dan Stein, "Population, Migration, and America: Is Immigration a Threat to National Security?" A Speech to the National War College Class of 1995, August 24, 1994, 27–28.

78. James W. Olson and Judith E. Olson, *Cuban Americans: From Trauma to Triumph* (New York: Twayne, 1995), 81–84.

79. CIS, *Scope*, Spring 1990, 5.

80. John Tanton and Wayne Lutton, "Immigration and Criminality in the U.S.A." *Journal of Social, Political and Economic Studies*, Summer 1993, 217.

81. *Border Watch*, December 1995.

82. FAIR, *Immigration Report*, June 1996.

83. *New York Times*, Sept. 10, 1995; Feb. 24, 1996.

84. Ibid., Sept. 11, 1995.

85. Ibid., Nov. 11, 1995; Feb. 11, 1996.

86. Lutton and Tanton, "Immigration and Criminality in the U.S.A.," 234.

87. William Kleinknect, *The New Ethnic Mobs: The Changing Face of Organized Crime in America* (New York: Free Press, 1996), vii.

88. "Infamous Immigrants," *The Social Contract*, Fall 1995, 3–22.

89. GAO, *Criminal Aliens: INS' Investigative Efforts in the New York City Area* (Washington D.C.: GPO, 1986), 3.

90. *Bergen (County) Record*, March 24, 1986.

91. U.S. Congress, Senate, *Criminal Aliens in the United States*, S. Rept., 104–48, Committee on Governmental Affairs, 104th Cong., 1st sess. (Washington D.C.: GPO, 1995), 1.

92. Ibid., 3.

93. U.S. Congress, House, *Criminal Aliens*, Hearing before the Subcommittee on International Law, Immigration, and Refugees of the Committee on the Judiciary, 103rd Cong., 2d sess. (Washington D.C.: GPO, 1994), 1.

94. *New York Times*, Sept. 13, 1994.

95. Handbill, "Barbara Coe for Assembly, 67th State Assembly District," December 1995.

96. *Miami Herald*, Feb. 5, 1995.

97. *New York Times*, July 9, 1996.

98. Ibid., June 9, 1994.

99. Ibid., August 29, 1995 *Bergen (County) Record*; August 30, 1995; *San Francisco Chronicle*, May 23, 1995.

100. *San Francisco Chronicle*, May 23, 1995; INS, *News Release*, Feb. 10, 1997; *Washington Times*, May 14, 1997. These were persons deported from the interior. The vast majority of those deported are persons caught trying to cross the southern border.

101. Alan Kraut, *Silent Travelers: Germs, Genes, and the 'Immigrant Menace'* (New York: Basic Books, 1994), book jacket.

102. *Border Watch*, April 1991.

103. Brimelow, *Alien Nation*, 187.

104. Kraut, *Silent Travelers*, 261–72. See also Palmer Stacy and Wayne Lutton, *The Immigration Time Bomb* (Monterey, Va.: AICF, 1985), chapter 13.

105. Kraut, *Silent Travelers*, 160–61.

106. *New York Times*, Feb. 28, 1990; Oct. 29, 1990; Nov. 5, 1990.

107. See also U.S. Congress, House, *HHS Authority Over Immigration and Public Health*, Hearing before the Subcommittee on Health and the Environment of

the Committee on Energy and Commerce, 101st Cong., 1st sess. (Washington D.C.: GPO, 1990).

108. *New York Times,* May 26, 1991.

109. Ibid., March 12, 1993.

110. *Congressional Record* (daily digest), Feb. 18, 1993, S 1762.

111. Ibid., March 11, 1993, H 1204.

112. *Time,* Feb. 22, 1993, 45.

113. Letter to the *New York Times,* March 12, 1996.

114. Ibid., Feb. 8, 1997. These figures, of course, were only estimates.

## 5. Old Wine in New Bottles: The Economic Debate

1. Vernon Briggs, Jr., *Mass Immigration and the Public Interest* (Armonk, N.Y.: M. E. Sharpe, 1992), 43–58.

2. Ibid., 92.

3. Ibid., 105.

4. Ibid., 250.

5. *San Francisco Examiner,* June 13, 1993.

6. See Peter Brimelow, *Alien Nation: Common Sense About America's Immigration Disaster* (New York: Random House, 1995), 167–75.

7. Roy Beck, *Re-Charting America's Future: Responses to Arguments Against Stabilizing U.S. Population and Limiting Immigration* (Petoskey, Mich.: Social Contract Press, 1994), 87–102.

8. Roy Beck, *The Case Against Immigration: The Moral, Economic, Social, and Environmental Reasons for Reducing U.S. Immigration Back to Traditional Levels* (New York: Norton, 1996), 102. Two of his chapters are devoted to the impact of immigration upon black Americans.

9. Ibid., 128.

10. George Borjas, *Friends or Strangers: The Impact of Immigrants on the U.S. Economy* (New York: Free Press, 1990), 80.

11. Ibid., 87.

12. *Wall Street Journal,* April 26, 1996; *Business Week,* June 20, 1994, 76.

13. *Business Week,* June 20, 1994, 76. For a statement of his general views see George Borjas, "Know the Flow" *The National Review* (April 17, 1995), 44–50.

14. *New York Times,* July 4, 1996.

15. A report by the Labor Department found that many persons permitted an amnesty by IRCA were not doing well. U.S. Department of Labor, *Effects of the Immigration and Reform and Control Act: Characteristics and Labor Market Behavior of the Legalized Population Five Years Following Legalization* (Washington D.C.: GPO, 1996), 83.

16. William H. Frey, "Immigration and the Internal Migration 'Flight' from US Metropolitan Areas: Toward a New Demographic Balkanization," *Urban Studies* 32 (nos. 4–5, 1995): 733–57; "Immigration and Internal Migration 'Flight': A California Case Study," *Population and Environment: A Journal of Interdisciplinary Studies* 14 (March 1995): 353–75.

17. William H. Frey, "Immigrant and Native Migrant Magnets," *American Demographics* (November 1996), 39.

18. David Jaeger, *Skill Differences and the Effect of Immigrants on the Wages of Natives* (Bureau of Labor Statistics, Working Paper, 1995).

19. Roger Waldinger, "Who Makes the Beds? Who Washes the Dishes? Black/Immigrant Competition Reassessed." paper, Dept. of Sociology, UCLA, February 1992.

20. *New York Times*, March 11, 1996. Waldinger thinks that alleviating the economic distress of low-skilled blacks requires attacking the unwillingness of employers to hire them and improving their training. It should be noted that the scholarly work of Frey and Jaeger do not advocate immigration cuts.

21. See Richard Mines and Jeffrey Avina, "Immigrants and Labor Standards: The Case of California Janitors," in Jorge A. Bustamante et al., ed., *U.S. Mexican Relations: Labor Market Interdependence* (Stanford: Stanford University Press, 1993), 429–48.

22. Jacquelyn Johnson Jackson, "Competition Between Blacks and Immigrants," *The Social Contract* (Summer 1995), 248–49.

23. Michael Lind, *The Next American Nation: The New Nationalism and the Fourth American Revolution* (New York: Free Press, 1995), 320.

24. Martin Conroy, *Faded Dreams: The Politics and Economics of Race in America* (New York: Cambridge University Press, 1994), 170; Stephen Steinberg, *Turning Back; The Retreat from Racial Justice in American Thought and Policy* (Boston: Beacon Press, 1995), 193.

25. James S. Robb, "Affirmative Action for Immigrants: The Entitlement Nobody Wanted," *The Social Contract* (Winter 1995), 96, 86.

26. Ibid., 87.

27. Ibid., 86–87 and 91–96; Joel Millman, *The Other Americans: How Immigrants Renew Our Country, Our Economy, and Our Values* (New York: Viking, 1997), 168.

28. Robb, "Affirmative Action for Immigrants," 96.

29. Beck, *The Case Against Immigration*, 187.

30. Internet. www5@netcom.com (Pauline Rizzuti). March 18, 1995. See also U.S. Congress, House, *Impact of Illegal Immigration on Public Benefit Programs and American Labor Policy*, Hearing before the Subcommittee on Immigration and Claims of the Committee on the Judiciary, 104th Cong., 1st sess. (Washington D.C.: GPO, 1996), 122–33.

31. Donald Barlett and James Steele, "America: Who Stole the Dream," *Philadelphia Inquirer*, Sept. 15, 1996.

32. *Los Angeles Times*, July 15, 1996.

33. Ibid. In the mid-1990s young American Ph.D's in mathematics and physics urged Congress to cut down on the number of foreigners in their fields. *Wall Street Journal*, Sept. 4, 1996; *Sacramento Bee*, March 27, 1994.

34. U.S. Congress, House, *The American Math and Science Student Support Act*, Hearings before the Subcommittee on Science of the Committee on Science, Space, and Technology, 102d Cong., 2d Sess. (Washington: GPO, 1992), 166.

35. See David North, *Soothing the Establishment: The Impact of Foreign-Born Scientists and Engineers in America* (Lanham, Md.: University Press of America, 1995), for a discussion of this issue. North did find some areas that indicated foreign-born students were favored over blacks.

36. Norman Matloff, "How Immigration Harms Minorities," *Public Interest*, Summer 1996, 63–64.

37. U.S. Dept. of Labor, *The Effects of Immigration on the U.S. Economy and Labor Market* (Washington D.C.: GPO, 1989), 126–31.

38. Theo J. Majka and Linda C. Majka, "Mexican Immigration, Transformation of California's Farm Labor, and the Decline of Unionization Since 1980," paper presented at the 1996 meetings of the Social Science History Association. Philip Martin and Elizabeth Midgley, "Immigration to the United States: Journey to an Uncertain Destination," *Population Bulletin*, September 1994, 30–31. Overall, they believe the labor market impacts are small.

39. *Wall Street Journal*, April 26, 1996.

40. John Martin, *What is the Relationship Between Income Inequality and Immigration?* (Washington D.C.: FAIR, 1996), 24.

41. FAIR, *Behind the Curtain: Julian Simon's Manipulation of Immigration Studies* (Washington D.C.: FAIR, 1996), 30.

42. *Border Watch*, November 1990. This issue featured an essay by Donald Huddle arguing that immigration causes unemployment.

43. Ibid., September 1993, See also ibid., April 1994, May 1995, February 1996.

44. CCN, *Clearing House Bulletin*, November 1993.

45. Population-Environment Balance, *Balance*, September 1993.

46. Leon Bouvier, *Peaceful Invasions: Immigration and Changing America* (Lanham, Md.: University Press of America, 1992), 74. For Lamm and Imhoff, see *The Immigration Time Bomb* (New York: Truman Talley Books, 1985), 125; for Tanton and Lutton, see their *The Immigration Invasion* (Petoskey, Mich.: Social Contract Press, 1994), 46.

47. Beck, *The Case Against Immigration*, 248.

48. Donald Huddle, *National Net Cots of Immigration*, study released by CCN, June 27, 1994.

49. *New York Times*, Sept. 3, 1993.

50. U.S. Congress, House, *Impact of Illegal Immigration on Public Benefit Programs and American Labor Policy*, Hearing before the Subcommittee on Immigration and Claims of the Committee on the Judiciary, 104th Cong., 1st sess. (Washington D.C.: GPO, 1996), 27.

51. Don Huddle, *The Net Costs of Immigration: The Facts, the Trends, and the Critics* (Washington D.C.: CCN, 1996), i.

52. New York State Committee on Cities, *Our Teeming Shores* (Albany: N.Y. State Senate, 1994), 46–57.

53. New York State Senate Majority Task Force on Immigration, *Our Teeming Shore, 2* (Albany: N.Y. State Senate, 1995), 20–24.

54. Los Angeles County Board of Supervisors, *Impact of Undocumented Persons and Other Immigrants on Costs, Revenues, and Services in Los Angeles County*, November 1992.

55. State of California, Assembly Office of Research, *Summary Report Prepared for the Assembly Select Committee on Statewide Immigration Impact* (Sacramento: California Assembly, 1994).

56. See testimony in U.S. Congress, House, *Impact of Federal Immigration Policy and INS Activities on Communities*, Hearings before the Subcommittee on Information, Justice, Transportation, and Agriculture, 103d Cong., 1st and 2d sess. (Washington D.C.: GPO, 1995); U.S. Congress, House, *Impact of Immigration on Welfare Programs*, Hearings before the Subcommittee on Human Resources of the Committee on Ways and Means, 103d Cong., 1st sess. (Washington D.C.: GPO, 1993).

57. Quoted in Lorraine M. McDonnell and Paul T. Hill, *Newcomers in American Schools: Meeting the Education Needs of Immigrant Youth* (Santa Monica: Rand, 1993), 101.

58. *New York Times*, Sept. 15, 1994; Michael Fix and Jeffrey Passel, "Setting the Record Straight: What are the Costs to the Public? *Public Welfare* (Spring 1994), 6–15.

59. Los Angeles County, *Impact*.

60. Center for Immigration Studies, *Announcement*, Sept. 22, 1994.

61. FAIR, *Immigration Report*, April 1995. It should be noted that GAO has been critical of Huddle's work.

62. Brimelow, *Alien Nation*, 152.

63. Imhoff and Lamm, *The Immigration Time Bomb*, chapter 7; Lutton and Tanton, *The Immigration Invasion*, chapter 1; and Palmer Stacy and Wayne Lutton, *The Immigration Time Bomb* (Alexandria, Va.: AICF, 1985), chapter 10.

64. California Coalition for Immigration Reform, *911*, Jan., 1995.

65. *Border Watch*, April, 1991; July, 1991; Nov., 1992; May, 1994; April, 1995; and May, 1995.

66. *New York Times*, April 16, 1995.

67. GAO, *Supplemental Security Income: Recent Growth in the Rolls Raises Fundamental Program Concerns* (Washington D.C.: GPO, 1995).

68. Robert Rector, "The U.S.—Retirement Home for Immigrants," *The Social Contract* (Summer, 1996), 279.

69. Borjas, "Know the Flow," 46; "The Welfare Magnet," 49.

70. Ibid., 46; George Borjas and Lynette Hilton, "Immigration and the Welfare State: Immigrant Participation in Means-Tested Entitlement Programs, *Quarterly Journal of Economics*, May, 1996.

71. George Borjas, "The New Economics of Immigration," *Atlantic Monthly*, (Nov., 1996), 80.

72. *Business Week*, June 20, 1994, 76.

73. Borjas, "The Welfare Magnet," 50.

74. *New York Times*, Nov. 21, 1995; Sept. 10, 1995; *Washington Times*, Jan. 12, 1995; *Los Angeles Times*, Nov. 14, 1994; *Hispanic*, April 1995, 18–22.

75. *Miami Herald*, May 24, 1996.

76. Ibid., March 13, 1995; *Orlando Sentinel*, Sept. 10, 1995; Jan. 18, 1996.

77. *Miami Herald*, March 13, 1995; *Orlando Sentinel*, Sept. 10, 1995; Jan. 18, 1996; Aug. 9, 1996. The two organizations managed to gather only one tenth of the required signatures to place the issues on the ballot.

78. *Miami Herald*, Aug. 9, 1996.

79. *Los Angeles Times*, July 15, 1996.

80. *Orlando Sentinel*, July 16, 1994.

81. *San Francisco Chronicle*, March 13, 1995; *Sacramento Bee*, Feb. 14, 1995.

82. *Orange County Register*, June 13, 1996; *San Francisco Chronicle*, Jan. 8, 1997; *San Diego Union-Tribune*, June 4, 1997.

83. *Sacramento Bee*, Dec. 6, 1996.

84. Ibid.

85. *Research Perspectives on Migration* (September/October 1996), 4.

86. *New York Times*, July 24, 1994.

87. *Congressional Quarterly*, April 15, 1995, 1069.

88. GAO, *Welfare Reform: Implications of Proposals on Legal Immigrants' Benefits* (Washington D.C.: GPO, 1995), 10. The *New York Times* study revealed a similar finding. *New York Times*, April 16, 1995.

89. *New York Times*, April 16, 1995.

90. *Congressional Record* (daily digest), August 1, 1996, S 9345–6.

91. Ibid., S 9354.

92. Ibid., S 9360.

93. *New York Times*, July 31, 1996; *Congressional Quarterly*, August 3, 1996, 2193–4.

94. *Research Perspectives on Migration* (September/October 1996).

95. *New York Times*, July 29, 1996.

96. Huddle, *The Net Costs of Immigration*, 12.

97. *New York Times*, Sept. 4, 1996.

98. *Miami Herald*, Sept. 18, 1996.

99. Most states indicated that they would help elderly disabled immigrants, but considerable confusion was reported about the forthcoming changes. *New York Times*, April 20, 1997.

100. Ibid., May 4, 1997; AP Story, May 6, 1997. Congressional Republicans were responding to Republican governors's complaints about the new costs for their states and to reports of the elderly disabled fearing that they would be thrown out of nursing homes.

101. *Washington Post*, May 1, 1997.

102. *New York Times*, Sept. 13, 1996.

103. *San Jose Mercury News*, Oct. 24, 1996. A number of states said they would help immigrants become citizens. So did New York City. *New York Times*, May 6, 1997.

104. *Washington Post*, Sept. 24, 1996; Oct. 6, 1996.

105. *Border Watch*, January 1994. AICF was also worried about an alleged campaign to make noncitizen voters. Ibid., February 1996.

106. Georgie Anne Geyer, *Americans No More: The Death of Citizenship* (New York: Atlantic Monthly Press, 1996), chapters 1–2.

107. Ibid., 52. See an excellent summary of the naturalization process in John Miller, "The Naturalizers," *Policy Review*, July 1996, 50–53.

108. *Chicago Tribune*, Sept. 22, 1996; *Washington Post*, Sept. 11, 1996.

109. Washington State Citizens for Immigration Control, *News and Views*, September 1996.

110. *Washington Post*, Sept. 11, 1996; Oct. 25, 1996; *Washington Times*, Oct. 24, 1996; *Sacramento Bee*, Sept. 24, 1996.

111. *New York Times*, Oct. 30, 1996; May 24, 1997; *San Francisco Chronicle*, April 19, 1997; GAO, *Naturalization of Aliens: Assessment of the Extent to Which Aliens Were Improperly Naturalized* (Washington D.C.: GPO, 1997); *Washington Post*, May 1, 1997.

112. *New York Times*, Oct. 8, 1996.

113. *Los Angeles Times*, Oct. 27, 1996.

114. Ibid., Oct. 23, 1996. See also *Washington Post*, Sept. 26, 1996; FAIR, *Immigration Report*, October 1996.

115. *Los Angeles Times*, Nov. 8, 1996.

116. Ibid.

117. *MCRI Immigration News*, October 1996.

**6. Why Can't They Be Like Us? The Assimilation Issue**

1. Southern Poverty Law Center, *Intelligence Report*, August 1994, 2–3; David Bennett, *The Party of Fear: From Nativist Movements to the New Right in American History* (Chapel Hill: University of North Carolina Press, 1989), 346–92. See also Dorothy Nelkin, "Biological Categories and Border Controls: The Revival of Eugenics in Anti-Immigration Rhetoric," paper for the International Center for Migration, Ethnicity, and Citizenship of the New School for Social Research, Oct. 24, 1995.

2. *The New American*, Feb. 19, 1996, entire issue.

3. *New York Times*, August 28, 1995.

4. Ibid. See also American-Muslim Research Center, *The Price of Ignorance: The Status of Muslim Civil Rights in the United States* (Washington D.C.: AMRC, 1996); American-Arab Anti-Discrimination Committee, *1995 Report on Anti-Arab Racism: Hate Crimes, Discrimination, and Defamation of Arab Americans* (Washington D.C.: AAAD, 1995).

5. *New York Times*, Feb. 10, 1997.

6. See Jack G. Shaheen, *The TV Arab* (Bowling Green, Ohio: Bowling Green University, 1984).

7. *New York Times*, August 28, 1995.

8. Council on American-Islamic Relations, *A Special Report on Anti-Muslim Stereotyping, Harassment and Hate Crimes Following the Bombing of Oklahoma City's Murrah Federal Building* (Washington D.C.: CAIR, 1995).

9. *New York Times*, August 28, 1995.

10. *Border Watch*, November 1990.

11. John Tanton and Wayne Lutton, *The Immigration Invasion* (Petoskey, Mich.: Social Contract Press, 1994), 134.

12. Oral History, 1989, John Tanton, Offices of FAIR.

13. Palmer Stacy and Wayne Lutton, *The Immigration Time Bomb* (Alexandria, Va.: AICF, 1985), 148.

14. AICF maintains that it does not necessarily endorse the views of the authors. *Border Watch's* tone is little different, however, and it publishes books by its head, John Vinson.

15. Lawrence Auster, *The Path to National Suicide: An Essay on Immigration and Multiculturalism* (Monterey, Va.: AICF, 1990), 45.

16. Ibid., 53.

17. Ibid., 75.

18. Peter Brimelow, *Alien Nation: Common Sense About America's Immigration Disaster* (New York: Random House, 1995), xv.

19. Ibid., 264.

20. David Gutierrez, *Walls and Mirrors: Mexican Americans, Mexican Immigrants, and the Politics of Ethnicity* (Berkeley: University of California Press, 1995), 184.

21. Ibid., 185.

22. VCT, *Newsletter*, February/March/April 1997. Spencer also thinks that "the Chinese are increasing their invasion of our nation," making southern California trapped between Mexicans and Chinese.

23. Ibid., June 1996.

24. Brent Nelson, *America Balkanized: Immigration's Challenge to Government* (Monterey, Va.: AICF, 1994), 40.

25. *Border Watch*, December 1993.

26. Ibid., October 1995.

27. Ibid., February 1996; Brimelow, *Alien Nation*, 193–94.

28. *Border Watch*, July, 1995.

29. John Vinson, *Immigration Out of Control: The Interests Against America* (Monterey, Va.: AICF, 1990), 15.

30. See Dinesh D'Souza, *Illiberal Education: The Politics of Race and Sex on Campus* (New York: Random House, 1991).

31. Francis Fukuyama, "Immigrants and Family Values," *Commentary*, May 1993, 26–32. See also the comments of Richard Bernstein in *Dictatorship of Virtue: Multiculturalism and the Battle for America's Future* (New York: Knopf, 1994); and liberal Arthur Schlesinger, *The Disuniting of America* (New York: Norton, 1992).

32. Roy Beck, *The Case Against Immigration: The Moral, Economic, Social and Environmental Reasons for Reducing U.S. Immigration Back to Traditional Levels* (New York: Norton, 1996), 192–208.

33. Leon Bouvier, *Fifty Million Californians?* (Washington D.C.: FAIR, 1991), 75. See also his *Peaceful Invasions: Immigration and Changing America* (Lanham, Md.: University Press of America, 1992), chapter 2.

34. See Gary Imhoff and Richard Lamm, *The Immigration Time Bomb: The Fragmenting of America* (New York: Truman Talley Books, 1985), 97–98.

35. Tanton and Lutton, *The Immigration Invasion*, 48. See also Brent Nelson, *Assimilation: The Ideal and the Reality* (Monterey, Va., 1987); and Nelson, *American Balkanized*.

36. *Wall Street Journal*, July 2, 1992.

37. Bouvier, *Peaceful Invasions*, 113–15.

38. Ibid., 117.

39. Ibid., 124.

40. Tanton and Lutton, *Immigration Invasion*, 152–53. See also Beck, *The Case Against Immigration*, 251–52; Brimelow, *Alien Nation*, 211.

41. FAIR, *Immigration Report*, April 1994; Balance, *The Balance Activist*, June 1996; CCN, *Clearing House Bulletin*, April/ May 1995; June/July 1995.

42. Advertizement by Negative Population Growth, 1995. Ad placed in popular and environmental organizations journals.

43. *Border Watch*, March 1991. For Brimelow's view see *Alien Nation*, 10–11.

44. *Business Week*, Nov. 7, 1994, 36; Charles Lane, "The Tainted Sources of the 'Bell Curve' " *New York Review of Books*, Dec. 1, 1994, 14–18.

45. James Crawford, *Hold Your Tongue: Bilingualism and the Politics of "English Only"* (New York: Addison-Wesley, 1992), 159–62; *Business Week*, Nov. 7, 1994, 36; letter to the *New York Times*, Feb. 24, 1996, by Harry F. Weyher, president of the Pioneer Fund.

46. U.S. Congress, House, *Cuban and Haitian Immigration*, Hearings before the Subcommittee on International Law, Immigration, and Refugees of the Committee on the Judiciary, 102d Cong., 1st. sess. (Washington D.C.: GPO, 1991), 182.

47. Crawford, *Hold Your Tongue*, 160. Information from IRS on foundation grants, reports for 1993 FAIR received $108,500 in 1993 and $150,000 in 1992. AICF received only $10,000 in 1993.

48. Jean Raspail, *The Camp of the Saints* (Petoskey, Mich.: Social Contract Press, 1995), viii.

49. FAIR, *Immigration Report*, February 1995.

50. Bouvier, *Peaceful Invasions*, 187.

51. Washington State Citizens for Immigration Control, *News and Views*, June, 1996.

52. *Border Watch*, September 1995.

53. Bruce Cain, Karin Mac Donald, and Kenneth F. McCue, "Nativism, Partisanship, and Immigration: Analysis of Prop 187." Paper presented at the 1996 meeting of the American Political Science Association, San Francisco, 5 and 8. See also Raymond Tatalovich, *Nativism Reborn? The Official English Language Movement and the American States* (Lexington: University of Kentucky Press, 1995), 170–80.

54. Newt Gingrich, *To Renew America* (New York: Harper/Collins, 1995), 159–62.

55. *New York Times*, Jan. 1, 1997.

56. William G. Ross, *Forging New Freedoms: Nativism, Education, and the Constitution, 1917–1927* (Lincoln: University of Nebraska Press, 1994), 94.

57. Ibid., 1–5.

58. Tatalovich, *Nativism Reborn?*, 84–94.

59. *Washington Post*, May 19, 1993; Tatalovich, *Nativism Reborn*, 84–94; James Crawford, ed., *Language Loyalties: A Source Book on the Official English Controversy* (Chicago: University of Chicago Press, 1992), 131.

60. Crawford, *Language Loyalties*, 125.

61. *Congressional Record* (daily digest), August 13, 1988, S21071 and 21662.

62. Crawford, *Hold Your Tongue*, 152–53.

63. Heidi Tarver, "Language and Politics in the 1980s: The Story of U.S. English," *Politics and Society*, June 1989, 227.

64. Ibid., 228.

65. *U.S. News and World Report*, Sept. 25, 1995, 40; ad in national media for U.S. English, 1995.

66. Tatalovich, *Nativism Reborn?*, 10; Crawford, *Hold Your Tongue*, 168–69 and 268–69. Larry Pratt later became Patrick Buchanan's campaign manager during

the 1996 primaries. He was forced to resign when it was revealed that he had spoken to several militia-type groups, including the Aryan Nation, and used rather explosive language. *Washington Times*, Feb. 16, 1996; Feb. 17, 1996.

67. Tatalovich, *Nativism Reborn?*, 103–122.

68. Crawford, *Hold Your Tongue*, 158–59.

69. Ibid., 157–58; Tatalovich, *Nativism Reborn?* 140–43.

70. *Washington Post*, Nov. 6, 1988; Crawford, *Hold Your Tongue*, 153–55.

71. Crawford, *Hold Your Tongue*, 155; Tatalovich, *Nativism Reborn?*, 142–43; *Washington Post*, Oct. 23, 1988.

72. Robert Park, "The Battle for Official English," *The Social Contract* (Summer 1996), 244–46. The amendment provided for exemptions in the case of medical care, federal government mandates, protecting the rights of criminal defendants and the teaching of foreign languages.

73. Crawford, *Hold Your Tongue*, 169–75.

74. Park, "The Battle for Official English," 246.

75. Ibid., 248; *New York Times*, August 31, 1996.

76. *San Francisco Examiner*, Dec. 3, 1996.

77. English First, *Members' Report*, Summer, 1994; telephone conversation with Mountjoy's staff, Feb. 10, 1996.

78. *New York Times*, March 4, 1997.

79. English First, *Members' Report*, Feb. 28, 1997. The Equal Employment Opportunity Commission also reported a number of cases in the private sector involving language discrimination. *New York Times*, April 23, 1997.

80. Monterey Park is part of Los Angeles County.

81. John Horton, *The Politics of Diversity: Immigration, Resistance, and Change in Monterey Park, California* (Philadelphia: Temple University Press, 1995), 10–11. The discussion of Monterey Park's ethnic conflict is drawn from Horton's careful study.

82. Ibid., 94–95.

83. Irgrid Betancourt, " 'Babel Myth'; The English-Only Movement and Its Implications for Libraries," *Wilson Library Bulletin*, February 1992, 39.

84. Horton, *The Politics of Diversity*, chapters 5–6. Lowell, Massachusetts, involving Asians, was also split by an English-only proposition. *New York Times*, Nov. 7, 1989; Crawford, *Hold Your Tongue*, 136–47.

85. *New York Times*, April 9, 1996.

86. The county failed again in 1996 to become an official English body. Ibid., August 14, 1996; Sept. 14, 1996.

87. English First, *Members' Report*, December 1994.

88. *New York Times*, May 10, 1996.

89. Ibid., July 25, 1996; July 28, 1996.

90. *Congressional Record* (daily digest), August 1, 1996, H 9740.

91. Ibid.

92. *New York Times*, August 31, 1996.

93. English First, "Statement of U.S. Senator Alan Simpson on Bill to Reauthorize the Use of Bilingual Ballots in the United States," from *Congressional Record* (daily digest), August 6, 1993.

94. Abigail Thernstrom makes the point that the sole purpose of Voting Rights Act was to help African Americans vote. Abigail M. Thernstrom, *Whose Votes Count?: Affirmative Action and Minority Voting Rights* (Cambridge: Harvard University Press, 1987), 3–4. This account of bilingual ballots relies on Thernstrom's thorough book.

95. Ibid., chapter 2.

96. Crawford, *Hold Your Tongue*, 192–96. Judicial rulings also brought the federal government into issue of bilingual ballots.

97. English First, *Bilingual Ballots: Election Fairness or Fraud?*, Statement by English First (no date).

98. Ibid.; *New York Times*, August 14, 1994

99. Imhoff and Lamm, *The Immigration Time Bomb*, 116–17.

100. *Los Angeles Times*, Nov. 7, 1984.

101. Schlesinger, *The Disuniting of America*, 108.

102. Bee Gallegos, *English: Our Official Language?* (New York: Wilson, 1994), 98–101.

103. Susan Schneider, *Revolution, Reaction, or Reform: The 1974 Bilingual Education Act* (New York: Las Americas, 1976), 22–25.

104. For the 1974 act see ibid.

105. Gallegos, *English*, 102–3.

106. Quoted in ibid., 104. See also his statement in U.S. Congress, Senate, *Bilingual Education Act, Amendments of 1986*, Hearing before the Subcommittee on Education of the Committee on Labor and Human Resources, 99th Cong., 2d sess. (Washington D.C.: GPO, 1986), 12–16; Crawford, *Hold Your Tongue*, 217–18.

107. *Washington Post*, June 6, 1986.

108. U.S. Congress, House, *Bilingual Education*, Hearings before the Subcommittee on Elementary, Secondary, and Vocational Education of the Committee on Education and Labor, 98th Cong., 2d sess. (Washington D.C.: GPO, 1984), 63–66; Crawford, *Hold Your Tongue*, 217–32.

109. English First, *Special Report on Bilingual Education Submitted to President Bill Clinton* (1993); *Evaluations of Current Bilingual Programs* (no date); Gary Imhoff, "The Position of U.S. English on Bilingual Education," *Annals of the American Academy of Political and Social Science*, March 1990, 48–61.

110. *Border Watch*, September 1995.

111. See Rosalie Porter, *Forked Tongue: The Politics of Bilingual Education* (New York: Basic Books, 1990).

112. *Washington Post*, August 13, 1987.

113. Tanton and Lutton, *Immigration Invasion*, 57.

114. Imhoff and Lamm, *The Immigration Time Bomb*, 118. See also Brimelow, *Alien Nation*, 265 and the critique by moderate Leon Bouvier, in *Peaceful Invasions*, 188.

115. *New York Times*, Jan. 4, 1993.

116. Ibid., June 19, 1996.

117. Crawford, *Hold Your Tongue*, 217–23; 228–32.

118. *U.S. News and World Report*, Sept. 25, 1995, 44–46; Peter Skerry, *Mexican Americans: The Ambivalent Minority* (New York: Free Press, 1993), 283–91; Rodolfo

O. de la Garza et al., *Latino Voices: Mexican, Puerto Rican, and Cuban Perspectives on American Politics* (Boulder: Westview Press, 1992), 99.

119. Skerry, *Mexican Americans*, 285.

120. Ibid., 289.

121. *New York Times*, Jan. 4, 1993.

122. Imhoff and Lamm, *The Immigration Time Bomb*, 109.

## 7. A New Immigration Policy: 1994–1997?

1. FAIR, *Immigration Report*, September 1993.

2. *Congressional Record* (daily digest), March 10, 1994, S 2799.

3. *Los Angeles Times*, August 10, 1994.

4. CIS, *Immigration Review*, Spring 1994.

5. *Christian Science Monitor*, April 21, 1994.

6. Quoted in FAIR, *Immigration Report*, July 1995.

7. Quoted in Fragomen, Del Rey, and Bernsen, *Immigration Law Report*, Feb. 15, 1995, 39.

8. *Washington Times*, March 20, 1996.

9. *Washington Post*, Nov. 19, 1994.

10. FAIR, *Immigration Report*, January 1955.

11. Ibid., March 1995.

12. Public Papers of the Presidents of the United States, *William J. Clinton*, Book 1, 1995 (Washington D.C.: GPO, 1996), 80–81.

13. *Congressional Record* (daily digest), March 19, 1996, H 2373–74.

14. It had been supported by Pete Wilson of California and by the Republican party in 1996, but this support was largely symbolic.

15. CIR, *U.S. Immigration Policy: Restoring Credibility* (Washington D.C.: GPO, 1994), ii.

16. CIR wanted elimination of the category for brothers and sisters of U.S. citizens, and cuts in employment visas and refugees. *New York Times*, June 5, 1995; FAIR, *Immigration Report*, July 1995.

17. *Wall Street Journal*, July 11, 1995.

18. Ibid., May 26, 1995.

19. *New York Times*, Sept. 9, 1995.

20. *Congressional Quarterly*, July 15, 1995, 2073.

21. Ibid., 2073–75; *New York Times*, June 22, 1995.

22. *New York Times*, Oct. 11, 1995.

23. *Wall Street Journal*, July 11, 1995; June 9, 1995.

24. *Congressional Quarterly*, Oct. 21, 1995, 3211–12; *New York Times*, Nov. 2, 1995; FAIR, *Immigration Report*, November 1995.

25. Center for Immigration Studies, *Announcement*, Nov. 15, 1995.

26. *Congressional Quarterly*, Nov. 25, 1995, 3600.

27. *New York Times*, March 8, 1996.

28. *Washington Post*, March 15, 1996.

29. *New York Times*, March 14, 1996; March 15, 1996.

30. *Washington Post*, March 15, 1996; *Congressional Quarterly*, March 16, 1996, 698–99.

31. *Congressional Record* (daily digest), April 25, 1996, S 4150.

32. Ibid., March 21, 1996, H 2593.

33. *New York Times*, March 22, 1996.

34. Ibid,, March 8, 1996.

35. *Boston Globe*, Jan. 17, 1997.

36. Ibid.

37. Ibid.

38. *Washington Post*, March 28, 1996.

39. *Washington Times*, April 26, 1996.

40. Ibid.

41. *Washington Post*, Nov. 18, 1996; April 23, 1997. These figures do not include a few thousand paroled into the United States or those requesting asylum. Nor do they include illegal aliens.

42. *Washington Times*, Sept. 29, 1996; *New York Times*, Sept. 29, 1996; *Congressional Quarterly*, Sept. 28, 1996, 2755–59.

43. *Washington Times*, March 26, 1996.

44. *New York Times*, March 21, 1996.

45. Ibid.

46. Ibid.

47. Ibid., June 11, 1996.

48. President Clinton did not request the authorized amount in his first budget of 1997.

49. *New York Times*, Sept. 29, 1996; March 16, 1997.

50. Ibid., July 11, 1997.

51. Ibid., Jan. 3, 1995.

52. John Juddis, "Huddled Elites," *The New Republic*, Dec. 23, 1996, 23–26.

53. Letter to Congress, March 20, 1996, entitled "Keep Families Together," from the Christian Coalition.

54. Sara Diamond, "Right-Wing Politics and The Anti-Immigration Cause," *Social Justice*, Fall 1966, 166.

55. National Immigration Forum, *The Golden Door*, Winter 1996.

56. Ad placed in the *Washington Times*, Aug. 25, 1996. The ad appeared before the final bill was passed, but it was clear by then that legal immigration would not be touched.

57. National Immigration Forum, *The Golden Door*, Winter 1996.

58. CCN, Letter to supporters, December 1996. See also column by Ben J. Seeley in *Los Angeles Times*, Oct. 30, 1996.

59. *Congressional Record* (daily digest), March 21, 1996, H 2597.

60. Ibid., April 25, 1996, S 4135.

61. *Washington Times*, April 1, 1996.

62. Peter Salins, *Assimilation American Style* (New York: New Republic Books, 1997), 40.

63. Ibid., 18.

64. *Sacramento Bee*, Jan. 15, 1997.

65. *Washington Times*, Feb. 1, 1997.

66. *San Francisco Chronicle*, Feb. 1, 1997.

67. *New York Times*, Feb. 4, 1997; *Daily News of Los Angeles*, Feb. 3, 1997.

68. *The Seattle Times*, June 16, 1997. Restrictionists complained about the questions asked.

69. *New York Times*, Jan. 17, 1997.

70. Ibid.

71. *San Jose Mercury News*, Jan. 15, 1997; *San Francisco Chronicle*, Jan. 15, 1997.

72. *Congressional Quarterly*, May 4, 1995, 1222.

73. *San Jose Mercury News*, Jan. 15, 1997.

74. *New York Times*, Jan. 17, 1997.

## Conclusions

1. *Detroit Free Press*, March 14, 1997.

2. FAIR, *Immigration Report*, June 1997.

3. *Washington Post*, June 6, 1997; *New York Times*, June 5, 1997; June 19, 1997; July 30, 1997.

4. *New York Times*, April 2, 1997.

5. *Los Angeles Times*, June 30, 1997. The most likely result would be a drop in immigration from Mexico and Central America.

6. *Washington Post*, June 7, 1997.

7. National Research Council, *The New Americans: Economic, Demographic, and Fiscal Effects of Immigration*, preliminary report (Washington: National Academy Press, 1997).

8. FAIR, *Immigration Report*, June 1997.

9. *Immigration Impact*, June 1997. This newsletter, which ceased publication in 1997, was edited by Gerri Williams, a member of FAIR. See also the opposing comments of FAIR's John L. Martin and professors James F. Hollifield and Dennis D. Cordell in *Plano Star Courier*, June 8, 1997.

10. The two volumes consumed 2,600 pages. Immigration was only one issue; most articles deal with the environment.

11. Peter Brimelow and Ed Rubenstein, "Electing a New People," *The National Review*, June 16, 1997, 32–34. Borjas went over familiar territory but he did not support immigration cuts, only changes in how newcomers were selected.

12. Juan F. Perea, ed., *Immigrants Out! The New Nativism and the Anti-Immigrant Impulse in the United States* (New York: New York University Press, 1997), 5. See also Bill Ong Hing, *To Be An American: Cultural Pluralism and the Rhetoric of Assimilation* (New York: New York University Press, 1997), and Thomas J. Espenshade, ed., *Keys to Successful Immigration: Implications of the New Jersey Experience* (Washington D.C.: Urban Institute, 1997).

13. Joel Millman, *The Other Americans: How Immigrants Renew Our Country, Our Economy, and Our Values* (New York: Viking, 1997), 316–17. Millman is a writer for the *Wall Street Journal*.

14. *New York Times*, Feb. 17, 1996.

15. *Seattle Times*, July 6, 1997. WSCIC did not limit its discussions to Wenatchee. It pointed to other Washington towns experiencing change. See, for example, its discussion of conditions in the City of Mattawa, WSCIC, *News and Views*, February 1997.

# Some Special Reading Lists

## Selected Books and Pamphlets in the Immigration Debate

Abernethy, Virginia. *Population Politics: The Choices That Shape Our Future*. New York: Insight Books, 1993.

Auster, Lawrence. *The Path to National Suicide: An Essay on Immigration and Multiculturalism*. Monterey, Va: AICF, 1990.

Beck, Roy. *The Case Against Immigration: The Moral, Economic, Social, and Environmental Reasons for Reducing U.S. Immigration Back to Traditional Levels*. New York: Norton, 1996.

——. *Re-Charting America's Future: Responses to Arguments Against Stabilizing U.S. Population And Limiting Immigration*. Petoskey, Mich.: Social Contract Press, 1994.

Briggs, Vernon M. Jr. *Mass Immigration and the National Interest*. Armonk, N.Y.: M. E. Sharpe, 1996.

Brimelow, Peter. *Alien Nation: Common Sense About America's Immigration Disaster*. New York: Random House, 1995.

Bouvier, Leon F. *Floridians in the 21st Century: The Challenge of Population Growth*. Washington D.C.: Center for Immigration Studies, 1992.

——. *Fifty Million Californians*. Washington D.C.: FAIR, 1991.

——. *Peaceful Invasions*. Lanham, Md.: University Press of America, 1992.

Bouvier, Leon F. and Lindsey Grant. *How Many Americans? Population, Immigration, and the Environment*. San Francisco: Sierra Books, 1994.

Bouvier, Leon F. and Dudley L. Boston Jr. *Thirty Million Texans?* Washington D.C.: Center for Immigration Studies, 1993.

Chronicles. *Immigration and the American Identity*. Rockford, Ill.: Rockford Institute, 1995.

Cose, Ellis. *A Nation of Strangers: Prejudice, Politics, and the Populating of America*. New York: Morrow, 1992.

Dalton, Humphrey, ed. *Will America Drown? Immigration and the Third World Population Explosion*. Washington D.C.: Scott-Townsend, 1993.

Espenshade, Thomas, ed. *Keys to Successful Immigration: Implications of the New Jersey Experience*. Washington D.C.: Urban Institute Press, 1997.

Geyer, Georgie Anne. *Americans No More: The Death of Citizenship*. New York: Atlantic Monthly Press, 1996.

Grant, Lindsey, ed. *Elephants in the Volkswagen: Facing Tough Questions About Our Overcrowded Country*. New York: Freeman, 1992.

——. *Juggernaut: Growth on a Finite Planet*. Santa Ana, Calif.: Seven Locks Press, 1996.

Hardin, Garrett. *The Immigration Dilemma: Avoiding the Tragedy of the Commons*. Washington D.C.: FAIR, 1995.

Hawkins, William R. *Importing Revolution: Open Borders and the Radical Agenda*. Monterey, Va.: AICF, 1994.

Heer, David. *Immigration in America's Future*. Boulder: Westview Press, 1996.

Hing, Bill Ong. *To Be An American: Cultural Pluralism and the Rhetoric of Assimilation*. New York: New York University Press, 1997.

Isbister, John. *The Immigration Debate: Remaking America*. West Hartford, Conn.: Kumarian Press, 1996.

Lamm, Richard and Gary Imhoff. *The Immigration Time Bomb*. New York: Truman Talley Books, 1985.

Lutton, Wayne. *The Myth of Open Borders: The American Tradition of Immigration Control*. Monterey, Va.: AICF, 1988.

Lutton, Wayne and John Tanton. *The Immigration Invasion*. Petoskey, Mich.: Social Contract Press, 1994.

Millman, Joel. *The Other Americans: How Immigrants Renew Our Country, Our Economy, and Our Values*. New York: Viking Press, 1997.

Mills, Nicholaus, ed. *Arguing Immigration: Are the New Immigrants a Wealth of Diversity . . . or a Crushing Burden?*. New York: Touchstone, 1994.

Nelson, Brent. *America Balkanized: Immigration's Challenge to Government*. Monterey, Va.: AICF, 1994.

Perea, Juan F., ed. *Immigrants Out: The New Nativism and the Anti-Immigrant Impulse in the United States*. New York: New York University Press, 1997.

Raspail, Jean. *The Camp of the Saints*. Petoskey, Mich.: Social Contract Press, 1994.

Salins, Peter D. *Assimilation American Style: An Impassioned Defense of Immigration and Assimilation As the Foundation of American Greatness and the American Dream*. New York: Basic Books, 1997.

Simon, Julian. *The Ultimate Resource*. Princeton: Princeton University Press, 1981.

Stacy, Palmer and Wayne Lutton. *The Immigration Time Bomb*. Alexandria, Va: AICF, 1985.

Ungar, Sanford J. *Fresh Blood: The New American Immigrants*. New York: Simon and Schuster, 1995.

Vinson, John. *Immigration Out of Control: The Interests Against America*. Monterey, Va.: AICF, 1992.

Williamson, Chilton Jr. *The Immigration Mystique*. New York: Basic Books, 1996.

**Interviews**

Betsy Ballash, February 5, 1997
Barbara Coe, January 12, 1996
Daniel Elliott, January 12, 1996
Maria Sepulveda Flynn, December 16, 1996
C. Scipio Garling, December 17, 1996
Leon Kolanliewicz, December 16, 1996
Judith Kunofsky, January 5, 1996
Alan Kuper, August 13, 1996
Ed Levy, July 12, 1996
Yeh Ling-Ling, April 18, 1997
Charles Scott, January 1, 1996
Patrick Skain, January 4, 1996
Dan Stein, December 17, 1997
Dr. John Tanton, February 11, 1997
John Vinson, September 5, 1996
Pat Walk, June 20, 1996

**Selected Organizations for Immigration Restriction or Official English**

American Immigration Control Foundation, Monterey, Va.
Bay Area Coalition for Immigration Reform, San Francisco.
California Coalition for Immigration Reform, Huntington Beach, Calif.
Californians for Population Stabilization, Sacramento, Calif.
Carrying Capacity Network, Washington D.C.
Diversity Coalition for an Immigration Moratorium, San Francisco.
English First, Springfield, Va.
The Federation for American Immigration Reform, Washington D.C.
Midwest Coalition to Reform Immigration, Chicago.
Negative Population Growth, Teaneck, N.J.
Population-Environment Balance, Washington D.C.
The Social Contract Press, Petoskey, Mich.
U.S. English, Washington D.C.
Voices of Citizens Together, Sherman Oaks, Calif.
Washington State Citizens for Immigration Control, Wenatchee, Wash.

# Index